C000242921

GCSE 9-1 CHEMISTRY

REVISION AND EXAM PRACTICE

FOR ALL EXAM BOARDS

Sarah Carter,
Darren Grover and
Mike Wooster

Authors Sarah Carter, Darren Grover and Mike Wooster
Editorial team Haremi Ltd
Series designers emc design ltd
Typesetting York Publishing Solutions Pvt. Ltd., INDIA
Illustrations York Publishing Solutions Pvt. Ltd., INDIA and Newgen KnowledgeWorks (P) Ltd, Chennai, India
App development Hannah Barnett, Phil Crothers and Haremi Ltd

Designed using Adobe InDesign
Published by Scholastic Education, an imprint of Scholastic Ltd, Book End, Range Road, Witney, Oxfordshire, OX29 0YD
Registered office: Westfield Road, Southam, Warwickshire CV47 0RA
www.scholastic.co.uk

Printed by Bell & Bain Ltd, Glasgow
© 2017 Scholastic Ltd
1 2 3 4 5 6 7 8 9   7 8 9 0 1 2 3 4 5 6

British Library Cataloguing-in-Publication Data
A catalogue record for this book is available from the British Library.
ISBN 978-1407-17694-9

Acknowledgements

The publishers gratefully acknowledge permission to reproduce the following copyright material:

p11 Hurst Photo/Shutterstock; p13 bszef/Shutterstock; p15 PR Image Factory/Shutterstock; p23 Djordje Konstantinovic/Shutterstock; p26 Daxiao Productions/Shutterstock; p29 Andraž Cerar/Shutterstock; p41 chromatos/Shutterstock; p42 108MotionBG/Shutterstock; p45 top Billion Photos/Shutterstock; p45 bottom Fablok/Shutterstock; p47 Andrey Kucheruk/Shutterstock; p54 alice-photo/Shutterstock; p56 honglouwawa/Shutterstock; p61 Smith1972/Shutterstock; p68 Natalia Evstigneeva/Shutterstock; p70 left My name is boy/Shutterstock; p82 Stocksnapper/Shutterstock; p89 joker1991/Shutterstock; p106 Alexey Stiop/Shutterstock; p114 Perry Harmon/Shutterstock; p119 Pix One/Shutterstock; p125 Aun Photographer/Shutterstock; p129 PhotostockAR/Shutterstock; p130 Saroj Khuendee/Shutterstock; p132 PK289/Shutterstock; p140 exopixel/Shutterstock; p144 Italianvideophotoagency/Shutterstock; p148 IPCC, from Carbon Dioxide and Global Warming Case Study, Purdue University, http://iclimate.org/ccc/Files/carbondioxide.pdf; p149 steveball/Shutterstock; p154 kunmanop/Shutterstock; p156 PhotoStock10/Shutterstock; p164 Cory Seamer/Shutterstock; p165 Arjen Dijk/Shutterstock.

Every effort has been made to trace copyright holders for the works reproduced in this book, and the publishers apologise for any inadvertent omissions.

Note from the publisher:

Please use this product in conjunction with the official specification that you are following and sample assessment materials. Ask your teacher if you are unsure where to find them. Mapping grids showing you which content you need to know for the main specifications are found online at www.scholastic.co.uk/gcse.

In the Exam Practice section of the book, the marks and star ratings have been suggested by our subject experts, but they are to be used as a guide only.

Answer space has been provided, but you may need to use additional paper for your workings.

How to use this book

Inside this book you'll find everything you need to help you succeed in the GCSE 9–1 chemistry specifications. It combines revision and exam practice in one handy solution. Broken down into topics and subtopics, it presents the information in a manageable format. Work through the revision material first or dip into the exam practice as you complete a topic. This book gives you the flexibility to revise your way!

SNAP IT!

Use the Snap It! feature in the revision app to take a picture, film a video or record audio of key concepts to help them stick. Great for revision on the go!

DO IT!

Activities that get you to turn information from one form into another so that it really embeds in your memory.

Callouts Step-by-step guidance to build understanding.

WORK IT!

Worked examples with model solutions to help you see how to answer a tricky question.

NAIL IT!

Tips written by subject experts to help you in the revision process.

MATHS SKILLS

To help you with those tricky bits of maths that you need to know and remember.

 ## Practical Skills

Revisit the key practicals in your specification.

 ## STRETCH IT!

Questions or concepts that stretch you further and challenge you with the most difficult content.

CHECK IT!

Check your knowledge at the end of a subtopic with the Check It! questions.

Consolidate your revision with the Review It! questions at the end of every topic.

REVIEW IT!

For mapping grids to show you exactly what you need to know for your specification, go to www.scholastic.co.uk/gcse

MARKS (5 marks)

Each question has the number of marks available to help you target your response.

EXAM-STYLE QUESTIONS

Exam-style questions for each subtopic ramped in difficulty.

★ STAR RATING ★

A quick visual guide to indicate the difficulty of the question, with 1 star representing the least demanding and 5 stars signposting the most challenging questions.

■ PRACTICE PAPERS

Full mock-exam papers to enable you to have a go at a complete paper before you sit the real thing! Find Paper 2 online at www.scholastic.co.uk/gcse

Revision Guide contents

Exam Practice contents

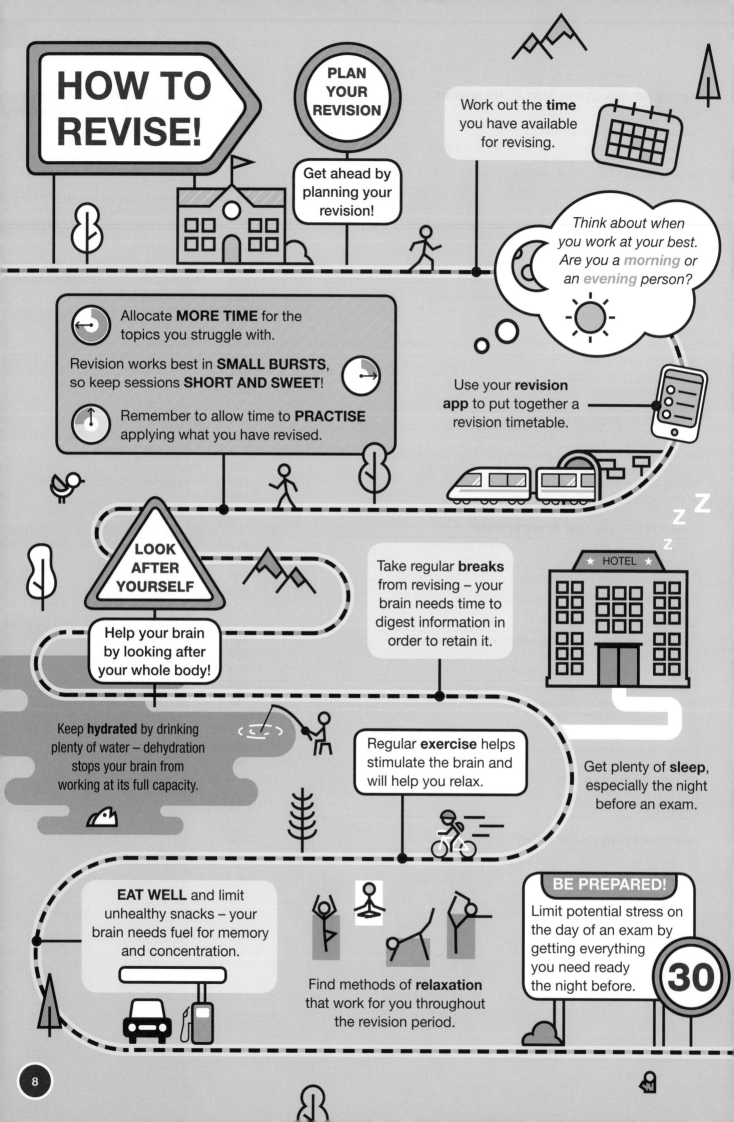

HOW TO REVISE!

PLAN YOUR REVISION

Get ahead by planning your revision!

Work out the **time** you have available for revising.

Think about when you work at your best. Are you a morning or an evening person?

Allocate **MORE TIME** for the topics you struggle with.

Revision works best in **SMALL BURSTS**, so keep sessions **SHORT AND SWEET**!

Remember to allow time to **PRACTISE** applying what you have revised.

Use your **revision app** to put together a revision timetable.

LOOK AFTER YOURSELF

Help your brain by looking after your whole body!

Take regular **breaks** from revising – your brain needs time to digest information in order to retain it.

HOTEL

Keep **hydrated** by drinking plenty of water – dehydration stops your brain from working at its full capacity.

Regular **exercise** helps stimulate the brain and will help you relax.

Get plenty of **sleep**, especially the night before an exam.

EAT WELL and limit unhealthy snacks – your brain needs fuel for memory and concentration.

Find methods of **relaxation** that work for you throughout the revision period.

BE PREPARED!

Limit potential stress on the day of an exam by getting everything you need ready the night before.

30

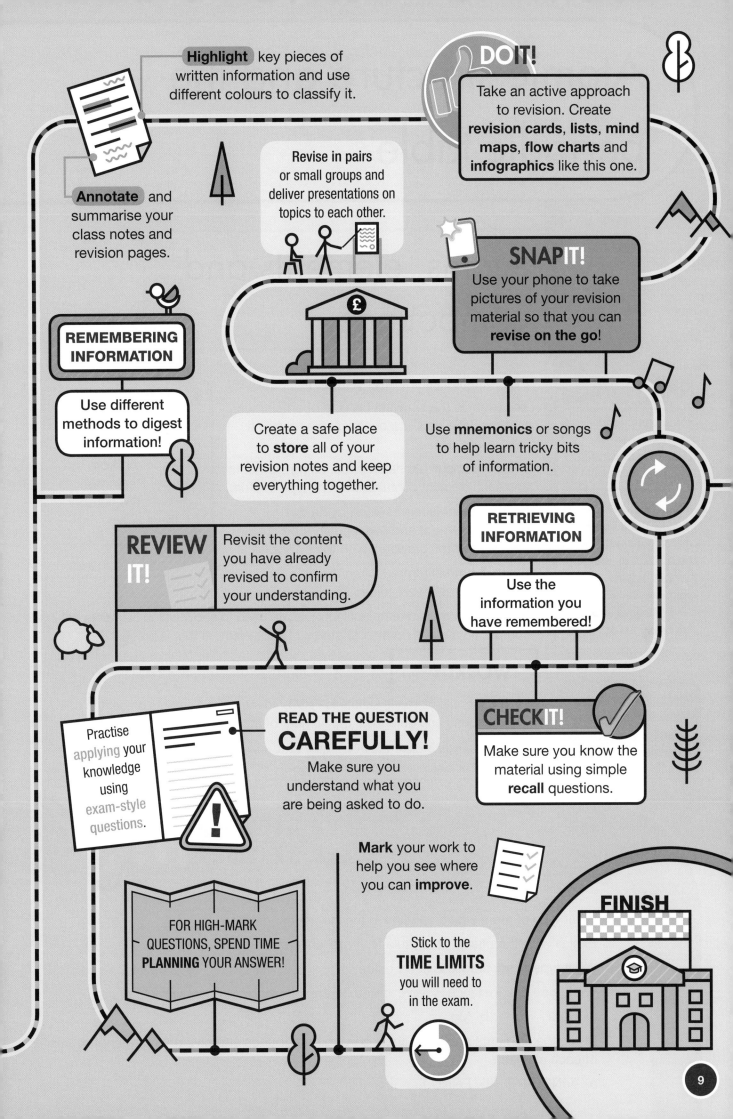

Highlight key pieces of written information and use different colours to classify it.

DO IT!
Take an active approach to revision. Create **revision cards**, **lists**, **mind maps**, **flow charts** and **infographics** like this one.

Annotate and summarise your class notes and revision pages.

Revise in pairs or small groups and deliver presentations on topics to each other.

SNAP IT!
Use your phone to take pictures of your revision material so that you can **revise on the go**!

REMEMBERING INFORMATION

Use different methods to digest information!

Create a safe place to **store** all of your revision notes and keep everything together.

Use **mnemonics** or songs to help learn tricky bits of information.

RETRIEVING INFORMATION

REVIEW IT! Revisit the content you have already revised to confirm your understanding.

Use the information you have remembered!

Practise applying your knowledge using exam-style questions.

READ THE QUESTION CAREFULLY!
Make sure you understand what you are being asked to do.

CHECK IT!
Make sure you know the material using simple **recall** questions.

Mark your work to help you see where you can **improve**.

FOR HIGH-MARK QUESTIONS, SPEND TIME **PLANNING** YOUR ANSWER!

Stick to the **TIME LIMITS** you will need to in the exam.

FINISH

Atomic structure and the periodic table

Atoms, elements and compounds

NAILIT!

Some compounds have formulae containing brackets. When you work out the number of atoms in the compound you multiply the number of atoms inside the bracket by the number outside. For example, $Ca(NO_3)_2$ has 2 nitrogen atoms and 6 oxygen atoms.

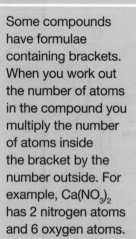

The Roman numerals represent the charge on the first ion in the compound.

All substances are made up of particles.

The atom is the smallest particle of an element that can take part in a chemical reaction and exist on its own.

There are about 100 naturally occurring elements and each element contains only one type of atom.

Each element is represented by its own chemical symbol and has its own atomic number (proton number), with the symbol A_r.

A compound is formed when the atoms of two or more elements are joined by chemical bonds.

Molecular formula or empirical formula are used to show which elements are in a compound and the number of atoms of each element that is present.

MATHS SKILLS

You will need to read the number of atoms in a compound from the formula. Remember to leave out the number 1 if there is only one atom in the formula of a compound.

WORKIT!

The formula of iron(II) sulfate is $FeSO_4$. Identify the elements present in this compound and determine the number of atoms of each element.

The elements present are iron, sulfur and oxygen. There is 1 atom of iron, 1 atom of sulfur and 4 atoms of oxygen.

CHECKIT!

1. What type of atom would you find in the element sodium?
2. Explain why the chemical formula H_2 represents an element.
3. What type of substance is silver oxide?
4. What type of substance is represented by the following chemical formulae?
   a $CuBr_2$ b Mg
5. Name the elements present in the following compounds and give the number of atoms of each element.
   a $AgNO_3$ b $Fe(NO_3)_3$

Mixtures and compounds

A physical property of a substance is one which you can measure or observe without changing the substance. Two examples of physical properties are melting point and appearance.

A chemical property of a substance is one which you can only observe by changing the substance.

A mixture is formed whenever elements or compounds are together but **not** joined chemically. An example of a mixture is iron mixed with sulfur. If the substances in a mixture are not joined chemically they can be easily separated. For example, the iron and sulfur can be easily separated using a magnet.

Mixtures have different physical properties to the substances that make them up. When they are separate, the substances in a mixture still keep their chemical properties.

There are different types of mixture and this means that there are different separation methods. See the Snap It! box on page 12.

The elements in a compound are joined chemically and therefore cannot be separated by physical means. For example, the compound iron(II) sulfide cannot be separated into iron and sulfur using a magnet because they are combined chemically.

DO IT!

Start a list of definitions and keep your list on a spreadsheet. You can begin this with definitions of an atom and a compound.

Practical Skills

The practicals that use these methods are:

1   The preparation of a soluble salt from an insoluble base.

2   The distillation of salt solution.

3   The separation of coloured substances using paper chromatography.

In some practicals, you will use more than one separation method. For example, in the separation of a soluble salt from an insoluble base you will first use filtration to remove any unreacted insoluble base and then crystallisation to get the salt from the solution.

DOIT!

In the table below there is an empty column labelled 'Example'.

For each separation method, give an example of where it is used. The answers are given below. Just put each example in the right box.

Ethanol from ethanol and water; salt from salty water; chalk from chalk and water; water from salty water; colourings in sweets.

NAILIT!

Some of the marks (about 15%) will be allocated to questions about practical techniques. For some of the required practical experiments you use some of these methods. Make sure you know which separation method is used along with the apparatus that is required.

In the exam you may be given data on the different boiling points or solubilities of different substances and asked to explain how you could separate them.

SNAPIT!

A table to show methods for separating different mixtures

Mixture	Method used and why	Apparatus used	Example
Separating an insoluble solid from a liquid.	Filtration because the insoluble solid cannot pass through the filter paper.	Filter funnel, filter paper and beakers	
Separating the liquid from a solution of a solid in a liquid. The liquid is the distillate.	Simple distillation because the liquid has a much lower boiling point and so evaporates at a much lower temperature.	Flask, heating equipment and condenser	
Separating two or more miscible liquids. (miscible means they can mix)	Fractional distillation because the liquid with the higher boiling point evaporates then condenses on the column, as the one with the lower boiling point carries on up as a vapour.	Flask, heating equipment, thermometer, fractionating column and condenser	
Separating coloured substances.	Paper chromatography which relies on the substances having **different attractions** for the paper and the solvent.	Container and chromatography paper	
Separating the dissolved solid from a solution.	Crystallisation, which depends on the big differences in boiling points between the solvent and the dissolved solid.	Evaporating basin and heating equipment	

WORKIT!

The boiling points of two substances X and Y along with water are shown in the table below.

Substance	Boiling point/°C
X (X is a solid at room temperature)	1800
Y (Y is a liquid at room temperature)	67
Water	100

a Explain how you could get X from a solution of X in water.

Crystallisation. The water has a much lower boiling point and can be evaporated off to give solid X.

b Explain how you could get Y from a solution of Y in water.

Fractional distillation. Y and water are miscible (they mix), otherwise Y would not dissolve in water. Their boiling points are close so fractional distillation is needed.

CHECKIT!

1 Why is a mixture of iron and sulfur easy to separate but it is very difficult to separate iron from sulfur in iron(II) sulfide?

2 a Explain how you could separate a mixture of chalk and salt. Check the Snap It! on page 12 for ideas.

   b The table below shows the solubilities of two solid substances, Q and R, in petrol and water.

Substance	Q	R
Solubility in petrol	Soluble	Insoluble
Solubility in water	Insoluble	Insoluble

Explain how you could use filtration to separate a mixture of Q and R.

Pure substances and formulations

Pure substances are either single elements or single compounds.

Everyday descriptions of pure substances are inaccurate. For example, pure spring water is a solution of various minerals and gases.

Pure substances melt and boil at specific temperatures.

Mixtures melt and boil over a range of temperatures.

A formulation is a mixture that is designed as an improvement upon a pure substance on its own.

Examples of formulations are metal alloys, drugs and paints.

For example, a drug has in its formulation the active chemical and other substances that stop the drug from going off and make it easy to swallow.

DOIT!

Look up the ingredients of a simple over-the-counter drug. A painkiller like Nurofen is a good one to do. How do the ingredients of the formulation improve the drug? Research 'The ingredients of Nurofen'.

MATHS SKILLS

Using formulae and inserting values into them using percentages.

The formulae used are:

$$\text{Percentage} = \frac{\text{mass of component}}{\text{total mass}} \times 100\%$$

$$\text{Number of moles} = \frac{\text{mass}}{M_r}$$

WORKIT!

A drug formulation in tablet form weighs 500 mg. The two components are 350 mg of a stabiliser (X) with a relative formula mass 70, and the 150 mg of the active drug itself (Y) which has a relative formula mass of 125.

What is the percentage composition of the tablet in terms of:

a mass

The percentage by mass of $X = 350/500 = 70\% = 70\%$

Therefore the percentage by mass of $Y = 100 - 70 = 30\%$

b moles?

The number of moles of $X = \text{mass}/M_r = 350 \times 10^{-3}/70 = 5 \times 10^{-3}$ mol

The number of moles of $Y = \text{mass}/M_r = 150 \times 0^{-3}/125 = 1.2 \times 10^{-3}$ mol

Therefore the total number of moles $= 5 \times 10^{-3}$ mol $+ 1.2 \times 10^{-3}$ mol $= 6.2 \times 10^{-3}$ mol

Mole percentage for $X = (5 \times 10^{-3}/6.2 \times 10^{-3}) \times 100\% = 80.6\%$

This means that the mole percentage for $Y = 100 - 80.6\% = 19.4\%$

SNAPIT!

A distinctive melting point is a criterion for purity. The apparatus used is shown below along with a typical heating curve for a **pure** substance.

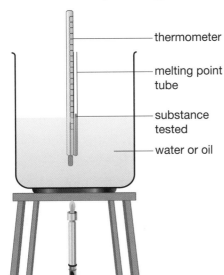

- thermometer
- melting point tube
- substance tested
- water or oil

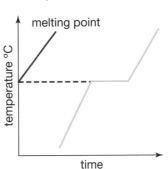

melting point

temperature °C

time

NAILIT!

A possible question on formulations is finding the percentage composition of a formulation and converting the masses present to moles.

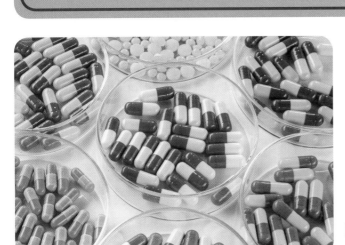

Drugs are formulations of chemicals

CHECKIT!

1 What is a pure substance?

2 Why isn't 'pure orange juice' scientifically pure?

3 What is a formulation?

4 Give one example of a product which is a formulation and give brief details of its composition.

Chromatography

NAILIT!

You should check your exam specification for which practicals you may be asked questions on.

This is one of the practicals you could be questioned on in your GCSE Chemistry exam. The practical emphasises that you carry out a practical safely and accurately, make measurements and make conclusions using these measurements.

Chromatography is a technique that can be used to separate mixtures into their components and identify these components.

MATHS SKILLS

Calculating the R_f value using experimental results.

When you express your answers for the R_f value you should give the answer to 3 significant figures unless asked to do otherwise. For example, if your calculation gives the answer as 0.65723 you should write down 0.657.

Using and rearranging the formula

$$R_f = \frac{\text{distance moved by spot}}{\text{distance moved by solvent}}$$

Chromatography involves two phases – a stationary phase and a mobile phase. In paper chromatography, paper is the stationary phase and a liquid solvent is the mobile phase.

When substances are added to the paper, the mobile phase carries them through the paper. The distance a compound moves on the paper depends on its relative attraction for the paper and the solvent. The R_f value for a substance is equal to the distance moved by its spot divided by the distance moved by the solvent.

Compounds that have a higher attraction for the paper and a low attraction for the solvent spend a lot of time on the paper and move up the paper slowly.

Compounds that have a higher attraction for the solvent and have less of an attraction for the paper move quickly up the paper.

At the end of the experiment the spots obtained after the solvent is run up the paper is called a **chromatogram**.

Mixtures give more than one spot and pure compounds give only one spot. If the substances being separated are colourless then a **locating agent** is needed to show how far they have moved. Sometimes a UV lamp can be used.

Practical Skills

Paper chromatography is often used to separate a mixture of coloured substances such as those found in inks and food colourings.

Chromatography requires a container, a supply of solvent(s), a ruler for measuring R_f values, chromatography paper and very thin capillary tubes for adding the test substances to the paper.

A pencil line is drawn a short distance from the bottom of the paper and this is called the baseline. The substances to be investigated are added at regular intervals along this line.

If the starting spots are too large then it will be very difficult to separate the mixture into easily identified substances. This is because the spots get larger as they rise up the paper.

The choice of solvent is not limited to water and should be chosen on the basis that it gives a good separation.

When measuring the R_f value of a substance the measurement is taken from the line where the substances are added to the paper and the middle of the spot obtained after the solvent has run up the paper.

SNAPIT!

A typical chromatogram using paper chromatography

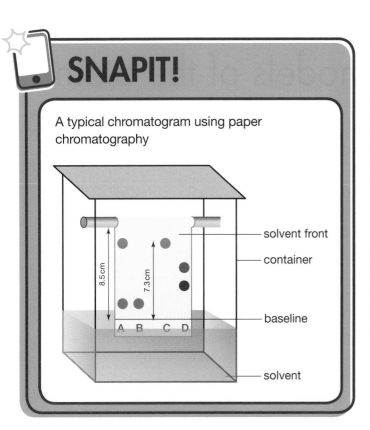

- solvent front
- container
- baseline
- solvent

8.5 cm

7.3 cm

A B   C D

WORKIT!

In a chromatography, experiment the spot for a substance X moved 12 cm and the solvent front moved 15 cm.

a What is the R_f value for X using this solvent?

The R_f value = 12/15 = 0.8

b In a second experiment under the same conditions, the solvent front moves 25 cm. What distance would the spot move in this second experiment?

$$R_f = \frac{\text{distance moved by spot}}{\text{distance moved by solvent}}$$

Rearrange this formula so that distance moved by spot = R_f × distance moved by solvent.

This means that the distance moved by spot = 0.8 × 25 cm = 20 cm.

Rearrange the formula

STRETCHIT!

Thin-layer and **gas chromatography** are two other types of chromatography. Thin-layer chromatography is similar to paper chromatography but with silica or alumina being the stationary phase. The solvent is the stationary phase. It has the advantage that more of the substance to be separated or identified can be loaded onto the thin-layer plate. It is also reproducible and you can compare between different plates. However, in paper chromatography there are more errors and we can only compare spots on the same chromatogram, not between different paper chromatograms.

Gas chromatography separates the components of a mixture by heating them so that they are gases. Then using an inert (unreactive) carrier gas like nitrogen (the **mobile phase**) they are pushed through a column containing a substance like silica which is coated with a liquid (the **stationary phase**).

If a substance has a high attraction for the stationary phase it stays on the column for a longer time than a substance that has a weaker attraction and the substances in the mixture separate. The time from when the mixture is injected onto the column to when it comes off the column is called its **retention time**. The **retention time** of a substance can be used to identify it in the same way as R_f values.

✓ CHECKIT!

1 In paper chromatography what is the stationary phase and what is the mobile phase?

2 Explain why pencil is used to draw the baseline on a chromatogram.

3 This question concerns the chromatogram shown in the Snap It! box.

Which of the three substances B, C and D is/are a pure substance? Explain your answer.

Scientific models of the atom

From the ancient Greeks up to the end of the 19th century, atoms were thought to be indivisible.

Joseph John Thomson discovered the electron and he suggested that the atom is a positive ball (the plum pudding) with negatively charged electrons (the currants) dotted around inside it.

A few years later, Ernest Rutherford showed that the atom has a central nucleus which contains positively charged protons with electrons orbiting around it.

It is now thought that the electrons are in energy levels or shells around the nucleus.

James Chadwick discovered the neutron (which is neutral) in the nucleus. This means that there are three sub-atomic particles – the electron, the proton and the neutron.

NAILIT!

The most important experiment is Rutherford's experiment. When Rutherford and his team fired high-energy positively charged alpha particles at gold foil they expected these particles to pass straight through. What they saw was that most of the particles did pass straight through but some were deflected or rebounded straight back.

Think about Rutherford's reasoning on his experimental results. The nucleus must be positive to repel the positive alpha particles and very dense because it had to withstand their high energy. As most of the alpha particles passed through the foil, most of the atom must be empty space.

DOIT!

Copy and complete the table below to show how scientists' vision of the atomic model atom has changed over time as new evidence became available.

Scientist	What they discovered	Comments

SNAPIT!

The diagram below shows the model of the atom we now use.

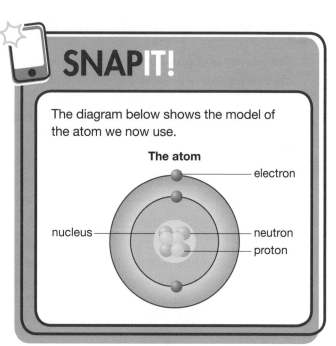

The atom

CHECKIT!

1 What does indivisible mean?

2 State the three main sub-atomic particles.

3 Describe the structure of the atom.

Atomic structure

In an atom, the protons and neutrons are in the central nucleus and the electrons move around the nucleus in electron shells.

The charges and masses of the three sub-atomic particles are very small and because of this we use their relative charges and relative masses. See the table below for a summary of their properties.

Each of the atoms of an element contains the same number of protons. This is called the atomic number.

For each element the atomic number is fixed and cannot change.

In a neutral atom, the number of protons equals the number of electrons.

Ions are charged atoms and are formed when atoms of an element react with atoms from another element.

An ion is positive (a cation) if electrons are lost and the number of positive charges on the ion is equal to the number of electrons lost.

An ion is negative (an anion) if electrons are gained and the number of negative charges is equal to the number of electrons gained.

The mass number of an atom is the sum of the number of protons and neutrons in the nucleus. The mass number can also be called the nucleon number, you may hear it called this in physics.

A table showing properties of sub-atomic particles

Name of sub-atomic particle	Where is it in the atom?	Relative charge	Relative mass
Proton	In the nucleus	+1	1
Neutron		0	1
Electron	In shells around the nucleus	−1	Very small (1/1836)

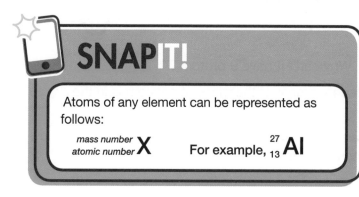

SNAPIT!

Atoms of any element can be represented as follows:

$^{\text{mass number}}_{\text{atomic number}}X$ For example, $^{27}_{13}Al$

DOIT!

Draw a diagram of an atom, label each sub-atomic particle in your diagram and write a short note to describe its relative mass and its relative charge.

Use the words electron, proton, neutron, atomic number, mass number, nucleus and neutral in your notes.

NAIL IT!

You must remember that the number of protons (the atomic number) in atoms of the same element never changes. If its atomic number were to change, it would be a different element.

MATHS SKILLS

You can work out the number of each sub-atomic particle in an atom by using its atomic number and mass number.

In a **neutral atom** the atomic number = number of protons = number of electrons

The mass number = number of protons + number of neutrons = atomic number + number of neutrons

This means that: the number of neutrons = mass number − atomic number

In a **positive ion** (cation) the number of electrons = atomic number − the number of charges on the ion

In a **negative ion** (anion) the number of electrons = atomic number + the number of charges on the ion

WORKIT!

1 An atom of potassium has the atomic number 19 and mass number 39. What are the number of electrons, protons and neutrons in an atom of potassium?

The number of protons and electrons are equal to the atomic number = 19

The number of neutrons = mass number − atomic number = 39 − 19 = 20

2 How many electrons are there in a calcium ion Ca^{2+}? [Atomic number of calcium = 20]

For Ca^{2+} number of electrons = 20 − 2 = 18

3 How many electrons are there in N^{3-} ion? [Atomic number of nitrogen = 7]

For N^{3-} number of electrons = 7 + 3 = 10

CHECKIT!

1 An oxygen atom contains 8 protons. Why can't it have 9 protons?

2 Explain why scientists have concluded that most of the mass of an atom is in the nucleus.

3 A phosphorus atom (symbol P) has an atomic number 15 and a mass number 31. Show how you could represent the phosphorus atom.

4 How many electrons are there in an Al^{3+} ion? [Atomic number of aluminium = 13]

5 An atom of sodium can be represented as shown below. Give the number of protons, electrons and neutrons in a sodium atom. $^{23}_{11}Na$

Isotopes and relative atomic mass

The atomic number of an element cannot change. It is fixed.

Therefore the number of protons is also fixed.

However, the mass number of an element can have different values and so the number of neutrons must also vary in number.

Atoms of the same element with different mass numbers are called isotopes.

Isotopes of an element have the same number of protons but different numbers of neutrons.

Examples of isotopes are the three naturally occurring isotopes of magnesium:

a $^{24}_{12}Mg$ **b** $^{25}_{12}MG$ **c** $^{26}_{12}Mg$

These all have 12 protons in the nucleus but atom **a** has 12 neutrons, **b** has 13 neutrons and **c** has 14 neutrons in the nucleus.

For any element there are different amounts of each isotope and this has to be taken into account when calculating the relative atomic mass of an element.

The units of atomic mass are atomic mass units (amu).

MATHS SKILLS

The amount of an isotope in terms of its percentage is its percentage abundance.

When you work out the relative atomic mass of an element, you start off by saying 'Let there be 100 atoms'. The percentage abundance of an isotope is the number of atoms out of the 100 which are that isotope.

You then multiply the percentage abundance of the isotope by its mass number to give the mass due to its atoms.

Repeat this for the other isotopes and add up all the masses due to all the isotopes.

Finally, divide the total mass by 100 to get the average mass which is the relative atomic mass.

NAILIT!

The relative atomic mass is a weighted average, which means that we don't just add up the mass numbers of the isotopes and find the average. We have to take into account the abundance of each isotope. If you consider the two isotopes of chlorine $^{35}_{17}Cl$ and $^{37}_{17}Cl$, the average is $(35 + 37)/2 = 36$ but this does not take into account that there is more of the $^{35}_{17}Cl$ isotope, and that is why the relative atomic mass is 35.5 atomic mass units – the average is nearer to 35.5. This means that when working out the relative atomic mass its value should be near the most abundant isotope. The Work It! on the next page explains how to work this out.

DOIT!

The mass numbers for the isotopes of chromium are shown below. Estimate the relative atomic mass of chromium to the nearest whole number and then look up the relative atomic mass in the periodic table.

Element	Mass number for each isotope with percentage abundance in brackets
Chromium	50 (4.31%); 52 (83.76%); 53 (9.55%) and 54 (2.36%)

WORKIT!

1 One example of an isotope is chlorine with its two isotopes $^{35}_{17}Cl$ and $^{37}_{17}Cl$. The isotope $^{35}_{17}Cl$ makes up 75% of the atoms and the $^{37}_{17}Cl$ isotope 25%. Calculate the relative atomic mass of chlorine.

Let there be 100 atoms. 75 of these are the $^{35}_{17}Cl$ isotope and they have a total mass of 75 × 35 = 2625 amu

The total mass of the $^{37}_{17}Cl$ isotope = 25 × 37 = 925 amu

The total mass of 100 atoms of all the isotopes = 2625 + 925 amu = 3550 amu

> This stands for atomic mass units.

The average mass = 3550/100 = 35.5 amu = the relative atomic mass of chlorine.

2 There are three naturally occurring isotopes of magnesium $^{24}_{12}Mg$ (78.6% of total); $^{25}_{12}Mg$ (10.11% of total) and $^{26}_{12}Mg$ (11.29% of total). What is the relative atomic mass of magnesium?

> Even though the percentages are not whole numbers just use the same method as for chlorine. One way of checking your answer is to estimate which number the relative atomic mass would be nearest to. In this case the most abundant isotope is magnesium-24 and therefore you expect the relative atomic mass would be nearer to 24 than the others.

Let there be 100 atoms. Mass of magnesium-24 isotope = 78.6 × 24 amu = 1886.4 amu

Mass of magnesium-25 isotope = 10.11 × 25 amu = 252.8 amu

Mass of magnesium-26 isotope = 11.29 × 26 amu = 293.5 amu

The total mass of 100 atoms = 2432.7 amu

Therefore the relative atomic mass is the average mass of each atom = 2432.7/100 = 24.3 amu (to 3 significant figures).

As expected, this is near to 24 which is the mass number of the most abundant isotope.

CHECKIT!

1 a Explain why the two atoms represented by $^{38}_{18}Ar$ and $^{40}_{18}Ar$ are isotopes.

b Give the numbers of electrons, protons and neutrons in these two atoms.

2 a There are two naturally occurring isotopes of copper. Their mass numbers and percentage abundance are given in this table.

Mass number	Percentage abundance/%
63	69
65	31

Use this data to calculate the relative atomic mass of copper to 3 significant figures.

b The atomic number of copper is 29. How many electrons, protons and neutrons are there in each isotope of copper?

The development of the periodic table and the noble gases

The periodic table was first written by Dmitri Mendeleev and has developed over time with new discoveries.

At the time, Mendeleev organised the elements in order of their atomic weights and he placed elements with similar properties in groups.

He did not place elements where they did not fit and left spaces for elements that he thought had not yet been discovered.

He also predicted the properties of these missing elements. When they were discovered his predictions were found to be very accurate.

Today the elements are placed in order of ascending atomic number. If the elements were placed in order of their relative atomic mass the elements iodine and tellurium would be placed in the wrong groups. The same applies to argon and potassium.

Vertical columns of elements are called groups and horizontal rows of elements are called periods.

The number of electrons in the outer shell of an element is its group number.

The number of occupied electron shells is the period number.

The first of the noble gases to be discovered was argon. This new element had completely different properties to those elements already discovered.

Due to Mendeleev's concept of grouping elements with similar properties, argon's discoverers then started looking for other elements with similar properties. This led to the discovery of the other noble gases: helium (in the Sun) and neon, krypton and xenon from the fractional distillation of liquid air.

The noble gases are very unreactive because they have full outer electron shells which are stable electron arrangements.

As you go down the group, the noble gases become denser.

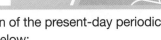

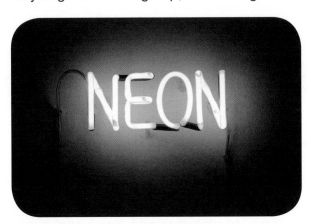

Neon gas is often used in lights

Write a short description of the present-day periodic table using the words below:

- groups
- similar
- period
- columns
- electron shells
- properties
- atomic number
- horizontal rows.

SNAPIT!

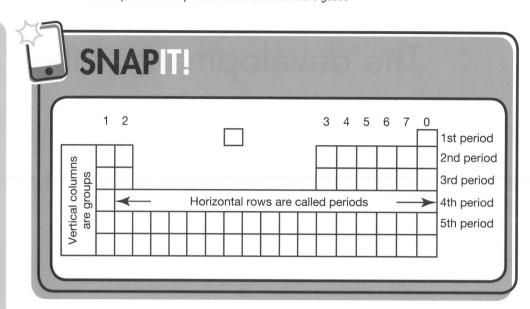

NAILIT!

- Once you have located an element in the periodic table you will probably need to select information about the element.
- Remember, the top number above the symbol is the relative atomic mass and the number below the symbol is the atomic number.
- The first row of elements consists of hydrogen and helium. These are easily missed because the hydrogen is placed on its own because it does not fit into a particular group.
- The groups you should concentrate on are the ones featured in this book. These are group 1– the alkali metals, group 7 – the halogens and group 0 – the noble gases.

The periodic table of the elements

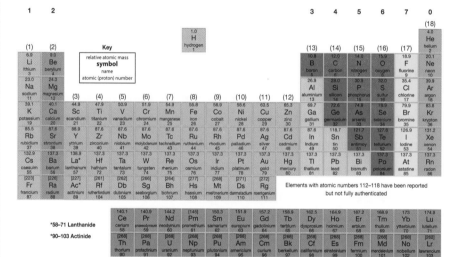

CHECKIT!

1 What are the names given to vertical columns and horizontal rows in the periodic table?

2 Name the element that is in group 3 and period 3 of the periodic table.

3 Explain why Mendeleev left spaces in his original periodic table.

4 Look at the pairs of elements potassium and argon, and tellurium and iodine. Use these examples to explain why we do not arrange the elements in order of their atomic mass.

Electronic structure and the periodic table

The electrons in atoms are arranged in electron shells.

The first shell can take a maximum of 2 electrons, the second shell holds 8 electrons and the third shell can also hold 8 electrons.

The number of electrons in the outer shell of an element is its group number.

The number of occupied electron shells is the period number.

The electronic structures with full outer shells are particularly important because they are very stable. These structures are the electronic structures of the noble gases — 2 and 2,8 and 2,8,8.

SNAPIT!

The diagram below gives two ways to represent the electronic structure of an element. In this case the elements carbon and chlorine.

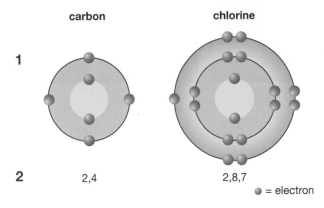

As you can see, one way shows the electrons in their orbits. The second way is a shorthand way and just gives the number of electrons in each shell.

DOIT!

Suppose you were given the atomic number of an element. Describe to a revision partner two ways you could locate an element in the periodic table. (Hint: number of protons and electrons.)

Alternatively, record a short MP3 of your explanation on your phone and check its accuracy by playing it back and comparing it with your notes or your textbook.

NAILIT!

Electronic structure is very important. If you can work out the electronic structures of different atoms you can then go on to work out the type of bond formed between them.

The electronic structures with full outer shells are particularly important because they are stable arrangements. These are sometimes called the noble gas arrangements.

You only need to be able to write out the electronic structures of the first 20 elements such as those for the elements hydrogen to calcium.

You will need to work out the electronic structure of an element. You do this by filling the shells up starting from the first or innermost shell which takes up to 2 electrons. You then fill up the second shell until it is full (8 electrons) and so on.

WORKIT!

Phosphorus has 15 electrons. Only 2 electrons go into the first shell, leaving 13 electrons. Only 8 can go into the second shell leaving 5 electrons for the outermost shell which can take up to 8.

Write out the electronic structure of phosphorus.

The electronic structure or electron arrangement of phosphorus is written as 2,8,5.

If we use the periodic table we can check this is right by looking at the third period (third row) and group 5. If we look here we find phosphorus.

Match heads contain phosphorous

CHECKIT! ✓

1 Describe where electrons are found in an atom.

2 State the maximum number of electrons that can be held in the second electron shell.

3 An element has 19 electrons. State its electron arrangement and describe its position on the periodic table.

Metals and non-metals

Metals are found on the left-hand side of the periodic table and non-metals on the right-hand side.

Most elements (about 92 out of 118) are metals.

The two types of element are different in their appearance, electrical conductivity, malleability and ductility. These differences are shown in the table below.

When metals react with non-metals their atoms lose electrons to form positive ions (cations).

When non-metals react with metals their atoms gain electrons to form negative ions (anions).

Physical property	Metals	Non-metals
Electrical conductivity	Electrical conductors	Electrical insulators
Malleability and ductility	Malleable and ductile	The solids are brittle. They snap when you try to bend or stretch them.
Appearance	All shiny	The solids are dull in appearance.

A table that shows differences between the physical properties of metals and non-metals

SNAP IT!

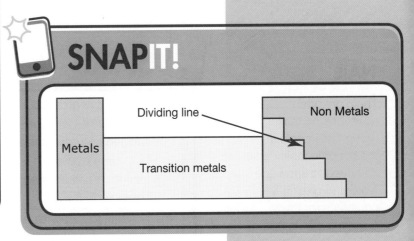

CHECK IT!

1 Calcium is a metal. Describe where you would find calcium in the periodic table.

2 Classify the elements sulfur and sodium as metals or non-metals. You should explain your answer by referring to some of their physical properties.

3 State the charge on a sodium ion and explain how it forms.

4 Black phosphorus is a form of phosphorus that conducts electricity. By referring to the periodic table explain why this is unusual.

27

Group 1 – the alkali metals

DO IT!

You can find videos of the reactions of the alkali metals on the internet. They will show what happens when they are added to water. Just do a search for 'alkali metals reactions with water'.

This is a balanced chemical equation. If you need to revise how to balance equations look at page 52.

The alkali metals are all in group 1 because they have one electron in their outer electron shell.

They are typical metals because they are shiny and good electrical conductors.

But, unlike most other metals, they are soft and have low densities. The first three, lithium, sodium and potassium, are less dense than water.

They all react with water to give hydrogen gas and an alkaline solution of the metal hydroxide. For example, sodium gives hydrogen and sodium hydroxide when it reacts with water.

sodium(s) + water(l) → hydrogen(g) + sodium hydroxide(aq)

$2Na(s) + 2H_2O(l) \rightarrow H_2(g) + 2NaOH(aq)$

When they react they all lose their outer electron to form a +1 ion (for example, Na^+). This gives them a stable full outer shell of electrons.

They get more reactive as you go down the group because it gets easier to lose their outer electron. See the table below to help you remember.

NAIL IT!

There are often questions on the group 1 elements in the periodic table. You need to know the word and chemical equations for their reactions with water.

You should also be able to predict the reactions of rubidium and caesium using what you know about the first three elements in the group.

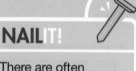

SNAP IT!

Li	Hardest in group but can be cut with a knife, tarnishes (goes dull) in air. When added to water, it floats and fizzes because hydrogen is released and leaves an alkaline solution of lithium hydroxide (LiOH).	They all have 1 electron in their outer electron shell and this is why they are in group 1. They are all soft and easily cut with a knife. They all react with air and water and this is why they have to be stored carefully. The first three are stored under oil, the rest are stored in sealed vials in a protective atmosphere. As you go down the group, their reactions with water get more and more violent. Each reaction produces hydrogen and an alkaline solution of the metal hydroxide.
Na	Easier to cut with a knife than lithium, tarnishes quickly. When added to water, it moves around on the surface of the water and gets hot enough to melt, giving hydrogen gas and alkaline sodium hydroxide (NaOH) solution.	
K	Even softer and tarnishes immediately. With water, it whizzes around the surface and melts, and the hydrogen given off burns producing a lilac flame. The solution remaining contains potassium hydroxide (KOH).	
Rb Cs	Look at videos from the internet to see their reaction with water.	

WORKIT!

What is the electron arrangement of sodium?

Sodium has the atomic number 11. This means that it has 11 electrons. 2 electrons go in the first shell, 8 in the second and this leaves 1 for the outer third shell. Its electronic structure is 2,8,1.

MATHS SKILLS

You should be able to work out the electron arrangements of the first three alkali metals. Remember 2 electrons can go in the first shell, 8 in the second and 8 in the third.

A piece of sodium, the outer layer has reacted with the air to form sodium bicarbonate. The newly exposed side is still a silvery-grey colour.

NAILIT!

Make sure you can explain why the elements get more reactive as you go down the group:

- They all lose their outer single electron when they react to give a stable electron arrangement.

- This gets easier as you go down the group for two reasons:

    1 The outer electron gets further from the positive nucleus and so it feels less of an attractive force and can leave the atom more easily.

    2 As you go down the group there are more electron shells between the nucleus and the outer electron. This also lowers the attractive force from the nucleus.

✓ CHECKIT!

1 a State the electron arrangements of lithium (atomic number 3) and potassium (atomic number 11).

  b Use your answers to explain why they are in the same group of the periodic table.

2 List four physical properties of sodium.

3 Write the word equation and balanced chemical equation for the reaction of potassium with water.

4 Why is sodium more reactive than lithium?

5 a Predict the observations you would make if rubidium was added to water.

  b Write the balanced chemical equation for the reaction of rubidium with water.

6 Explain why the alkali metals are always found in compounds never uncombined.

Group 7 – the halogens

The halogens are all in group 7 because they have 7 electrons in their outer electron shell.

As elements they exist as molecules of 2 atoms (diatomic molecules) for example, Cl_2 and Br_2.

When they react with metals, they all gain 1 electron to form a −1 ion. These ions are called halide ions.

As you go down the group the:

- Elements get heavier as the relative molecular masses increase.

- Elements get less reactive because it gets harder to gain an extra electron (see Snap It! box below).

- More reactive halogens displace less reactive ones from solutions of their salts (see next subtopic).

DOIT!

Using the Snap It! box, describe the properties of the elements as you go down the group. Predict the properties of astatine and then look it up on the internet. How many did you get right?

SNAPIT!

Pale yellow gas	F	Halogens all have 7 electrons in their outer shell and this is why they are in group 7.
Pale green gas	Cl	Halogens get darker as you go down the group and their melting points and boiling points increase.
Dark red liquid	Br	Halogens all exist as molecules of 2 atoms and form -1 ions when they react with metals.
Dark grey solid	I	Halogens get **less reactive** as you go down the group.
Black solid	At	This is because it gets harder to gain an extra electron to become stable.

NAILIT!

There are often questions on the group 7 elements in the periodic table.

You should also be able to predict the reactions of fluorine and astatine using what you know about the middle three elements in the group: chlorine, bromine and iodine.

Of the group 7 elements, you will only be asked to work out the electron arrangements (or draw the electron structure) for fluorine and chlorine. However, you should be able to work out that the electron arrangement of iodine and bromine also end in 7.

One common error is to use chlo**ride** instead of chlo**rine**. Chloride is used when chlorine is part of a compound. You can have sodium chloride but not sodium chlorine. The element 'chloride' does not exist.

WORKIT!

Bromine is in group 7. It has two isotopes $^{79}_{35}\text{Br}$ (50.5%) and $^{81}_{35}\text{Br}$ (49.5%).

a   Calculate the relative atomic mass of bromine.

The first step to remember is to let there be 100 atoms and then work out the mass of each isotope in the 100 atoms.

Mass of bromine — 79 isotopes = 50.5 × 79 = 3990 amu ◄——— amu = atomic mass units

Mass of bromine — 81 isotopes = 49.5 × 81 = 4010 amu

The total mass of 100 atoms = 3990 + 4010 = 8000 amu

This makes the relative atomic mass = 80

b   Calculate the number of electrons, protons and neutrons in the bromine-79 isotope.

The atomic number is 35 and this means that there must be 35 electrons and 35 protons.

The mass number = 79 and the number of neutrons = 79 – 35 = 44

c   How many electrons are there in a Br⁻ ion?

As the ion is 1⁻ it must have 1 extra electron compared with the neutral atom. The number of electrons = 35 + 1 = 36 electrons.

NAILIT!

Make sure you can explain why the elements get less reactive as you go down the group:

- They all gain an extra electron when they react to give a stable electron arrangement.

- This gets harder as you go down the group for two reasons:

  1   The outer electron shell gets further from the positive nucleus and so any electron feels less of an attractive force and this makes it harder to gain an electron.

  2   As you go down the group, there are more electrons between the nucleus and the outer electron. This also lowers the attractive force from the nucleus and makes it harder to gain an electron.

✓ CHECKIT!

1   State the number of outer shell electrons a bromine atom has.

2   When chlorine reacts with sodium what ion is formed, Cl⁺ or Cl⁻?

3   Draw the electron arrangement of a chloride ion.

Displacement reactions in group 7

DO IT!

Write word equations using the results table in the Snap It! box and use these to explain the observations for each reaction. Then give the order of reactivity from your observations.

A displacement reaction is a chemical **reaction** in which a more reactive element takes the place of a less reactive element from its compound.

In group 7, a displacement reaction takes place when a more reactive halogen takes the place of another less reactive halogen in a compound.

A halide is a compound formed between a halogen and another element.

The more reactive halogen displaces a less reactive halogen ion in a solution of a metal halide (a salt).

For example, when bromine is added to a solution of sodium iodide, the more reactive bromine displaces the iodide ion to form sodium bromide and iodine.

This is because bromine accepts an electron more easily than iodine so the iodide ion donates its extra electron to a bromine atom.

SNAP IT!

The results table below shows what happens in some of the halogen displacement reactions. Try and work out the order of reactivity. Check your answer online to see if you were correct.

Halogen	Sodium chloride solution	Sodium bromide solution	Sodium iodide solution
Chlorine	X	turns yellow/ pale orange	turns brown
Bromine	No change	X	turns brown
Iodine	No change	No change	X

In solution, chlorine is very pale green; bromine is pale yellow to orange and iodine is brown or purple depending on the solvent.

X is placed where there is no experiment. For example, you cannot displace a chloride using chlorine!

MATHS SKILLS

You should be able to balance the equations for displacement.

First, write down the word equation, then the chemical equation, and then balance it.

WORK IT!

The word equation for reacting sodium bromide with chlorine is:
sodium bromide + chlorine → sodium chloride + bromine

Write a balanced chemical equation for this reaction.

Write symbols $NaBr + Cl_2 \rightarrow NaCl + Br_2$

Balance equation $2NaBr + Cl_2 \rightarrow 2NaCl + Br_2$

Practical Skills

When you do displacement reaction experiments, you must always add the halogen to water as a control. This means you can compare it with the reaction mixture to see if there is a change.

Sometimes cyclohexane is added to the mixture and shaken. Any halogen formed dissolves more in the cyclohexane than the water. This helps because in water, bromine and iodine are not very different in colour (depending on their concentrations). In cyclohexane bromine is still orange/red in colour whilst iodine is purple. So this can be used to confirm the identity of the halogen produced.

STRETCH IT!

You could be asked to write ionic equations for the displacement reactions that take place. The simple rule for these is that the salts exist as ions and the halogen molecules do not. For example, the reaction between chlorine and potassium iodide solution gives iodine and potassium chloride solution.

Symbol equation: $2KI + Cl_2 \rightarrow 2KCl + I_2$

The potassium iodide and potassium chloride can be written as ions:

$2K^+ + 2I^- + Cl_2 \rightarrow 2K^+ + 2Cl^- + I_2$

The K^+ ions do not change and can be cancelled out because it does not take part in the reaction. The K^+ ion is called a **spectator ion** (it just looks on).

So the final equation is $2I^-(aq) + Cl_2(g) \rightarrow 2Cl^-(aq) + I_2(s)$

The letters in brackets are state symbols, these are explained on page 36.

For more information on ions, see page 38 and 39.

CHECK IT!

1 State the formula of a fluorine molecule.

2 Describe the observations when chlorine is added to an aqueous solution of sodium iodide.

3 a Write the word and balanced chemical equation for the reaction between bromine and sodium iodide (NaI).

  b Describe what you would see happen when the bromine is added to the sodium iodide. Explain this observation.

  c Write the ionic equation for this reaction.

4 When bromine is added to a solution containing sodium chloride no change is observed.

  a What would be the control for this reaction?

  b Explain the observation.

NAIL IT!

When you write the formulae for the halogens remember they are diatomic molecules, X_2. So, for example, chlorine is Cl_2 and bromine is Br_2. The general formula of all the sodium halides is NaX.

The transition metals

DO IT!

Draw a rough outline of the periodic table. Write where you would find the alkali metals, the halogens, the noble gases and the transition elements.

Write a short list of the properties of each group on sticky notes or on your outline.

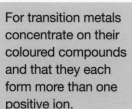

NAIL IT!

For transition metals concentrate on their coloured compounds and that they each form more than one positive ion.

The transition metals are found in the middle block of the periodic table.

They have typical metal properties. They are shiny, malleable and ductile. They are also good electrical and thermal conductors.

Unlike the group 1 metals, transition metals are hard and dense.

They are not as reactive as the group 1 metals. Their reactions with oxygen, water and chlorine are not as vigorous as the reactions of the group 1 metals.

As for all metals, the atoms of transition metals lose electrons when they react to form positive ions (cations). The difference is that each transition metal forms ions with different charges. For example, iron forms Fe^{2+} and Fe^{3+} ions.

The different metal ions of each transition metal have different colours. For example, Fe^{2+} ions are green and Fe^{3+} ions are orange-brown.

This means that transition metals form coloured compounds. Non-transition metal compounds are all white in colour.

Transition metals and their compounds form good catalysts. Examples include iron in the Haber process, platinum in the catalytic converter in car exhausts and vanadium pentoxide in the manufacture of sulfuric acid.

SNAP IT!

There are only a few coloured compounds that you need to know about.

Colours of compounds containing transition metal ions.

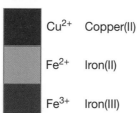

Cu^{2+}	Copper(II)
Fe^{2+}	Iron(II)
Fe^{3+}	Iron(III)

Later on in the course, you will be asked to identify the transition metal ion in a compound and you will have to use the colours to confirm they are present when sodium hydroxide is added to a solution of their ions.

CHECK IT!

1 Predict four properties of the transition metal chromium.

2 Classify calcium, nickel and iron as either transition or non-transition metals.

3 You have been given unlabelled samples of copper chloride and sodium chloride. Describe how you could tell which is which.

1 a Balance the chemical equation below for the reaction between sodium and chlorine.

$$Na(s) + Cl_2(g) \rightarrow NaCl(s)$$

   b i How can you tell from the symbols in the equation that this is a reaction between two elements?

      ii Describe the appearance of each reactant.

      iii In the product the two types of particle formed are Na^+ and Cl^-. What is the name given to these charged particles?

   c Explain why sodium chloride solution in water is a mixture.

2 In the periodic table, what is a group and what is a period?

3 Sodium has the atomic number 11. Explain why sodium cannot have the atomic number 12.

4 Sulfur has the atomic number 16. Describe its position in the periodic table.

5 a A metal X forms a green compound and a blue compound. Explain where you would find X in the periodic table.

   b Predict four physical properties of the element X.

6 a When group 7 elements react with metals they form ions. What is the charge on these ions?

   b Explain why the group 7 elements get less reactive as you go down the group.

7 Magnesium has the atomic number 12 but has atoms with three different mass numbers, 24, 25 and 26.

   a What does the atomic number 12 tell you about an atom of magnesium?

   b How is it possible for magnesium atoms to have three mass numbers?

   c Gallium has two isotopes, gallium-69 (60%) and gallium-71(40%). Use these figures to calculate the relative atomic mass of gallium.

8 Describe two things that Mendeleev did to make his version of the periodic table work.

9 Explain why the elements in group 1 get more reactive as you go down the group.

10 Explain why the noble gases are so unreactive.

11 a When the element argon was discovered it had very different properties to any other element. Why do you think scientists went on to look for other elements like it?

    b Why was this element so hard to discover?

12 The element astatine is in group 7. It is so rare that most of its chemistry has been guessed at from its position below iodine in group 7.

    a Why do we think it is black in colour?

    b The symbol for astatine is At. What is the formula of an astatine molecule?

    c Predict the formula of sodium astatide.

    d What is the charge on an astatide ion?

Bonding, structure and the properties of matter

Bonding and structure

Strong attractive forces between the particles in a substance make its melting and boiling point high. This is because more energy is needed to overcome these forces.

You can work out the state of a substance at room temperature or any other temperature using its melting and boiling points (see Work It! box below).

When a substance melts, attractive forces between the solid particles are broken as the particles break away from the solid lattice and become liquid particles. The temperature remains constant until all these bonds are broken.

In the same way, when a liquid boils the particles overcome the attractive forces between the liquid particles to become a gas. The temperature stays constant at the boiling point until all these attractive forces are overcome.

The state of a substance at room temperature and pressure (RTP) can be shown in a chemical equation by using the state symbol for the substance.

These state symbols are (s) for solids; (l) for liquids and (g) for gases. The extra symbol (aq) is for substances dissolved in water to give an aqueous solution.

DOIT!

Imagine yourself as a particle. Write a short account of what it would feel like if you were in a solid, a liquid and a gas. What would happen to you if you were a particle in the solid and you were heated until the solid melted?

WORKIT!

A substance X melts at 250°C and boils at 890°C. What state is X in at **a** 140°C and **b** 723°C?

a   140°C is below the melting point of X so it hasn't melted and is a solid.

b   723°C is above the melting point so X would have melted but it is below the boiling point and this means that it has not boiled and at this temperature X is a liquid.

MATHS SKILLS

You could be asked to work out what state a substance is in at a given temperature. You will be given the melting point and boiling point of the substance.

To work out the state you have to answer two questions. These are:

- At this temperature has it melted?
- At this temperature has it boiled?

SNAPIT!

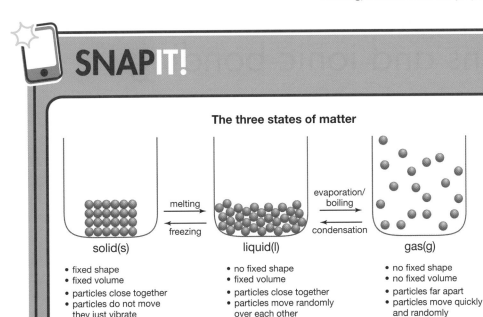

The three states of matter

melting →
← freezing

evaporation/boiling →
← condensation

solid(s)

- fixed shape
- fixed volume
- particles close together
- particles do not move they just vibrate
- this state has the lowest energy of three states

liquid(l)

- no fixed shape
- fixed volume
- particles close together
- particles move randomly over each other

gas(g)

- no fixed shape
- no fixed volume
- particles far apart
- particles move quickly and randomly
- this state has the highest energy

NAILIT!

The three states of matter can be represented by a simple model, as shown in the Snap It! box. This particle model can help to explain melting, boiling, freezing and condensing. Depending on your specification and whether you are sitting the Higher or Foundation Tier, you may be expected to understand the limitations of this model:

- The model assumes that the particles are spheres.

- Many particles are not spheres, for example, polymers.

- In the model there are no forces between the particles, which is not correct!

STRETCHIT!

OCR Gateway only

One way of demonstrating that the way the particle theory is inaccurately represented is to show the ratio of particle spacing to particle diameter. When aluminium is a gas at 2800 K the average distance between each particle is equal to 7.26×10^{-9} m = 7.26 nm. The diameter of each aluminium particle is 0.25×10^{-9} m = 0.25 nm.

This means that the ratio $\dfrac{\text{average distance between each particle}}{\text{diameter of each particle}} = \dfrac{7.26\,\text{nm}}{0.25\,\text{nm}} = 29.$

This shows that when we represent the particles in the gaseous state we do not represent the situation accurately.

CHECKIT!

1 Which state of matter could be described as having a fixed volume but no fixed shape?

2 If a substance has a low melting point, what can you say about the forces of attraction between its particles?

3 Describe what happens to the particles in a substance as they melt, in terms of movement and arrangement.

4 A substance Y has a melting point of −25°C and a boiling point of 135°C.

   a In which state of matter is Y at **i** 20°C and **ii** 250°C?

   b Which state symbol could you use for Y in a chemical equation.

5 The particle theory states that particles are solid spheres. Give two reasons why this statement is incorrect.

Ions and ionic bonding

In general ions are formed when metal atoms transfer their outer electrons to the outer shells of non-metal atoms. This electron transfer forms charged particles called ions.

Metal atoms form positive ions (cations) because they have lost one or more negatively charged electrons. The positive charge on the ion is the same as the number of electrons that are lost.

Non-metal atoms form negative ions (anions) because they have gained one or more negatively charged electrons. The negative charge on the ion is the same as the number of electrons that are gained by the atom.

The elements in groups 1 and 2 of the periodic table are metals and they form positive ions.

Each group 1 atom forms a 1+ ion by losing 1 electron from its outer shell, and each group 2 atom forms a 2+ atom by losing 2 electrons from its outer shell.

The elements in groups 6 and 7 are non-metals and they form negative ions.

Each group 6 atom gains 2 electrons to form a 2− ion and each group 7 atom gains 1 electron to form a 1− ion.

All the ions formed have the same electronic structure as the nearest noble gas because these are stable electron arrangements.

The ionic bond is the electrostatic attraction between the positive and negative ions.

You can work out the formula of an ionic compound by balancing the charges on the ions (see Work It! box on page 39).

DO IT!

The atomic number of lithium is 3 and fluorine's is 9. Draw diagrams of the atoms including their nuclei before reaction and diagrams of the ions after reaction. Use your diagrams to explain why the lithium ion is Li⁺ and the fluoride ion is F⁻.

SNAP IT!

The **dot-and-cross** diagrams below show the outer electronic structures of some atoms and ions before and after electron transfer. Take a picture so you have an example to revise from.

In the third example, each chlorine can accept just 1 electron and the magnesium has to lose 2 electrons. This means that each magnesium has to react with 2 chlorines.

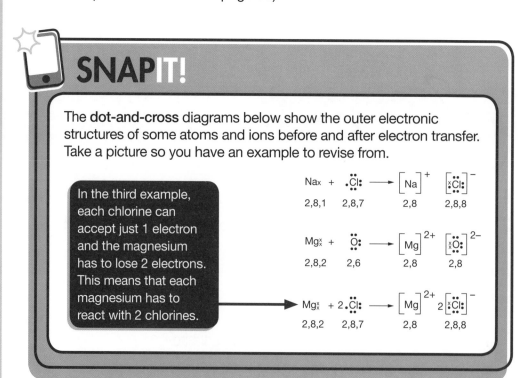

NAILIT!

When you draw the ions and their electronic structures, you only have to give the outer electrons, as these are the only ones involved in bonding. For the positive metal ions, you do not have to draw any dots or crosses because they have lost their outer electrons.

You must also remember to draw the electrons gained by the non-metal atom as different to the ones already there. For example, if you look at the chloride ion in the Snap It! box the electron gained from the sodium is written as an $\times$ when the chlorine electrons are given as $\bullet$.

You can also identify whether or not a compound is ionic by looking at the elements. A compound is ionic if one element comes from either group 1 or 2 and the other one comes from either group 5, 6 or 7.

As far as hydrogen is concerned, it resembles group 7 elements because it has to gain 1 electron to be stable.

WORKIT!

1   Calculate the formula of the compound sodium oxide.

Sodium is in group 1 which means that its ion is Na^+. Oxygen is in group 6 which means the oxide ion is O^{2-}.

To make the charges add up to zero we need 2 of the Na^+ ions and 1 of the O^{2-} ion.

The formula is therefore Na_2O.

A dot-and-cross diagram could also be used to find the formula. The sodium atom needs to lose 1 electron and the oxygen needs to gain 2 electrons. Therefore to make this happen there needs to be 2 sodium atoms combining with 1 oxygen and the formula is therefore Na_2O.

2   Calculate the formula of strontium fluoride.

Strontium is in group 2 and this means that its ion is Sr^{2+}. Fluorine is in group 7 so its ion is F^-. To make the charges add up to zero we need 1 strontium ion and 2 fluoride ions. The formula is SrF_2.

MATHS SKILLS

When you work out the formula of an ionic compound you have to make the charges on the ions add up to zero. Let's suppose you have a compound containing M^{2+} ions and X^- ions. To make the charges add up to zero we need 2 of the $1-$ ions and 1 of the $2+$ ions. This means that the formula is MX_2.

✓ CHECKIT!

1   The list below shows the formulae of six compounds. From the list choose the three ionic compounds.

   LiCl CS_2 NH_3 $BaBr_2$ CO_2 NaH

2   Draw dot-and-cross diagrams for the three ionic compounds you have chosen.

3   Explain how group 1 elements form 1+ ions.

4   State the formula of a sulfide ion.

5   Explain how the ions in NaCl stay together.

6   State the formula of the ionic compounds potassium sulfide and magnesium iodide.

The structure and properties of ionic compounds

The ions in ionic compounds are held together because of the strong electrostatic attraction between the oppositely charged ions.

The electrostatic forces around each ion extend in all directions so each ion attracts several oppositely charged ions around it. This results in a giant lattice where the ions are regularly arranged in a repeating pattern.

The diagrams below showing the structure of sodium chloride illustrate this.

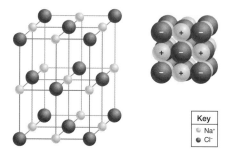

Key
○ Na+
● Cl-

Even though there are many ions in a giant ionic lattice the numbers of each ion are in the same ratio as they are in the formula of the compound. For example, in NaCl the number of sodium and chloride ions are equal in number. In $CaBr_2$ there are twice as many bromide ions as there are calcium ions. For ionic compounds the simplest whole number ratio of ions is used as the formula, which is the empirical formula.

Ionic compounds have high melting and boiling points because the ionic bonds are **strong** and in the giant lattice there are lots of them to break. A lot of energy is needed to break these bonds.

Ions are charged particles and when they move (in aqueous solution or as a liquid) they can carry an electric current.

In solid form ionic compounds do not conduct electricity because the ions are fixed in a lattice and do not move and therefore they cannot carry the current.

If an ionic compound is dissolved in water or is in molten form, then the ions are no longer fixed in a lattice and can move. This means that the ionic compound will conduct electricity.

DO IT!

You may be asked to complete part of an ionic lattice by placing the ions in their places on the grid. The one most usually asked is NaCl because it is 1:1 in terms of positive and negative ions

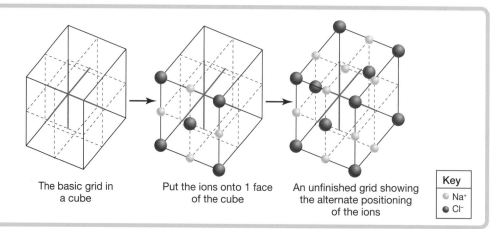

The basic grid in a cube

Put the ions onto 1 face of the cube

An unfinished grid showing the alternate positioning of the ions

Key
○ Na+
● Cl-

NAILIT!

With a few exceptions, all giant structures have high melting and boiling points because they have lots of bonds that have to be broken. The attraction between ions increases as the charges on the ions increase. For example, the attraction between magnesium ions Mg^{2+} and oxide ions O^{2-} is greater than the attraction between sodium ions Na^+ and chloride ions Cl^-. This means that the melting point of magnesium oxide is higher than that of sodium chloride.

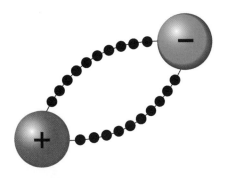

SNAPIT!

Property	Ionic compounds	Explanation
Melting and boiling point	High	Strong electrostatic attraction between the ions and there are lots of bonds to be broken.
Electrical conductivity of solid	Poor	The ions cannot move and cannot carry the current.
Electrical conductivity of liquid	Good	The ions can move and can carry the current.

CHECKIT!

1 Describe what keeps the ions together in an ionic lattice.

2 Explain why the melting point of sodium chloride is very high.

3 Explain why sodium chloride does not conduct electricity as a solid but it does conduct electricity when it is dissolved in water.

4 What can you say about the number of fluoride ions compared to magnesium ions in the ionic lattice of magnesium fluoride (MgF_2)?

5 Explain which of potassium bromide (KBr) and calcium oxide (CaO) has the higher melting point.

Covalent bonds and simple molecules

A covalent bond is formed when a pair of electrons is **shared** between the atoms of two non-metal atoms.

The number of covalent bonds formed by an atom is equal to the number of electrons it needs to gain.

After forming the bonds each atom has the same electronic structure as the nearest noble gas.

Covalent bonds are strong and require a lot of energy to break.

Covalent bonding can be represented by dot-and-cross diagrams or straight lines drawn between atoms. For example:

HCl can be represented by H——Cl or H $\overset{\bullet\bullet}{\underset{\bullet\bullet}{\overset{\times}{Cl}}}$

CH_4 can be represented by

$$H\text{——}\overset{\displaystyle H}{\underset{\displaystyle H}{C}}\text{——}H \quad \text{or} \quad H\overset{\times}{\underset{\times}{\overset{\bullet}{C}}}{}^{\displaystyle H}_{\displaystyle H}H$$

Covalently bonded substances can exist as simple molecules, giant covalent structures or polymers.

Simple molecules are neutral particles and have no charges or free electrons. This means they cannot carry an electric current either in liquid or solid form, as they do not have any delocalised electrons or ions that are free to move and carry the electric charge.

Simple molecular substances have weak intermolecular forces between the molecules. These weak attractive forces need little energy to break them. This means that simple molecular substances have low melting and boiling points and quite often, they are liquids or gases at room temperature.

The intermolecular forces increase as the molecular size **increases** and this means that the melting and boiling points also increase.

DO IT!

Use your notes, textbook or the internet to find five substances that are either gases or liquids at room temperature. At the same time, find out the bonding present.

NAIL IT!

When a simple molecular substance melts or boils, the weak intermolecular forces are broken **not** the strong covalent bonds.

SNAPIT!

See the examples below:

Nitrogen 2,5
needs to gain 3
electrons so forms
3 covalent bonds
per atom

Hydrogen 1
needs to gain 1
electron so forms
1 covalent bond per
atom

Ammonia NH_3

Oxygen 2,6
needs to gain
2 electrons so
forms 2 covalent
bonds per atom

Carbon 2,4
needs 4 electrons
so forms 4 covalent
bonds per atom and
because it needs to gain
more electrons it is the
central atom of the
molecule

Carbon dioxide CO_2

$$O=C=C$$

Each oxygen shares two
pairs of electrons with
the carbon and this means
there are double covalent
bonds between the carbon
and each oxygen

NAILIT!

Check your specification and the tier you are following as you may need to concentrate on drawing dot-and-cross diagrams for compounds containing hydrogen. For example, H_2O and NH_3.

You may be asked to draw dot-and-cross diagrams for compounds containing hydrogen, as well as for more complicated covalent bonding such as that shown in carbon dioxide where multiple bonds are involved (see Snap It! box).

Remember only the outer electrons are shown in dot-and-cross diagrams. The element which has to gain the most electrons is always the central atom in a molecule.

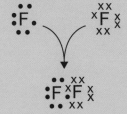

Some elements also exist as simple diatomic molecules. These elements are H_2, O_2, and N_2 and all the halogens (see group 7 on page 30) F_2, Cl_2, Br_2, I_2 and At_2. This is because they can form stable electron arrangements by bonding with each other. For example, fluorine F_2 as shown in the dot-and-cross diagrams to the right.

CHECKIT!

1 Explain what is meant by a covalent bond.

2 What type of element has atoms that form covalent bonds?

3 Draw a molecule of water (H_2O) using a dot-and-cross diagram and using straight lines for the covalent bonds.

4 Draw dot-and-cross diagrams and line diagrams for   **a** HF   **b** CF_4

5 CF_4 is a compound with a simple molecular structure. Predict some of its physical properties such as melting point, electrical conductivity, and so on.

Diamond, graphite and graphene

Diamond, graphite and graphene are all made of carbon atoms, these atoms are linked together by strong covalent bonds.

Diamond and graphite exist as giant covalent structures.

In diamond, each carbon atom is covalently bonded to four other carbon atoms in a giant repeating pattern. This forms a tetrahedral shape. Each covalent bond is strong and difficult to break, these combined properties make diamond **very hard**.

As diamond has strong covalent bonds in a giant structure it has very high melting and boiling points.

There are no delocalised electrons or ions that are free to move in diamond, therefore it is an electrical insulator.

In graphite, the carbon atoms are in layers of hexagonal rings where each carbon atom is covalently bonded to three other carbons. This means that each carbon has a spare electron which is free to move through the layers so graphite conducts electricity both as a solid and as a liquid. These are delocalised electrons.

The covalent bonds in the layers are strong but between the layers there are only weak intermolecular forces. These are easy to break and so the layers can slide over each other easily, making graphite very soft and slippery. This means it can be used in industry as a lubricant.

Graphite also has high melting and boiling points because to melt graphite all of its strong covalent bonds have to be broken and this requires lots of energy.

Graphene has an identical structure to a single layer of graphite. This means that it is one atom thick.

It also means that graphene has identical properties to one layer of graphite, making it strong, flexible, transparent and a good electrical conductor. These properties give it lots of potential uses in, for example, electrical circuits, medical applications, displays and solar cells.

DOIT!

Redraw this table. Compare the physical properties of a simple molecular and a giant covalent.

	Physical property	Simple molecular	Giant covalent
Diamond			
Graphite			
Graphene			

SNAPIT!

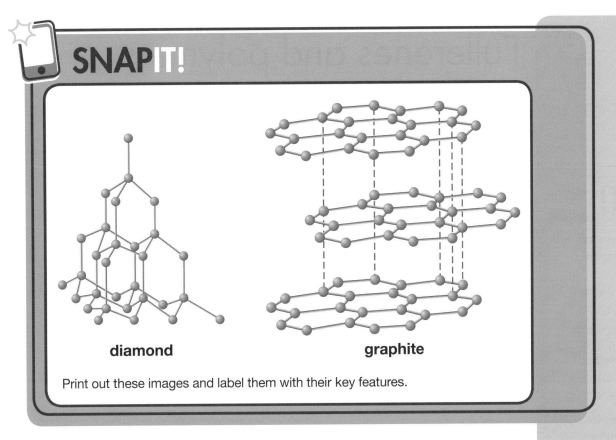

diamond   graphite

Print out these images and label them with their key features.

Diamonds

Graphite

NAILIT!

You should be able to recognise the diagrams of diamond and graphite and understand that they are examples of giant covalent structures.

Describing or recognising the structures of diamond and graphite is not a high-level skill and would only get you a few marks in a question. The same applies to simply describing the properties. It is using the structure to explain the bulk properties that is a high-level skill.

CHECKIT!

1 Describe the structure found in graphite and diamond.

2 Explain why the melting points of graphite, diamond and graphene are very high.

3 Explain why graphite is very soft.

4 Explain why diamond does not conduct electricity but graphite does.

5 Graphene is one layer of graphite. Describe this layer.

6 Silicon dioxide has a structure which is similar to diamond. Predict the properties of silicon dioxide.

Fullerenes and polymers

The smallest example of a spherical fullerene is buckminsterfullerene which is a large but simple molecular substance with the formula C_{60}. These spheres contain mostly 6-carbon rings but there are also small numbers of 5- and 7-carbon rings.

These spherical fullerenes can be used to trap drugs and deliver them to parts of the body. They are also used in industry as lubricants and catalysts.

Carbon nanotubes are cylindrical fullerenes which have a high length to diameter ratio. Due to the strong covalent bonds between the carbons in the layers they have a high tensile strength. They are good electrical and heat conductors.

Polymers are very large molecules which are made up of long chains of carbon atoms joined by strong covalent bonds. As the chains are very long, the intermolecular forces between each chain are quite large and this means polymers are solids at room temperature.

DO IT!

You may have used a key in biology to identify plants or animals. You can use a key to identify lots of different things. A key will usually ask questions based on easily identifiable features of something.

Draw out a key for carbon structures which can be used to identify them using the structures and properties. The key should include graphite, diamond, polymers, graphene and fullerenes (spherical and nanotubes).

SNAP IT!

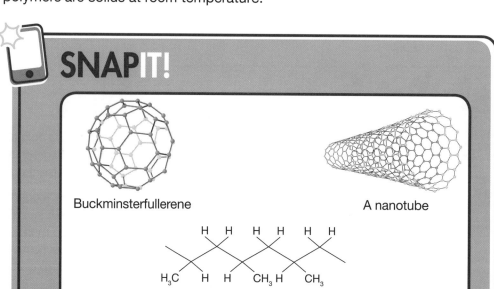

Buckminsterfullerene

A nanotube

A section of the polymer polypropene

CHECK IT!

1 a State how many carbon atoms there are in the smallest molecule of the buckminsterfullerene series of structures.

   b This substance has a simple molecular structure. Predict some of its physical properties.

2 Describe the properties of nanotubes.

3 Explain why nanotubes are used to reinforce tennis rackets.

4 State a use for buckminsterfullerene.

Giant metallic structures and alloys

Metals form a giant lattice of layers of positive metal ions (cations) in a sea of delocalised electrons which are free to move.

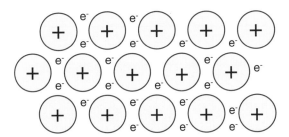

This diagram shows how the delocalised electrons can move around the positive metal ions.

The electrostatic attraction between the positive ions and the delocalised or free electrons is called a metallic bond. These metallic bonds are usually strong and need a lot of energy to overcome them, which is why most metals have high melting and boiling points.

The metallic bond is found in both pure metals and in alloys.

The layers of metal ions can slide over each other without disrupting the structure. This means that metals can be bent, shaped (they are malleable) and drawn into wires (they are ductile).

The delocalised electrons are free to move and can carry an electric current, so metals are good electrical conductors both as solids and liquids.

Metals are also good heat or thermal conductors because the electrons can transfer the heat along the metal.

Alloys are mixtures of metals.

Introducing different-sized metal atoms into a metal lattice makes it harder for the layers to slide over each other so alloys are harder than pure metals.

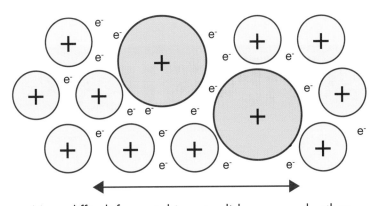

More difficult for metal ions to slide over each other

Car wheels are often made from alloys of magnesium or aluminium

DOIT!

Make a summary table for structure and fill it in. The headings are shown below:

Type of structure	Example	Particles present	Melting point and boiling point	Electrical conductivity	
				As solid	As liquid
Giant ionic					
Simple molecular					
Giant covalent					
Giant metallic					

NAILIT!

A common question is recognising the type of structure from the properties of a substance. These properties are usually melting points, boiling points and electrical conductivity in the solid and liquid states.

SNAPIT!

Property	For metals	Explanation
Melting and boiling point	Usually high	Strong metallic bonds in a giant lattice
Electrical conductivity as solid	Good	Delocalised electrons carry the current
Electrical conductivity as liquid	Good	Delocalised electrons carry current
Thermal (heat) conductivity	Good	Delocalised electrons transfer the heat energy
Malleability and ductility	Malleable (can be shaped) and ductile (can be drawn into wires)	Layers of metal ions can slide over each other without changing the structure

CHECKIT!

1 Describe a giant metallic lattice.

2 Explain why metals are good electrical conductors in both the solid and liquid form.

3 Explain the term alloy.

4 Explain why alloys are often harder than pure metals.

Nanoparticles

A nanometre (nm) is 1 billionth of a metre or 1×10^{-9} m.

Nanoparticles are 1 nm to 100 nm in size.

To get some idea of the size of nanoparticles, coarse particles or dust have diameters 1×10^{-5} m (10000 nm) and 2.5×10^{-5} m (25000 nm). This means that a small particle of dust has a diameter 100 times the diameter of the largest nanoparticle.

Fine particles have diameters between 100 nm and 2500 nm.

Nanoparticles have very high surface area to volume ratios.

Their large surface area means that they will react very quickly. It also means that they make very good catalysts.

Nanoparticles also have very different properties to the same substance in larger sized particles. For example, titanium dioxide is a dense white solid used in house paint because of its white colour. Titanium dioxide nanoparticles are so small they are transparent and do not reflect visible light. They are used in sunscreens.

Uses of nanoparticles include controlled delivery of drugs, cosmetics and sunscreen as well as antibacterial agents in clothing.

DOIT!

Research three uses of nanoparticles, especially noting the differences between the properties of the nanoparticles and the normal bulk properties.

WORKIT!

Suppose you have two cubes. The first cube has sides equal to 10 nm. The second smaller cube has sides equal to 1 nm. Work out the surface area to volume ratio of two cubes and explain what this tells us about the relationship between the size of particles and their surface area to volume ratio.

Cube 1 — its sides have an area of 100 nm^2. There are 6 sides so its total surface area is 600 nm^2.
Its volume = $10 \times 10 \times 10 \text{ nm}^3 = 1000 \text{ nm}^3$.
The surface area/volume ratio = $600/1000 = 0.6$.

Cube 2 — the second smaller cube has sides equal to 1 nm.
Its total surface area is 6 nm^2
Its volume is $1 \times 1 \times 1 = 1 \text{ nm}^3$.
The surface area/volume ratio = $6/1 = 6$. This is 10 times the surface area to volume ratio when the sides of the cube were 10 times bigger.

This shows that smaller particles have a greater surface area to volume ratio.

As the side of the cube decreases by a factor of 10 the surface area to volume ratio increases by a factor of 10.

MATHS SKILLS

You have to be aware of the high surface area to volume ratio of nanoparticles. To do this you must know how to work out areas and volumes.

If you have a cube with sides of length L, the area of each of its faces is L^2 and its volume is L^3.

CHECKIT!

1 Describe the range of sizes for nanoparticles.

2 List three uses for nanoparticles.

3 A cube has sides equal to 4 nm. What is its surface to volume ratio? What does this change to if the cubes are made smaller with 2 nm sides?

1 Explain how a lithium ion is formed from a lithium atom. [Atomic number of lithium = 3]

2 a State the size range for nanoparticles.

  b List three uses for nanoparticles.

3 When magnesium (atomic number 12) reacts with chlorine (atomic number 17) the ionic compound magnesium chloride is formed.

  a Showing the outer electrons only, draw dot-and-cross diagrams of magnesium and chloride ions.

  b State the formula of magnesium chloride.

  c Explain why magnesium chloride has a high melting point.

  d Why is solid magnesium chloride a poor electrical conductor?

4 Carbon (atomic number 6) and hydrogen (atomic number 1) combine to form methane (CH_4).

  a Draw a dot-and-cross diagram to show the bonding in methane.

  b Explain why methane is a gas at room temperature even though the bonds between the carbon and hydrogen are strong.

5 These diagrams show the structures of diamond and graphite.

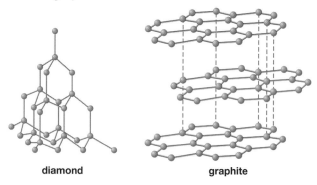

diamond   graphite

  a What type of structure do they both have?

  b Why do they both have high melting points?

  c Why is graphite slippery?

  d Explain why solid graphite is a good electrical conductor but solid diamond is a poor electrical conductor.

6 The table below shows the properties of four substances. The letters are not their symbols.

  Using the data in the table name the type of structure present in A to D.

Substance	Melting point /°C	Electrical conductivity	
		As solid	As liquid
A	−55	Poor	Poor
B	2015	Poor	Good
C	1897	Good	Good
D	2567	Poor	Poor

7 Using your knowledge of types of structure, explain the following observations:

  a Methane has a lower melting and boiling point than potassium chloride.

  b Magnesium oxide has a higher melting point than potassium chloride.

  c Brass (an alloy of copper and zinc) is harder than pure copper.

  d Sodium conducts electricity in both the solid and liquid state but sodium chloride only conducts electricity in the liquid state or in a solution.

Quantitative chemistry

Conservation of mass and balancing equations

In chemical equations the reactants are written on the left-hand side and the products on the right-hand side.

Chemical formulae are used to represent the substances in the reactants and the products.

The law of conservation of mass states that no atoms are lost or gained during a chemical reaction.

Therefore, when you represent chemical reactions by chemical equations there must be the same number of each type of atom on both sides of the equation. This means that the equation must be **balanced**.

One consequence of this is that the mass of the reactants is equal to the mass of the products.

If the chemical container is open and gas is consumed or produced in a reaction, the mass appears to go up or down respectively but in terms of the atoms taking part it really has not changed.

Example:

$CaCO_3(s) + 2HNO_3(aq) \rightarrow Ca(NO_3)_2(aq) + H_2O(l) + CO_2(g)$

The mass appears to diminish because the CO_2 gas comes off from the reaction.

NAILIT!

Chemical equations can also be called symbol equations. Make sure you know how to balance chemical equations as they are worth lots of marks in the exam.

SNAPIT!

The diagram below shows apparatus that could be used to prove that the law of conservation of mass is true. Your teacher may have demonstrated this in class. There is a bung in the top of the flask so that no substances can enter or leave. Once the reactants have mixed and the reaction has started the top-pan balance shows that the mass does not change.

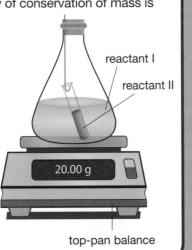

reactant I

reactant II

20.00 g

top-pan balance

DOIT!

Take the following equation and explain to a revision partner why the equation has to be balanced and show them how it should be balanced. If working alone, write down your notes and check against your textbook.

$Fe_2O_3 + Al \rightarrow Fe + Al_2O_3$

NAIL IT!

Balancing equations and being able to interpret them is one of the vital skills you need to get a good grade in chemistry. One thing that you may have to do is to balance equations that have in them negative acid groups such as nitrate (NO_3^-) and sulfate (SO_4^{2-}) or positive ammonium (NH_4^+). You must remember that if you have more than one of these groups in a compound then brackets are placed round the group.

For example, calcium nitrate contains the Ca^{2+} ion and the NO_3^- ion. Calcium nitrate's formula is therefore $Ca(NO_3)_2$.

When balancing equations like this treat the nitrate group like a single atom except when there is more than one, then they need brackets round them.

WORK IT!

The reaction between ammonia and copper(II) oxide gives nitrogen, copper and water as products. Write a balanced chemical equation for this reaction.

The unbalanced chemical equation may be written as
$$NH_3 + CuO \rightarrow N_2 + Cu + H_2O.$$

NH_3 and N_2 are both gases so are followed by (g); CuO and Cu are solids, followed by (s) and H_2O is a liquid (l).

The number of nitrogen and hydrogen atoms are unequal and so the equation needs balancing. To balance it you can balance the nitrogen atoms first to give 2 on each side. Then the hydrogen atoms – 6 on each side – followed by the oxygen atoms – 3 on each side and the copper atoms – 3 on each side.

The final equation is
$$2NH_3(g) + 3CuO(s) \rightarrow N_2(g) + 3Cu(s) + 3H_2O(l)$$

MATHS SKILLS

A balanced chemical equation has the same number of each type of atom in the reactants as there are in the products.

When you balance a chemical equation the first thing you must remember is **not to change the formulae!**

You can only write numbers in normal-sized writing **before the formulae.**

Stage 1 – work out which atoms are not equal in number on both sides of the equation. Balance these by putting numbers in the correct places.

Stage 2 – see which atoms are now wrong in number and balance them and continue until the atoms are equal in number on both sides.

CHECK IT! ✓

1 When magnesium is heated with aluminium oxide, magnesium oxide and aluminium are formed.

   a In this reaction, identify which are the reactants and which are the products.

   b If 72 g of magnesium completely reacts with 103 g of aluminium oxide, what is the total mass of aluminium and magnesium oxide formed?

2 a Write the word equation for the following **unbalanced** chemical equation:

   $$HCl + CaCO_3 \rightarrow CaCl_2 + H_2O + CO_2$$

   b Write out the balanced chemical equation.

   c Add state symbols to the equation.

   d If this reaction was carried out in an open container the measured mass would decrease. Explain why.

Relative formula masses

The relative atomic mass (symbol = A_r) of an element is the weighted average mass of its naturally occurring isotopes.

You calculate the relative formula mass (symbol = M_r) of a compound by adding up all the relative atomic masses of all the atoms present in the formula of the compound.

The elements hydrogen, oxygen, nitrogen, chlorine, bromine, iodine and fluorine exist as diatomic molecules. This means that in equations their relative formula masses are twice their relative atomic masses.

All other elements are represented by just their symbols in an equation. So their relative formula mass is equal to their relative atomic mass.

Using the law of conservation of mass we can say that in a chemical reaction the sum of the relative formula masses of the reactants is equal to the sum of the relative formula masses of the products.

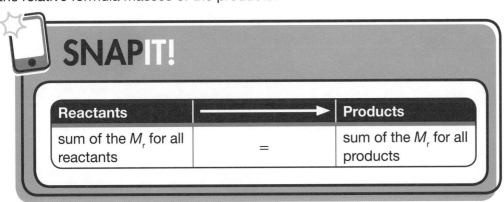

SNAPIT!

Reactants		Products
sum of the M_r for all reactants	$=$	sum of the M_r for all products

For example, when calcium carbonate (formula mass = 100) is heated it decomposes to calcium oxide (formula mass = 56) and carbon dioxide. This means that the formula mass of carbon dioxide equals 44.

MATHS SKILLS

In a chemical formula, the number to the right-hand side of an atom is the number of that type of atom in the compound. For example, in carbon dioxide CO_2 there is 1 carbon atom and 2 oxygen atoms.

Also, when there is a group of atoms such as hydroxide and there are brackets around the group in the formula, then you multiply whatever is inside by the number outside it.

For example, calcium hydroxide $Ca(OH)_2$ has 1 calcium, 2 oxygens and 2 hydrogens.

NAILIT!

The elements hydrogen, oxygen, nitrogen, chlorine, bromine, iodine and fluorine exist as diatomic molecules. This means that in equations hydrogen is written as H_2, oxygen as O_2, etc. They can be remembered as HONClBrIF. Say it as a way of remembering it.

DOIT!

If you do not like using HONClBrIF to remember the elements that exist as molecules of 2 atoms (diatomic molecules) then make up a mnemonic as an aid to remember it.

WORKIT!

a Find the relative formula mass of aluminium oxide Al_2O_3.

There are 2 aluminium atoms and 3 oxygen atoms. The relative
formula mass = $(2 \times 27) + (3 \times 16) = 102$.

b Find the relative formula mass of calcium nitrate $Ca(NO_3)_2$.

In this formula there is 1 calcium atom and 2 times whatever is inside the
brackets. This means there are 2 nitrogen atoms and 6 oxygen atoms so the
relative formula mass = $(1 \times 40) + (2 \times 14) + (6 \times 16) = 164$.

NAILIT!

You do not have to remember relative atomic masses of elements. You will be given a periodic table showing them. Make sure you use the right number. The relative atomic mass is the top one.

CHECKIT!

1 State the relative formula masses of the following compounds:

  a CaO

  b $MgCl_2$

  c KNO_3

  d $Al_2(SO_4)_3$

2 The balanced equation below represents the reaction taking place when silver carbonate is heated:

$$2Ag_2CO_3(s) \rightarrow 4Ag(s) + 2CO_2(g) + O_2(g)$$

  a If 552 g of silver carbonate is heated, 88 g of carbon dioxide and 32 g of oxygen are formed. Calculate the mass of silver produced by the reaction.

  b What law are you applying in your calculation?

The mole

The **amount** of a chemical substance is measured in moles (unit = mol).

The number of atoms, ions or molecules in a mole is equal to Avogadro's constant **(N_A)**. The value of this is 6.02×10^{23}.

This number applies to all particles. For example, there are the same number of CH_4 molecules in 1 mole of methane as there are sodium atoms in 1 mole of the element sodium.

The mass of 1 mole of any substance is its relative formula mass expressed in grams.

The number of moles of a substance is equal to its mass in grams divided by its relative formula mass.

SNAPIT!

The equations for moles and number of particles

$m = n \times M_r$ number of of particles = $n \times N_A$

$n = m \div M_r$

$M_r = m \div n$

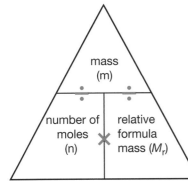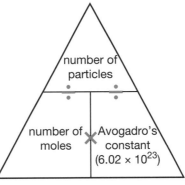

There are two ways of learning the equations – either using the triangles or learning one equation and then rearranging it.

Consider the left-hand triangle. You have to use the operations shown in the triangle. This means that the top quantity m = the product of the two bottom quantities $n \times M_r$. The bottom left-hand quantity n = the top quantity m divided by the bottom left, and so on.

DO IT!

Test out your understanding of putting numbers in standard form by writing 0.000065 in standard form.

Type 0.000065 into your calculator then press =. You should get 6.5×10^{-5}. Were you correct?

On some calculators you may need to press S↔D before getting your answer.

Test yourself on some other numbers. Remember, you will be asked to express answers to 3 significant figures.

MATHS SKILLS

Use the calculation triangles to construct formulae for your calculations.

$n = m/M_r$ $m = n \times M_r$ no. of particles = $n \times N_A$

When using Avogadro's constant you need to know how to use your calculator.

Type in 6.02 then press the [x10^x] button and then 23. You will get 6.02×10^{23}

NAIL IT!

Know the relationships:
$n = m/M_r$
$m = n \times M_r$
number of particles $= n \times N_A$.

You need to be able to write down large numbers like Avogadro's constant in **standard form**.

The same applies to very small numbers. For example 0.00041 is expressed as 4.1×10^{-4}.

WORKIT!

How many moles of carbon dioxide (CO_2) are there in 2.2 g of the substance?

The relative formula mass of carbon dioxide = 44

This means that ← (see left-hand triangle on page 55)
$n = m/M_r = 2.2/44 = 0.05$ mol

How many carbon dioxide particles are there in the same mass of the substance?

Number of CO_2 particles = number of moles × Avogadro's constant

$$= 0.05 \times 6.02 \times 10^{23}$$

$$= 3.1 \times 10^{22}$$

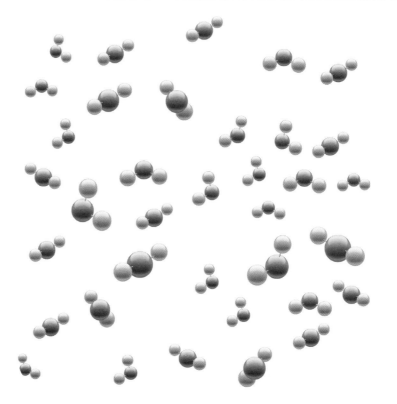

CHECKIT!

1 State how many particles of a substance are found in 1 mole of the substance.

2 Describe how you would find the mass of one mole of a compound.

3 a Calculate the relative formula mass of sulfur dioxide (SO_2).

   b Calculate how many moles there are in 1.6 g of sulfur dioxide.

   c Calculate how many sulfur dioxide molecules there are in 1.6 g of the substance.

Reacting masses and using moles to balance equations

You can tell how many moles of a substance react or are produced in a reaction from the numbers in front of the formulae in the balanced chemical equation.

When you are given the masses that react you can convert these into moles and then use the equation to find the masses of the substances produced by using the ratios in the equation.

The same applies to finding the mass of reactants needed to produce a certain mass of products.

If you know the masses of reactants and products in a reaction you can convert these to moles and use the results to balance the equation.

DO IT!

Have a go at calculating one of the Work It! questions from page 58 yourself. Record yourself explaining how you would work it out and compare to the solution given.

SNAP IT!

Finding masses produced in chemical reactions

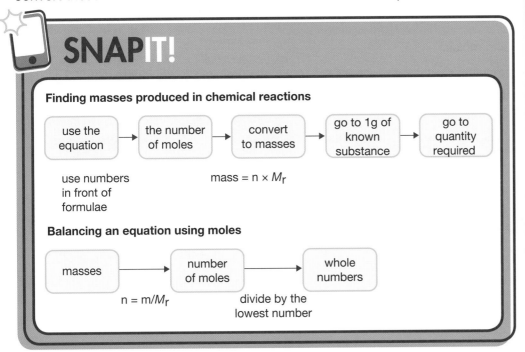

| use the equation | → | the number of moles | → | convert to masses | → | go to 1g of known substance | → | go to quantity required |

use numbers in front of formulae

$$mass = n \times M_r$$

Balancing an equation using moles

| masses | → | number of moles | → | whole numbers |

$$n = m/M_r$$

divide by the lowest number

MATHS SKILLS

1   To work out the **mass of a substance produced** see the first worked example in the Work It! on page 58.

2   To see how to **balance an equation** see the second worked example in the Work It! on page 58.

NAIL IT!

When you answer this type of numerical question and you are using a calculator, it is sometimes tempting to just write down the answer. This is not a good idea because if you make a mistake using the calculator and give the wrong answer without any working you will not get any marks. Always show your working and you will get credit for the correct approach.

You should also make sure your calculator will give an answer that enables you to quote your answer to 3 significant figures and will give the answer in standard form. For example:

$45 \div 4789$

If you use the scientific mode there is no problem. You can ask for 3 figures and you get 9.40×10^{-3}. So make sure you have it in this setup.

WORKIT!

1 Mass of a substance produced.

Calculate the mass of silver formed when 23.2 g of silver oxide is heated.

NOTE: Formula masses $Ag_2O = 232$; $Ag = 108$.

1. Write the balanced equation.	$2Ag_2O$	⟶	$4Ag$	$+ \; O_2$
2. Use the equation to find the number of moles of reactants and products.	2 moles of silver oxide	give	4 moles of silver	You are not asked about the oxygen.
3. Convert these moles to masses.	$2 \times 232g = 464g$	give	$4 \times 108g = 432g$	Remember a mole is the M_r in g.
4. IMPORTANT Go down to 1g of reactant to make calculation easier.	$1g$	give	$432/464g$	Divide both sides by 464.
5. Go to the desired quantity.	$23.2g$	give	$\dfrac{23.2 \times 432}{464}g$ $= 21.6g$	This will give 23.2 times whatever 1g gives.

2 Balancing equations using moles.

In the reaction between aluminium oxide and magnesium, 10.2 g of aluminium oxide reacts with 7.2 g of magnesium to give 5.4 g of aluminium and 12.0 g of magnesium oxide. Use these results to find the balanced equation for the reaction. [M_r $Al_2O_3 = 102$; $Mg = 24$; $Al = 27$ and $MgO = 40$]

Write word equation	Aluminium oxide +	magnesium ⟶	aluminium	+	magnesium oxide
Write down the masses	$10.2g$ +	$7.2g$	$5.4g$		$12.0g$
Convert these masses to moles	$\dfrac{10.2}{102} = 0.1\,mol$	$\dfrac{7.2}{24} = 0.3\,mol$	$\dfrac{5.4}{27} = 0.2\,mol$		$\dfrac{12.0}{40} = 0.3\,mol$
Divide by the lowest number which is 0.1 to give simplest whole-number ratio	$\dfrac{0.1}{0.1} = 1$	$\dfrac{0.3}{0.1} = 3$	$\dfrac{0.2}{0.1} = 2$		$\dfrac{0.3}{0.1} = 3$
Write out the balanced equation	Al_2O_3 +	$3Mg$ ⟶	$2Al$	+	$3MgO$

CHECKIT! ✓

1 Calculate the mass of silver that could be formed from 6.35 g of copper when copper is added to silver nitrate solution:

$Cu(s) + 2AgNO_3(aq) \rightarrow Cu(NO_3)_2(aq) + 2Ag(s)$

2 When 68 g of silver nitrate ($AgNO_3$) is heated it decomposes to form 43.2 g of silver (Ag), 18.4 g of nitrogen dioxide (NO_2) and 6.4 g of oxygen O_2.

Use this data to write a balanced equation for the reaction. You must show all your working.

[Relative formula masses: $AgNO_3 = 170$; $Ag = 108$; $NO_2 = 46$; $O_2 = 32$]

Limiting reactant

If there are two reactants in a chemical reaction and there is an excess (more than needed) of one of them then the other reactant is called the limiting reactant.

The amounts of the products formed depend on the amount of the limiting reactant.

The limiting reactant is identified by comparing the number of moles of each reactant with those required by the balanced chemical equation.

At the end of the reaction the limiting reactant is completely used up and the reactant in excess remains along with the products.

SNAPIT!

Identifying the limiting reactant in a reaction

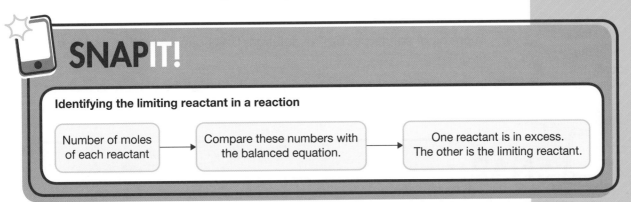

Number of moles of each reactant → Compare these numbers with the balanced equation. → One reactant is in excess. The other is the limiting reactant.

WORKIT!

The equation for the reaction between zinc and hydrochloric acid is
$Zn(s) + 2HCl(aq) \rightarrow ZnCl_2(aq) + H_2(g)$

If 0.10 mol of zinc is added to 0.3 mol of hydrochloric acid what is the limiting reactant?

From the equation 2 mol of hydrochloric acid react with 1 mol of zinc, and this means that 0.1 mol of zinc needs exactly 0.2 mol of hydrochloric acid to react.

This means that 0.3 mol of hydrochloric acid is in excess and the limiting reactant is zinc. As there is 0.1 mol of zinc this means that we will get 0.1 mol of hydrogen and 0.1 mol of zinc chloride.

MATHS SKILLS

To identify the limiting reactant, you work out the number of moles of each reactant and then compare with what is needed using the chemical equation for the reaction.

✓ CHECKIT!

1 Magnesium and sulfuric acid react as follows:

$Mg(s) + H_2SO_4(aq) \rightarrow MgSO_4(aq) + H_2(g)$

1.00 mol of magnesium is added to 0.90 mol of sulfuric acid.

a Identify the limiting reactant.

b Explain your answer.

c How many moles of hydrogen are produced in the reaction?

Concentrations in solutions

In a solution the substance being dissolved is called the solute and the liquid in which it dissolves is called the solvent.

A solution in water (a solvent) is described as an aqueous solution.

The greater the number of moles of solute dissolved in a solution, the more concentrated it is. If the amount of water is increased, then the solution becomes more dilute.

To compare the concentrations of solutions we use the amount of solute dissolved in 1 dm³ (1000 cm³).

The concentration of a solution can be expressed in two different ways:

1 In grams of solute per dm³ of solution. Units can be written as g per dm³ or g/dm³.

2 In moles of solute per dm³ of solution. Units can be written as mol per dm³ or mol/dm³.

DO IT!

Get all the 'calculation triangles' together and put them onto a sheet which you can put on your wall. Every so often when you take a break, look at the sheet. Gradually the information will sink in!

SNAPIT!

The equation triangles are shown below

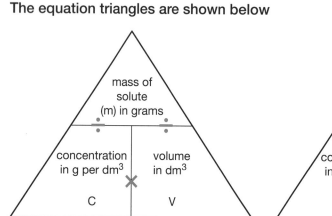
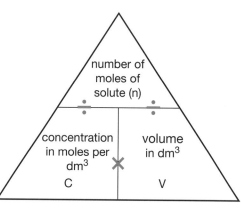

NAILIT!

Always convert the volume of a solution to dm³ if it is given as cm³.
1 cm³ = 1/1000 dm³
= 1 × 10⁻³ dm³
= 0.001 dm³.

MATHS SKILLS

Make sure you can use the formulae from these triangles:

C = m/V
m = C × V
V = m/C
C = n/V
n = C × V
V = n/C

NAILIT!

Remember that concentration is not the same as strength!

WORKIT!

A solution contains 0.400 g of sodium hydroxide (M_r of NaOH = 40) in 100 cm³ of solution. What is the concentration of the solution in both g per dm³ and moles per dm³?

Use the equations $C = m/V$; $n = m/M_r$ and then $C = n/V$.

$C = m/V$; $V = 100/1000 \, dm^3 = 0.100 \, dm^3$.

The concentration = 0.400/0.1 g
per dm³ = 4.00 g per dm³.

Use $n = m/M_r = 0.4/40 \, mol = 0.01 \, mol$.
The concentration = 0.0100/0.100 mol/dm³
= 0.100 mol/dm³

NAILIT!

If memorising the equation triangles is not your way of learning, then think of how we express concentration. The units of concentration are mol/dm³. Which is saying $C = n/V$. From there you can rearrange the equation to find V and n. The same applies to the formula $C = m/V$.

NAILIT!

As with all the other topics where calculations are made, make sure you show your working. Also, when the question is longer, highlight the part of the question that tells you what you have to find. Use questions in the Check It! box below as an example.

CHECKIT!

1 A solution of hydrochloric acid contains 0.1 mol in 500 cm³.

   What is its concentration?

   a in mol/dm³

   b in g/dm³

2 A solution has a concentration of 0.2 mol/dm³. Calculate many moles of solute there are in 250 cm³ of the solution.

Moles in solution

NAIL IT!

Do not forget to convert the volumes of the solution from cm³ to dm³. If you are asked to find the volume of a solution do not forget that your answer will give you the number of dm³ required. **Do not give it as cm³ unless the question asks for the volume in cm³ and then you must multiply your answer by 1000.**

Titrations are used to find the volumes of acids and alkalis that react together in a neutralisation reaction.

The reaction is complete when an indicator changes colour.

If you know the concentration of one of the two solutions, and the volumes of both, then you can find the concentration of the other solution.

The solution you know the concentration of is called the **standard solution**.

SNAP IT!

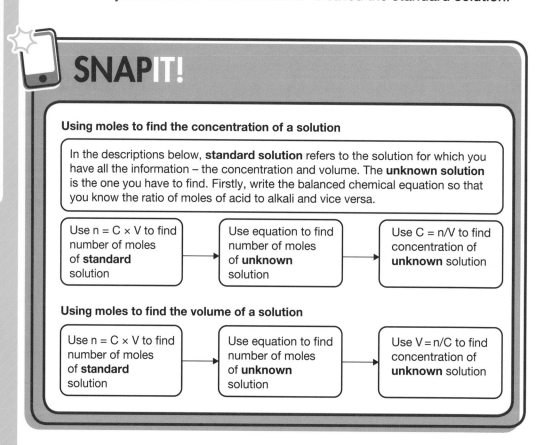

Using moles to find the concentration of a solution

In the descriptions below, **standard solution** refers to the solution for which you have all the information – the concentration and volume. The **unknown solution** is the one you have to find. Firstly, write the balanced chemical equation so that you know the ratio of moles of acid to alkali and vice versa.

| Use n = C × V to find number of moles of **standard** solution | → | Use equation to find number of moles of **unknown** solution | → | Use C = n/V to find concentration of **unknown** solution |

Using moles to find the volume of a solution

| Use n = C × V to find number of moles of **standard** solution | → | Use equation to find number of moles of **unknown** solution | → | Use V = n/C to find concentration of **unknown** solution |

MATHS SKILLS

Rearrange the equation for concentration with the three different quantities. See the Snap It! box above for the procedure.

Practical Skills

One of the practicals is the titration of a strong acid against a strong alkali. You will also have to determine the concentration of one of these solutions using the known concentration of the other. This practical technique is covered on page 90.

WORKIT!

The concentration of a solution of sodium hydroxide is 1 mole per dm^3.
In a titration experiment, $20\,cm^3$ of this sodium hydroxide solution needed
$40\,cm^3$ of sulfuric acid for complete reaction. What is the concentration of
the sulfuric acid?

Procedure

1. Write the equation.
$2NaOH(aq) + H_2SO_4(aq) \rightarrow Na_2SO_4(aq) + 2H_2O(l)$

2. Write down the information.

$V = 20\,cm^3$
$= 20/1000\,dm^3$
$= 0.02\,dm^3$
Concentration
$= 1\,mol\ per\ dm^3$

$V = 40\,cm^3$
$= 40/1000\,dm^3$
$= 0.04\,dm^3$
Concentration
unknown

3. Find the number of moles of NaOH.
$n = C \times V$
$= 1 \times 0.02$
$= 0.02\,mol$

4. Use the equation to find the number of moles of the H_2SO_4 by using the molar ratios of acid to alkali.

In the equation there are 2 of these to 1 of the H_2SO_4

Number of mol
$= \frac{1}{2} \times 0.02$
$= 0.01\,mol$

5. Now use $C = n/V$ to find the concentration of the H_2SO_4.

$C = n/V$
$= 0.01/0.04$
$= 0.25\,mol/dm^3$

✓ CHECKIT!

1 Potassium hydroxide (KOH) and nitric acid (HNO_3) react with each other as follows:

$HNO_3(aq) + KOH(aq) \rightarrow KNO_3(aq) + H_2O(l)$

A solution of potassium hydroxide has a concentration of $0.200\,mol/dm^3$. In an experiment to find the concentration of a solution of nitric acid, $20.0\,cm^3$ of the potassium hydroxide solution needed $30.0\,cm^3$ of the acid for complete reaction.
Calculate the concentration of the nitric acid.

2 When hydrochloric acid is added to a solution of sodium carbonate the following reaction takes place:

$2HCl(aq) + Na_2CO_3(aq) \rightarrow 2NaCl(aq) + H_2O(l) + CO_2(g)$

In an experiment the concentration of the sodium carbonate was $0.500\,mol/dm^3$ and the concentration of the hydrochloric acid was $1.00\,mol/dm^3$. What volume of the acid is required to react completely with $20\,cm^3$ of the sodium carbonate solution?

Moles and gas volumes

At the same temperature and pressure equal volumes of different gases contain the same number of molecules.

This means that under the same conditions equal volumes of gases have the same number of moles present.

At room temperature (20 °C or 293 k) and 1 atmosphere pressure (RTP), 1 mole of any gas occupies a volume of 24 dm³ (24 000 cm³).

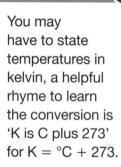

DO IT!

Your sheet of calculation triangles is almost complete. Review all the formulae and test yourself. Come back to them every so often. This will improve your recall.

STRETCH IT!

You may have to state temperatures in kelvin, a helpful rhyme to learn the conversion is 'K is C plus 273' for K = °C + 273.

SNAP IT!

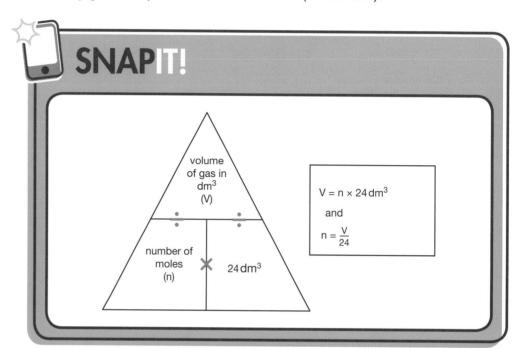

$$V = n \times 24\,dm^3$$

and

$$n = \frac{V}{24}$$

volume of gas in dm³ (V)

number of moles (n)   ✕   24 dm³

NAIL IT!

Remember all the rules we have about amounts of substances also apply to gases. This means that if we know the mass of a gas we can find its volume and if we know its volume we can find its mass.

(RTP = Room temperature and 1 atmosphere pressure)

Mass of gas (g) ⟶ Number of moles of gas ⟶ Volume at RTP (dm³)

$$n = \frac{m}{M_r}$$

$$V = n \times 24\,dm^3$$

Volume at RTP (dm³) ⟶ Number of moles of gas ⟶ Mass of gas

$$n = \frac{V}{24} \text{ (in dm}^3)$$

$$m = n \times M_r$$

WORKIT!

A gas occupies 800 cm³ at RTP. How many moles of gas is this?

Use the equation $n = \frac{V}{24}$. Remember 24 refers to dm³ and therefore we have to convert the 800 cm³ to dm³. This means that $V = \frac{800}{1000}$ dm³ $= 0.8$ dm³. Therefore the number of moles of gas $(n) = \frac{0.8}{24}$ mol
$$= 0.0333 \text{ mol or } 3.33 \times 10^{-2} \text{ mol}.$$

When hydrochloric acid is added to calcium carbonate it forms a solution of calcium chloride, water and carbon dioxide gas.

$$2HCl(aq) + CaCO_3(s) \rightarrow CaCl_2(aq) + H_2O(l) + CO_2(g)$$

a Calculate the volume of carbon dioxide gas given off at RTP when ◀ 0.2 mol of hydrochloric acid is added to an excess of calcium carbonate.

Limiting reactants are explained on page 59.

From the equation 2 mol of hydrochloric acid give 1 mol of carbon dioxide gas. This means that 0.2 mol of HCl will give 0.1 mol of CO_2. This amount of gas at RTP occupies 0.10×24.0 dm³ $= 2.40$ dm³.

b What is the mass of this volume of carbon dioxide?

Number of moles of gas = 0.10 mol

The relative formula mass of carbon dioxide = 44

The mass of $CO_2 = n \times M_r = 0.10 \times 44 g = 4.40 g$

✓ CHECKIT!

1 Give the formula to find the number of moles of a gas and its volume at RTP.

2 A gas occupies 120 cm³ at RTP. How many moles of gas is this?

3 What is the mass of oxygen (O_2) gas that occupies 480 cm³ at RTP? [M_r of $O_2 = 32$]

4 When silver oxide (Ag_2O ($M_r = 232$)) is heated the following decomposition reaction takes place:

$$2Ag_2O(s) \rightarrow 4Ag(s) + O_2(g)$$

a How many moles of silver oxide (Ag_2O) are there in 11.6 g of the compound?

b What is the volume of oxygen produced at RTP when 11.6 g of silver oxide is heated? [Hint: 2 mol of silver oxide give 1 mol of oxygen]

c What is the mass of this volume of oxygen?

d Using the law of conservation of mass calculate the mass of silver produced.

Percentage yield and atom economy

$$\text{Percentage yield} = \frac{\text{mass of product actually made}}{\text{maximum theoretical mass of product}} \times 100\%$$

The maximum theoretical yield is the maximum mass of product that could be made.

The percentage yield is an indication of the efficiency of a chemical process.

NAILIT!

There are a few reasons why the percentage yield drops to below 100%:

- Some of the product may be lost in the purification or separation process.
- The products may react back to give the reactants in a reversible process.
- There may be other reactions taking place that do not give the desired product.

The atom economy is a measure of how much of the reactants end up as useful products.

Atom economy = $\frac{\text{mass of wanted product(s)}}{\text{total mass of product(s)}}$ x 100%

If there is only one product then the atom economy is 100%.

WORKIT!

In an experiment to demonstrate the thermite reaction, excess aluminium reacted with 8.00 g of iron(III) oxide to give iron and 5.10 g of aluminium oxide.

The equation for the reaction is: $2Al(s) + Fe_2O_3(s) \rightarrow 2Fe(s) + Al_2O_3(s)$

a i What is the limiting reactant in this reaction?

The iron(III) oxide is the limiting reactant because the aluminium is in excess.

ii Calculate the maximum theoretical yield of iron in the reaction.

From the equation 1 mol of iron(III) oxide gives 2 mol of iron.

iii If 4.2 g of iron was formed, what is the percentage yield?

Therefore 160 g of iron(III) oxide gives $2 \times 56 = 112$ g of iron.

This means that 1 g of iron(III) oxide gives $\frac{112}{160}$ g of iron.

Therefore 8 g of iron(III) oxide should give $8 \times \frac{112}{160}$ g of iron = 5.6 g

The percentage yield = $\frac{\text{mass of product actually made}}{\text{maximum theoretical mass of product}} \times 100\%$

$= \frac{4.2}{5.5} \times 100\% = 75\%$

b What is the atom economy for this reaction if the desired product was iron?
[M_r Al = 27; Fe_2O_3 = 160; Fe = 56; Al_2O_3 = 102]

Atom economy of a reaction = $\frac{\text{relative formula mass of desired product in the reaction}}{\text{sum of relative formula masses of reactants}} \times 100\%$

In this reaction the atom economy = $\frac{2 \times 56}{2 \times 27 + 160} \times 100\% = \frac{112}{214} \times 100\%$

$= 52.3\%$

CHECKIT!

1 If the actual yield of product in a reaction is 24.0 g and the theoretical yield is 96.0 g, what is the percentage yield? Explain why it is not 100%.

2 The equations below show two methods to prepare ammonia (NH_3). Calculate the atom economy for both methods:

a $NH_4Cl(s) + NaOH(aq) \rightarrow NH_3(g) + NaCl(s) + H_2O(l)$

b $N_2(g) + 3H_2(g) \rightleftharpoons 2NH_3(g)$

Quantitative chemistry

For this set of questions you will need your periodic table. You will also need to use the following information:

Avogadro's constant $(N_A) = 6.02 \times 10^{23}$; 1 mole of any gas occupies $24\,dm^3$ at RTP.

You should also refer to the formulae sheets that you have been making during this topic. Have your list of formulae ready.

1 a Express the following numbers in standard form:

    i 0.0833   ii 223 000
    iii 856.1   iv 0.0000453

  b Write the following numbers in standard form and to three significant figures.

    i 4   ii 0.06572   iii 0.04550
    iv 0.0004389   v 567900

2 a Balance the following equations:

    i $H_2(g) + Cl_2(g) \rightarrow HCl(g)$
    ii $Na(s) + Br_2(l) \rightarrow NaBr(s)$
    iii $K(s) + N_2(g) \rightarrow K_3N(s)$
    iv $Mg(s) + AgNO_3(aq) \rightarrow Mg(NO_3)_2(aq) + Ag(s)$
    v $Na(s) + O_2(g) \rightarrow Na_2O(s)$

  b Explain why these equations have to be balanced.

3 Calculate the relative formula masses of the following compounds:

  a K_2O b $Ca(OH)_2$ c $Mg(NO_3)_2$ d $Al(OH)_2$
  e potassium sulfate   f copper(II) chloride
  g silicon dioxide

4 a Calculate the relative formula mass of CO_2.

  b How many moles of carbon dioxide are present in 4.4 g of CO_2?

  c How many CO_2 molecules are there in 4.4 g of CO_2?

  d What is the volume of this mass of CO_2 at RTP?

5 The equations below show two ways by which carbon dioxide can be prepared:

    i $2HCl(aq) + CaCO_3(s) \rightarrow CaCl_2(aq) + H_2O(l) + CO_2(g)$
    ii $C(s) + O_2(g) \rightarrow CO_2(g)$

  a Calculate the atom economies of both methods.

  b Why is atom economy important to chemists?

6 The equation below represents the reaction between sodium hydroxide and hydrochloric acid:

$HCl(aq) + NaOH(aq) \rightarrow NaCl(aq) + H_2O(l)$

In one experiment on this reaction $20.0\,cm^3$ of hydrochloric acid reacted with $30.0\,cm^3$ of NaOH which had a concentration of 1 mole per dm^3. What is the concentration of the acid?

7 Magnesium and hydrochloric acid react as follows:

$Mg(s) + 2HCl(aq) \rightarrow MgCl_2(aq) + H_2(g)$

6 g of magnesium are added to $200\,cm^3$ of hydrochloric acid with a concentration of 1 mole per dm^3.

  a How many moles of magnesium are there in 6 g of the metal?

  b How many moles of hydrochloric acid were used?

  c Explain which of the two reactants was the limiting reactant.

Chemical changes

Metal oxides and the reactivity series

Most metals react with oxygen to form metal oxides.

Gain of oxygen is oxidation and loss of oxygen is reduction.

The reactivity series (see Snap It! box on page 69) is an arrangement of the metals in order of their reactivity. The non-metals carbon and hydrogen are sometimes included for comparison.

When metals react they lose electrons to form positive ions (cations). The more reactive the metal the more easily it loses electrons.

Metals that react with water at room temperature give metal hydroxides and hydrogen gas is produced. For example, when calcium is added to water, calcium hydroxide is formed along with hydrogen.

$$Ca(s) + 2H_2O(l) \rightarrow Ca(OH)_2(aq) + H_2(g)$$

When metals react with dilute acids, metal salts are produced and hydrogen gas is given off. For example, when magnesium is added to hydrochloric acid the salt formed is magnesium chloride and hydrogen is also given off.

$$Mg(s) + 2HCl(aq) \rightarrow MgCl_2(aq) + H_2(g)$$

More reactive metals will displace less reactive metals from solutions of metal salts.

For example, magnesium is more reactive than iron. This means that if magnesium is added to a solution of iron(II) sulfate the iron is displaced to give a solution of magnesium sulfate and iron.

$$Mg(s) + FeSO_4(aq) \rightarrow Fe(s) + MgSO_4(aq)$$

NAIL IT!

Oxidation is also loss of electrons and loss of hydrogen, and reduction is also gain of electrons and gain of hydrogen. REDOX is oxidation and reduction happening in the same reaction.

NAIL IT!

Metal salts are formed when the hydrogen in an acid molecule is replaced by a metal atom. For example, sulfuric acid, H_2SO_4, has two replaceable hydrogens and either one or both of them can be replaced. This means that salts of sulfuric acid include $NaHSO_4$, Na_2SO_4 and $MgSO_4$.

Crystals of iron(II) sulfate

SNAPIT!

The reactivity series

This diagram shows the relative reactivity of some common metals. The way to remember the order is simply to say **PoSLiCaMZICSG**. The letter(s) representing the metals are not necessarily their usual symbols.

The reactivity series

MOST REACTIVE ⟶ LEAST REACTIVE

Potassium **S**odium **Li**thium **Ca**lcium | **M**agnesium **Z**inc **I**ron **L**ead | **C**opper **S**ilver **G**old

These metals react with cold water to give hydrogen and a metal hydroxide

These metals react with dilute acids to give a metal salt and hydrogen

Hydrogen

Carbon

Silver and gold are so unreactive they are found uncombined

DOIT!

If you do not like the **phonetic** method of remembering the reactivity series (PoSLiCaMZICSG), make up your own mnemonic.

CHECKIT!

1 State what is formed when a metal atom reacts.

2 Which is more reactive, carbon or copper?

3 List what is formed when lithium is added to water.

4 Write the word equation and balanced chemical equation for the reaction between hydrogen (H_2) and copper(II) oxide (CuO).

5 Write the word equation and balanced chemical equation for the reaction between magnesium (Mg) and copper sulfate ($CuSO_4$).

6 State what is formed when dilute hydrochloric acid is added to:

 a zinc metal

 b copper metal.

Extraction of metals and reduction

Metals in the Earth's crust are found in rocks called ores. These ores contain enough of the metal to make it worthwhile to use them.

Unreactive metals are known as native metals. These are gold, silver, platinum and copper. They are found uncombined with other elements and don't need chemical reactions to extract them.

If a metal is less reactive than carbon then it can be extracted by heating the metal oxide with carbon. The metal oxide is reduced by losing its oxygen, this process is known as smelting.

Iron is less reactive than carbon and iron(III) oxide (Fe_2O_3) is reduced to iron by heating with carbon in the blast furnace. In fact, the reducing agent is carbon monoxide (CO).

$$Fe_2O_3(s) + 3CO(g) \rightarrow 2Fe(s) + 3CO_2(g)$$

DO IT!

One way of getting the reactivity series into perspective and to see why it is useful is to consider the uses of some of the metals. For example, copper is very unreactive which makes it useful for pipes because it will not react with the water. Consider some of the other metals on the list like magnesium and sodium.

STRETCH IT!

Aluminium is a reactive metal but can be used for cooking foil and aeroplane fuselages. Do some research to find out why.

SNAP IT!

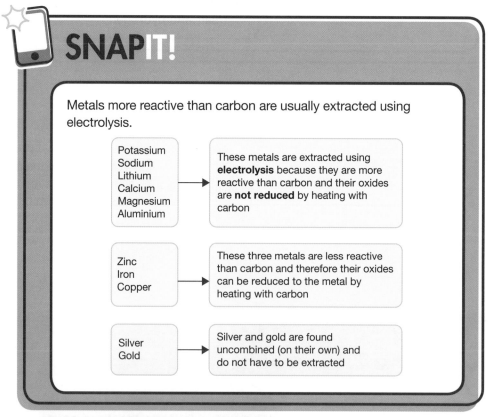

Metals more reactive than carbon are usually extracted using electrolysis.

| Potassium Sodium Lithium Calcium Magnesium Aluminium | → | These metals are extracted using **electrolysis** because they are more reactive than carbon and their oxides are **not reduced** by heating with carbon |

| Zinc Iron Copper | → | These three metals are less reactive than carbon and therefore their oxides can be reduced to the metal by heating with carbon |

| Silver Gold | → | Silver and gold are found uncombined (on their own) and do not have to be extracted |

Gold and silver can be found uncombined with other elements, while other elements are found in ores

STRETCH IT!

In compounds, metals exist as positively charged ions. This means that when they react they lose electrons. Another definition of oxidation is that **Oxidation Is Loss** of electrons.

The more reactive the metal the more easily they lose electrons and the less easily they take them back.

In electrolysis, electrons are gained by metal ions to form metal atoms. This is another version of reduction. **Reduction Is Gain** of electrons.

We remember this definition of oxidation and reduction by using the mnemonic **OILRIG**.

Oxidation **I**s **L**oss of electrons and **R**eduction **I**s **G**ain of electrons.

Examples of oxidation involving metals losing electrons are:

$Fe \rightarrow Fe^{2+} + 2e^-$ and $Al \rightarrow Al^{3+} + 3e^-$

Examples of reduction are the reverse of those above and $Na^+ + e^- \rightarrow Na$.

NAIL IT!

When metals oxides are reduced by carbon to the metal, carbon dioxide is usually formed.

For example, copper(II) oxide and carbon form copper and carbon dioxide.

$2CuO(s) + C(s) \rightarrow 2Cu(s) + CO_2(g)$

When carbon is heated with the oxide of a more reactive metal, there is no reaction.

$Al_2O_3(s) + C(s) \rightarrow$ No reaction

CHECK IT!

1 What term is used for the following?

   a a metal gaining oxygen

   b a metal losing oxygen

2 In the reaction shown below which metal is reduced and which metal is oxidised?

   $2Al(s) + Fe_2O_3(s) \rightarrow Al_2O_3(s) + 2Fe(s)$

3 a Lead is a more reactive metal than copper but less reactive than iron. Suggest a method for extracting lead from its ore.

   b Barium is more reactive than calcium. Suggest a method for extracting barium from its ore.

The extraction of iron in the blast furnace

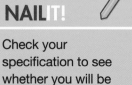

NAILIT!

Check your specification to see whether you will be tested on this in your exam.

Iron is the most commonly used metal and it is less reactive than carbon.

The main ore of iron is haematite which is mainly iron(III) oxide (Fe_2O_3).

The iron is extracted from haematite in a large tower-like structure called a blast furnace. A simplified diagram of the furnace is shown in the Snap It! box on page 73.

As it is less reactive than carbon, iron(III) oxide can be reduced to iron by heating with carbon but in the blast furnace the reducing agent is carbon monoxide.

There are three solids fed in at the top of the furnace. These are coke, limestone and iron ore. Their functions in the furnace are described in the table below:

Raw material	Reactant present	Function in the blast furnace
Coke	Carbon (C)	As a fuel and to form the compound carbon monoxide which is the reducing agent in the furnace.
Haematite (iron ore)	Iron(III) oxide (Fe_2O_3)	Source of iron
Limestone	Calcium carbonate ($CaCO_3$)	To react with acidic impurities in the iron ore such as sand (SiO_2) which are removed as slag (Ca_2O_4Si).

Near the bottom of the blast furnace hot air is blown into the furnace (mainly nitrogen and oxygen).

Reaction I

The oxygen in the air reacts with the coke (carbon) to form carbon dioxide in a very exothermic reaction. The heat from this reaction supplies most of the energy for the other reaction in the furnace to take place.

$$C(s) + O_2(g) \rightarrow CO_2(g)$$

Reaction II

The carbon dioxide then reacts with more carbon to form carbon monoxide. In this reaction the carbon dioxide is reduced (loses oxygen) and the carbon is oxidised (gains oxygen) to form carbon monoxide.

$$C(s) + CO_2(g) \rightarrow 2CO(g)$$

Reaction III

It is the carbon monoxide which then reduces the iron(III) oxide in the iron ore to give molten iron and carbon dioxide. The molten iron sinks to the bottom of the furnace where it is run off.

$$Fe_2O_3(s) + 3CO(g) \rightarrow 2Fe(l) + 3CO_2(g)$$

Reaction IV

The calcium carbonate from the limestone then reacts with acidic impurities like sand (SiO_2) to form calcium silicate or slag. This is an acid-base reaction. The slag is less dense than the iron and therefore floats on top of the molten iron and is run off separately.

$$CaCO_3(s) + SiO_2(s) \rightarrow CaSiO_3(s) + CO_2(g)$$

DOIT!

Plan a presentation about the blast furnace. How could you present it so that the facts are introduced gradually rather than all at once.

NAILIT!

The hardest equation to balance is the equation for the reaction between carbon monoxide and iron(III) oxide.

The key is to realise that the iron(III) oxide has to lose 3 oxygens and that each carbon monoxide molecule can only gain one oxygen atom in forming carbon dioxide. This means that we need 3 carbon monoxide molecules to reduce the iron(III) oxide to iron and the equation is: $3CO(g) + Fe_2O_3(s) \rightarrow 3CO_2(g) + 2Fe(l)$

SNAPIT!

A simplified diagram of the blast furnace is shown below:

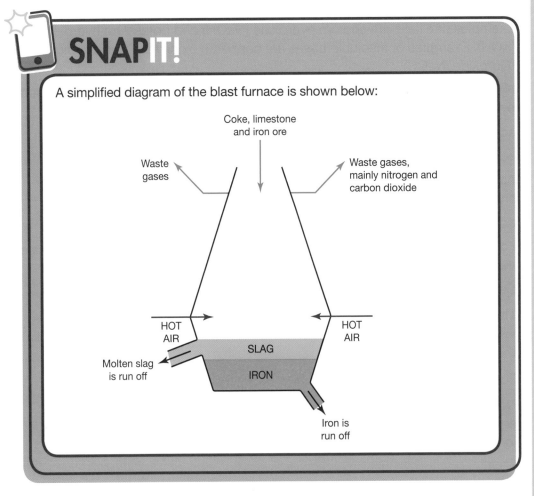

CHECKIT!

1 Explain why iron is represented as Fe(l) in the equation rather than the usual Fe(s).

2 Explain why the main gases in the waste gases leaving the furnace are nitrogen and carbon dioxide.

3 Explain why the coke fed into the furnace has two functions.

The reactions of acids

Acids are a group of substances with similar properties. This means that if you know the properties of one acid you can predict the properties of the others.

The reason all acids have similar properties is that they all contain hydrogen, and when in aqueous solution they all give hydrogen ions (H^+).

Hydrochloric acid (HCl) and sulfuric acid (H_2SO_4) react with metals to form salts and hydrogen.

Alkalis are soluble metal hydroxides; bases are insoluble metal oxides and hydroxides.

Examples of alkalis are sodium hydroxide (NaOH) and potassium hydroxide (KOH). Examples of insoluble bases are copper(II) oxide (CuO) and sodium hydroxide (NaOH).

Hydrochloric acid (HCl), nitric acid (HNO_3) and sulfuric acid (H_2SO_4) are all neutralised by alkalis and bases. Each neutralisation reaction forms a salt and water.

acid(aq) + alkali(aq) → salt(aq) + water(l)

acid(aq) + base(s) → salt(aq) + water(l)

All three of the acids above react with metal carbonates to give a salt, water and carbon dioxide gas. So the general equation is:

acid(aq) + carbonate(s) → salt(aq) + water(l) + carbon dioxide(g)

For example, calcium carbonate ($CaCO_3$) reacts with nitric acid (HNO_3) to produce the salt calcium nitrate ($Ca(NO_3)_2$), carbon dioxide (CO_2) and water (H_2O).

$$CaCO_3(s) + 2HNO_3(aq) \rightarrow Ca(NO_3)_2(aq) + CO_2(g) + H_2O(l)$$

The reaction between acids and metals is a redox reaction. The metal atoms lose electrons and are oxidised. The hydrogen (H^+) ions are reduced because they gain electrons.

For example, $Mg(s) + 2H^+(aq) \rightarrow Mg^{2+}(aq) + H_2(g)$

Note that the negative ions associated with the acid do not appear in these equations because they do not take part in the reaction. They are spectator ions ('they just look on').

DO IT!

Make up an exam question about the reactions of acids for a friend or revision partner.

- Each part of the question should be worth a certain number of marks.
- Write a mark scheme for your question.

NAIL IT!

One common problem associated with the writing of chemical equations involving acids is the writing of the formulae of the salt because of the negative ions in acids like sulfuric acid and nitric acid.

- The key to this is realising that the acids contain replaceable hydrogen ions.
- For example, sulfuric acid is H_2SO_4. It contains two replaceable hydrogen ions. Each of these has one positive charge. Therefore the sulfate ion must have two negative charges to balance out the positive charges from the hydrogen ions and its formula is SO_4^{2-}.
- If sulfuric acid forms a salt then we can use this information to write the correct formulae for the salt.
- For example, magnesium sulfate contains the magnesium Mg^{2+} ion (magnesium is in group 2). Therefore the formula of magnesium sulfate is $MgSO_4$ as the +2 on the magnesium ion cancels out the -2 on the sulfate ion.
- Similarly the nitrate ion is NO_3^- (only one replaceable hydrogen ion in nitric acid (HNO_3)). Therefore in magnesium nitrate we need two nitrate ions to cancel out the charges on the Mg^{2+}, so magnesium nitrate is written $Mg(NO_3)_2$.

SNAPIT!

This table shows salts formed by metals with different acids. Remember to find the formula of the salt the charges on the ions have to be balanced (see Ions and ionic bonding on page 38).

Metal in base; alkali etc.	Formula of metal ion	Acid	Ion from acid	Name of salt formed	Formula of salt
Magnesium	Mg^{2+}	Nitric (NHO_3)	NO_3^-	magnesium nitrate	$Mg(NO_3)_2$
Copper	Cu^{2+}	Sulfuric (H_2SO_4)	SO_3^{2-}	copper(II) sulfate	$CuSO_4$
Zinc	Zn^{2+}	Hydrochloric (HCl)	Cl^-	zinc chloride	$ZnCl_2$
Sodium	Na^+	Sulfuric (H_2SO_4)	SO_4^{2-}	sodium sulfate	Na_2SO_4

Practical Skills

There are two practicals associated with this topic. You can see them on pages 76 and 90. They are:

1 The preparation of a soluble salt by the reaction of a base with an acid.

2 The determination of the reacting volumes of a strong acid and an alkali by titration.

3 Using the results from the titration to find the concentration of either the acid or the alkali.

CHECKIT!

1 What is meant by the terms:

  a alkali

  b base?

2 Name the salts formed when sodium hydroxide reacts with:

  a hydrochloric acid

  b nitric acid

3 When copper carbonate is added to sulfuric acid, the mixture fizzes/effervesces. Explain this observation.

4 Nitric acid forms sodium nitrate ($NaNO_3$).

  a Give the formula of the nitrate ion.

  b Give the formula of magnesium nitrate.

5 **Complete** and **balance** the following chemical equations:

  a $MgO(s) + H_2SO_4(aq) \rightarrow$

  b $MgCO_3(s) + H_2SO_4(aq) \rightarrow$

  c $Mg(OH)_2(s) + HCl \rightarrow$

6 a Give the ionic equation for the reaction between an acid and magnesium.

  b Explain why this is a redox reaction.

The preparation of a soluble salt

A soluble salt is prepared by the neutralisation reaction between an insoluble base and an acid.

If a metal carbonate is used, then the only difference is that carbon dioxide is given off.

The metal ion needed to make the salt comes from the base and the negative ion (anion) in the salt comes from the acid.

The general equation for the reaction shows that the reaction gives a clear solution because there is only water and an aqueous solution of a salt formed.

Base(s) + acid(aq) → salt(aq) + water(l)

Therefore when the insoluble base stops dissolving we know all the acid has been used up.

Practical Skills

The skills/ techniques used are heating, filtration, evaporation and crystallisation.

Stage	What is done/action	Explanation of what is done
1	Heat up the acid.	Higher temperature means faster reaction.
2	Add excess of insoluble base.	Neutralisation reaction takes place between acid and base.
3	Stop adding the base when it stops dissolving, or if a carbonate is added it stops fizzing.	When the base stops dissolving or the carbonate stops fizzing it means that the acid has been used up.
4	Filter off the unreacted base or carbonate.	Remove unreacted insoluble base or carbonate, collect the filtrate which is just the aqueous solution of the salt.
5	Heat the salt solution on a steam bath.	Steam bath evaporates the water in the salt solution slowly so we get crystals and not powder.
6	Stop heating when solid salt starts to appear. You now have a saturated solution.	Saturated solution means that no more will dissolve in the solution at the higher temperature.
7	Leave the saturated solution to cool so that crystallisation can take place.	At a lower temperature the solid is less soluble so more crystals appear.

SNAP IT!

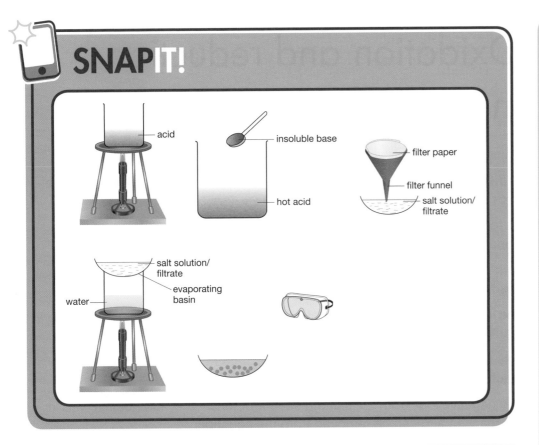

acid

insoluble base

hot acid

filter paper

filter funnel

salt solution/ filtrate

salt solution/ filtrate

evaporating basin

water

DO IT!

Write an account to go with the diagrams in the Snap It! box.

NAIL IT!

The reasons for not getting as much salt as theoretically possible are as follows:

- Some acid is lost when the insoluble base is added as spitting takes place.
- Some salt solution is left in the filter paper.
- Not all of the salt solution crystallises.

MATHS SKILLS

You might be asked to calculate the percentage yield for the preparation and account for any losses.

$$\text{Percentage yield} = \frac{\text{actual yield (what you get)}}{\text{theoretical yield (what you should get)}} \times 100\%$$

CHECK IT!

1 What reactants could you use to prepare the following soluble salts?

  a Copper sulfate

  b Zinc nitrate

  c Magnesium chloride

2 a Describe how an unreacted base is separated from the salt solution.

  b Why is this method of separation used?

3 In a salt preparation 4.5 g of the salt were prepared when 5 g was the theoretical yield. Calculate the percentage yield.

4 The preparation of magnesium nitrate can be made using two different reactions and the equations for these are shown below:

  A $MgO(s) + 2HNO_3(aq) \rightarrow Mg(NO_3)_2(aq) + H_2O(l)$

  B $MgCO_3(s) + 2HNO_3(aq) \rightarrow Mg(NO_3)_2(aq) + H_2O(l) + CO_2(g)$

  a Suggest **two** observations that suggest reaction B has been completed.

  b Assuming that magnesium nitrate is the desired product, calculate the atom economy for each method.

    [Relative formula masses MgO = 40; $MgCO_3$ = 84; HNO_3 = 63; $Mg(NO_3)_2$ = 148; H_2O = 18]

Oxidation and reduction in terms of electrons

In displacement reactions a reactive metal will displace a less reactive one from an aqueous solution of its salt.

As far as electrons are concerned, Oxidation Is Loss of electrons and Reduction Is Gain of electrons (remembered as OILRIG).

Ionic equations for displacement reactions will only involve metal atoms and positive metal ions (cations).

The ions of the less reactive metal gain electrons from the atoms of the more reactive metals.

This means that the less reactive metal ions are reduced and the more reactive metal atoms are oxidised.

The negative ions from the salt are spectator ions – they are not involved in the reaction and can be removed from the equation.

NAIL IT!

When you write the ionic equations **leave out the non-metal ions** and just put in the metal atoms and ions present. For example, the reaction between zinc metal and an aqueous solution of copper(II) sulfate:

$Zn(s) + Cu^{2+}(aq) \rightarrow Zn^{2+}(aq) + Cu(s)$

Note that the zinc has lost electrons and become more positive by forming a Zn^{2+} ion (oxidised) and at the same time the copper(II) ion has lost its +2 charge by accepting electrons and forming a neutral copper atom (reduced).

SNAP IT!

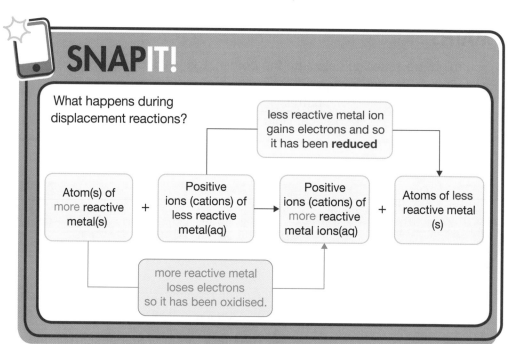

What happens during displacement reactions?

Atom(s) of more reactive metal(s) + Positive ions (cations) of less reactive metal(aq) → Positive ions (cations) of more reactive metal ions(aq) + Atoms of less reactive metal (s)

less reactive metal ion gains electrons and so it has been **reduced**

more reactive metal loses electrons so it has been oxidised.

CHECK IT!

1 State the definitions of reduction and oxidation in terms of loss and gain of electrons.

2 a Write the following reaction as an ionic equation:

$Mg(s) + ZnCl_2(aq) \rightarrow MgCl_2(aq) + Zn(s)$

b State and explain which species has been oxidised and which has been reduced in part a.

The pH scale and neutralisation

An aqueous solution is one formed when a substance dissolves in water. Its state symbol is (aq).

Acids are a group of substances with similar properties. This is because all aqueous solutions of acids produce H^+ ions.

In the same way aqueous solutions of alkalis all give OH^- ions.

In neutralisation reactions H^+ and OH^- ions react to give water. The ionic equation for this reaction is as follows:

$$H^+(aq) + OH^-(aq) \rightarrow H_2O(l)$$

The pH scale runs from 0 to 14 and is a measure of the acidity or alkalinity of a solution.

Acid solutions have a pH value less than 7. The lower the pH the more concentrated the H^+ ions are.

Neutral solutions such as pure water have a pH of 7.

SNAPIT!

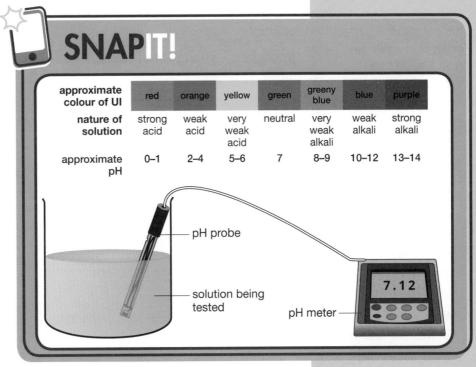

approximate colour of UI	red	orange	yellow	green	greeny blue	blue	purple
nature of solution	strong acid	weak acid	very weak acid	neutral	very weak alkali	weak alkali	strong alkali
approximate pH	0–1	2–4	5–6	7	8–9	10–12	13–14

pH probe

solution being tested

7.12

pH meter

Alkaline solutions have a pH value greater than 7 and the higher the pH the greater the concentration of OH^- ions.

The pH of a solution can be measured accurately using a pH probe or more approximately using the colour of universal indicator (UI) in the solution.

A pH probe measures the concentration of hydrogen ions accurately and the pH is read from a pH meter either digitally or on a scale.

✓ CHECKIT!

1 State the ions that would be found in aqueous solutions of both hydrochloric acid and sulfuric acid.

2 State the ions that would be found in aqueous solutions of both sodium hydroxide and calcium hydroxide.

3 Classify the reaction which takes place when hydrochloric acid is neutralised by an alkali.

4 The pH of a solution of hydrochloric acid is 1. Ethanoic acid of the same concentration has a pH of 3. Explain what conclusions you can draw from this data.

Strong and weak acids

Use your calculator to express concentrations (mol/dm³) in standard form. The numbers you need to look at are 1, 0.1, 0.001, etc.

Describe what happens to the order of magnitude n, in 1×10^{-n} as the concentration decreases 10-fold each time.

A concentrated solution of an acid has a greater amount (in moles) of the acid dissolved in the same volume of water than a dilute solution.

A strong acid like hydrochloric acid is completely ionised in aqueous solution.

A weak acid like ethanoic acid is only partially ionised in aqueous solution.

This means that 1000 molecules of the strong acid, hydrochloric acid, will all ionise to give 1000 H^+ ions in aqueous solution. On the other hand, only 4 out of 1000 molecules of the weak acid, ethanoic acid, will ionise in aqueous solution.

Important – strong is not the same as concentrated, and weak is not the same as dilute.

If the pH value of a solution decreases by 1 unit then the concentration of the H^+ ions increases by 10 times or 1 order of magnitude.

WORKIT!

As the pH decreases by 1 unit, the hydrogen ion concentration **increases by a factor of 10** or **1 order of magnitude**. On the other hand, if the pH increases by 1 then the hydrogen ion concentration decreases by a factor of 10 or has decreased by 1 order of magnitude to one-tenth of what it was before.

What happens to the pH as the concentration of H^+ ions goes from 0.1 mol per dm³ to 0.001 mol/dm³?

In going from 0.1 mol/dm³ to 0.001 mol/dm³ the concentration decreases 100 times.

A decrease in the hydrogen ion concentration of 100 times is a decrease of 2 orders of magnitude and this means the pH value goes up by 2.

MATHS SKILLS

Understand what is meant by order of magnitude.

An increase of 1 order of magnitude means that the value has increased 10 times. A decrease by 1 order of magnitude means that the value has decreased 10 times to one-tenth of the original value.

An increase of 100 times is 2 orders of magnitude and so on.

CHECKIT!

1 Explain the difference between a strong acid and a weak acid.

2 Explain the difference between a dilute and a concentrated solution.

3 If the pH of a solution goes down by 3, explain what has happened to the concentration of the H^+ ions in the solution.

The basics of electrolysis and the electrolysis of molten ionic compounds

Electrolysis is the splitting up of an ionic compound using electricity.

Electrolysis takes place when the ionic compounds are in the liquid state or in aqueous solution because the ions are free to move and carry the current.

The liquid that is decomposed by electrolysis is called the electrolyte.

When ions lose or gain electrons at the electrodes they are discharged.

During electrolysis, negative ions (anions) move towards the positive electrode (the anode (+)) and lose electrons to form non-metallic elements.

Positive ions (cations) move towards the negative electrode (cathode (−)) and gain electrons to form metallic elements (or hydrogen).

For example, molten potassium iodide forms iodine at the anode (+) and potassium at the cathode (−).

The reactions at electrodes can be represented using ionic half equations:

Generally at cathode (−) $M^{n+} + ne^- \rightarrow M$

At anode (+) $2X^{m-} \rightarrow X_2 + 2me^-$

These equations show that at the cathode the metal ions gain electrons and this is reduction. Also, at the anode the non-metal ions lose electrons and this is oxidation.

SNAPIT!

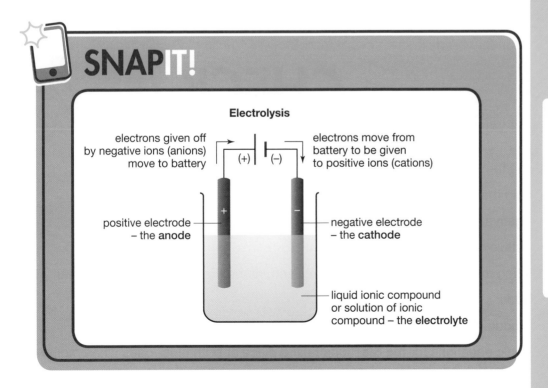

Electrolysis

electrons given off by negative ions (anions) move to battery

electrons move from battery to be given to positive ions (cations)

(+) (−)

positive electrode – the **anode**

negative electrode – the **cathode**

liquid ionic compound or solution of ionic compound – the **electrolyte**

DOIT!

Write a short account of what happens to the ions and the electrons at each electrode during electrolysis. You could copy out the diagram in the Snap It! box and complete it by putting in the ions and what happens at each electrode.

NAILIT!

Depending on your specification, you may need to learn how to balance ionic half equations.

Look back to your notes on ionic compounds – remember that group 1 elements form +1 ions, e.g. Na$^+$; group 2 elements form +2 ions: group 6 elements form 2– ions; and group 7 elements form 1– ions.

MATHS SKILLS

You need to balance the charges on both sides of the equation.

WORKIT!

What is formed at the cathode (−) and anode (+) when molten calcium chloride is electrolysed?

Calcium is formed at the cathode and chlorine at the anode.

Give the equations for the reactions at the electrodes.

At the cathode (−) $Ca^{2+} + 2e^- \rightarrow Ca$

At the anode (+) $2Cl^- \rightarrow Cl_2 + 2e^-$

Flakes of calcium chloride

CHECKIT! ✓

1 What is the term used for the following?

   a the liquid that is electrolysed

   b the negative electrode

   c the positive electrode

2 When molten magnesium chloride is electrolysed, name the substances formed at:

   a the anode

   b the cathode.

3 a Write ionic equations for the reactions taking place at both electrodes when molten magnesium chloride is electrolysed.

   b Explain why the reaction at the anode is oxidation.

The electrolysis of copper(II) sulfate and electroplating

When copper(II) sulfate solution is electrolysed using inert electrodes (for example, carbon or platinum electrodes) the rules are the same as for the electrolysis of all other aqueous solutions.

Copper is less reactive than hydrogen and the copper(II) ions are discharged at the cathode and copper metal is formed as a pink-brown solid. As copper(II) ions are removed from solution the blue colour of the copper(II) sulfate solution fades.

At the anode, hydroxide ions are discharged to give oxygen gas.

When copper electrodes are used the reaction at the cathode is identical but at the anode the copper metal dissolves to form copper(II) ions which transfer to the cathode. This means that the anode loses mass whilst the cathode gains mass by the same amount.

This means that for every copper(II) ion dissolving into the electrolyte, one is removed by being discharged at the cathode. Because of this, there is no net change in the concentration of the copper(II) ions and the intensity of the blue colour of the solution does **not** change.

The two half-reactions taking place in the electrolysis are shown below:

electrolysis

Copper(II) ions discharged at cathode to form copper

Copper anode dissolves to form copper(II) ions

Cu^{2+}

solution of copper(II) sulfate with the same intensity of colour because concentration of Cu^{2+} is unchanged

At anode	$Cu(s) \rightarrow Cu^{2+}(aq) + 2e^-$	**This is oxidation**
At cathode	$Cu^{2+}(aq) + 2e^- \rightarrow Cu(s)$	**This is reduction**

SNAP IT!

When copper electrodes are used the process can be summarised as follows, take a picture to revise on-the-go:

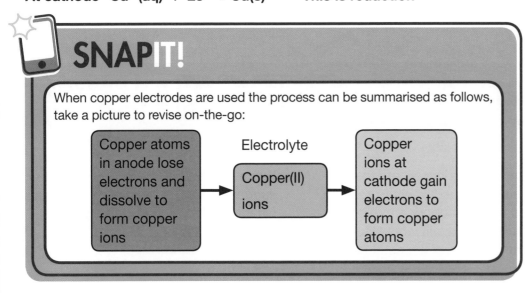

| Copper atoms in anode lose electrons and dissolve to form copper ions | Electrolyte
Copper(II) ions | Copper ions at cathode gain electrons to form copper atoms |

Practical Skills

You may have done an experiment on the electrolysis of copper(II) sulfate in class. Think about what you observed and explain why it happened. What would happen if you performed the experiment, then swapped the electrodes?

Electroplating

Electroplating is the coating of one metal with another metal using electrolysis. In electroplating the anode is the coating metal, the electrolyte contains the ions of this metal and the object being plated is the cathode. For example, when plating with chromium the anode is made from chromium and the electrolyte is chromium sulfate solution. This is shown in the diagram below:

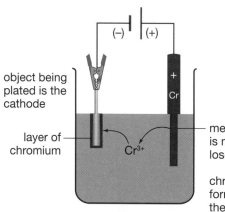

Electroplating is used for many reasons:

- Appearance – electroplating with gold or silver is commonly used to make jewellery look more expensive, and taps are often electroplated in chromium for a shiny finish.

- Protection from corrosion – electroplating can protect an easily eroded metal from environmental conditions. An example of this is coating steel with nickel or zinc-nickel alloys.

- Desired properties – electroplating can add properties to the original metal to help with its purpose, for example, copper connectors may be silver plated to increase electrical conductivity.

 **DOIT!**

Look online to find some more examples of objects that are electroplated.

You will learn more about protecting from corrosion in Rusting on page 164.

CHECKIT! ✓

1 In an experiment to investigate the electrolysis of copper(II) sulfate solution it is found that the copper anode loses 0.200 g in mass. Explain what would happen to the mass of the cathode.

2 When electroplating a spoon with silver, suggest a suitable electrolyte and predict what would form at each electrode.

The electrolysis of aqueous solutions

Water ionises to give hydrogen ions (H^+(aq)) and hydroxide ions (OH^-(aq)).

If the metal is more reactive than hydrogen in the reactivity series the hydrogen ion will be discharged. So, hydrogen (H_2) gas is produced.

If the electrolyte is not a halide then the hydroxide ion is discharged. So, oxygen gas is produced.

The presence of these two ions from the water means that there is a choice from two products at each electrode.

At the cathode, we have a choice between the metal ion and the hydrogen ion.

If the metal present is more reactive than hydrogen, then we get **hydrogen from the discharge of the hydrogen ions**.

At the anode (+), we have a choice between the discharge of the hydroxide ion and the other negative ion.

We get oxygen from the discharge of the hydroxide ion **unless** the other negative ion is a group 7 halide ion (Cl^-, Br^- or I^-). If so we get the halogen which is Cl_2, Br_2 or I_2.

NAILIT!

Remember that the product at the anode is always a diatomic molecule. The elements that form diatomic molecules are H_2, O_2, N_2, Cl_2, Br_2, I_2 and F_2.

STRETCHIT!

You may be asked to write half equations for the reactions at the electrodes. When aqueous solutions are electrolysed you may be asked to write the half equations for the discharge of the hydrogen (H^+) and the hydroxide (OH^-) ions.

The half equations for the reactions at each electrode are shown below.

At the negative cathode (−)

$2H^+$(aq) $+ 2e^- \rightarrow H_2$(g)

And at the positive anode (+)

$4OH^-$(aq) $\rightarrow 2H_2O$(l) $+ O_2$(g) $+ 4e^-$

This means that at the cathode, hydrogen ions gain electrons and are reduced. At the same time, at the anode hydroxide ions lose electrons and are oxidised.

Practical Skills

You will have performed electrolysis experiments in class. Make sure you can describe how to set up the experiment and explain what happened using **cations** and **anions**.

DO IT!

Choose a solution. Draw a diagram showing both electrodes and the ions that would be attracted to those electrodes. Write notes on your diagram to explain what happens to the ions.

WORKIT!

1 How can we predict which positive ion (cation) is discharged at the cathode (–) during the electrolysis of an aqueous solution?

The answer is hydrogen unless the metal is less reactive than hydrogen. Using the reactivity series (PoSLiCaMZIC) shows that only copper ions (CC in the list) would be discharged.

Cu^{2+} ions accept electrons to give Cu.

2 How can we predict which non-metal ion is discharged at the anode during electrolysis of an aqueous solution?

If the non-hydroxide ion (OH^-) is a halide ion (Cl^-, Br^- or I^-) then the halide ion is discharged to give the halogen Cl_2, Br_2 or I_2. If there is any other negative ion (such as SO_4^{2-} and NO_3^-) then we get oxygen given at the anode from the discharge of the hydroxide (OH^-) ion.

NAILIT!

When asked what products you would get from the electrolysis of an aqueous solution you should also be aware of what remains. For example, if you have a solution of copper(II) sulfate you will get copper at the cathode because copper is less reactive than hydrogen. At the anode you get oxygen from the hydroxide ion. This means that hydrogen ions and sulfate ions are left behind, which together make sulfuric acid.

Depending on your specification and tier, you may be asked to write the half equations for the reactions at the electrodes.

WORKIT!

When aqueous potassium chloride solution is electrolysed, what is formed at each electrode and what solution remains after the electrolysis?

Potassium is more reactive than hydrogen and this means that at the cathode (–) we will get hydrogen (H_2) as the product.

Chloride (Cl^-) is a halide ion so we will get chlorine (Cl_2) formed at the anode (+).

This means that the ions left behind are potassium (K^+) and hydroxide (OH^-) ions and the solution that remains is potassium hydroxide (KOH) solution.

CHECKIT! ✓

1 a State the formulae of the four ions present in an aqueous solution of sodium chloride.

  b Suggest the products at each electrode when aqueous sodium chloride solution is electrolysed.

  c What solution remains after the electrolysis is complete?

  d Write the half equations for the reactions at each electrode and explain whether oxidation or reduction has taken place.

The extraction of metals using electrolysis

If a metal is more reactive than carbon, then the metal oxide cannot be reduced to the metal by heating with carbon.

Electrolysis is used to extract metals **more reactive** than carbon. An example is aluminium.

To extract aluminium, the electrolyte used is aluminium oxide. Aluminium oxide has a very high melting point so to save energy and lower the operating temperature the aluminium oxide is dissolved in a compound called cryolite.

Carbon is used for both electrodes. Aluminium ions are discharged at the cathode (–) to give molten aluminium metal which is run off.

At the anode (+), oxide ions are discharged to form oxygen gas. This oxygen gas then reacts with the carbon anode to form carbon dioxide. The carbon anode (+) burns away and loses mass. This means that the anode (+) has to be replaced at regular intervals.

DOIT!

Write a brief description of how aluminium is extracted from aluminium oxide. Your description should include materials used for electrodes, how energy is saved and what happens at each electrode.

SNAPIT!

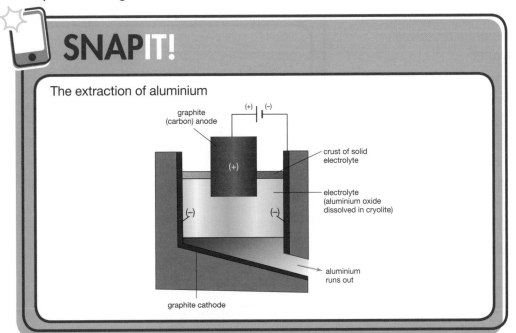

The extraction of aluminium

NAILIT!

At the cathode aluminium ions are **reduced** by gaining electrons.

$Al^{3+} + 3e^- \rightarrow Al$

At the anode (+) oxide ions are **oxidised** by losing electrons.

Remember OILRIG.

CHECKIT!

1 List the metals that are extracted using electrolysis.

2 Justify the use of electrolysis to extract aluminium from its ore.

3 Write a brief description of the electrolysis of aluminium oxide.

4 Sodium is extracted from molten sodium chloride. Write the half equations for the reactions at each electrode.

Investigation of the electrolysis of aqueous solutions

Part of the investigation is to predict the products formed by the electrolysis of various solutions. For more information on electrolysis of aqueous solutions see page 85.

You can make predictions about the identity of the solution that remains because you know that it is formed from the ions that do not react.

Universal indicator can be used to identify the pH of the solution.

The apparatus you will use is similar to that shown in the Snap It! box. The gas is collected by downward displacement of the solution used.

The volume of gas produced depends on the identity of the gas. If hydrogen and oxygen are formed, then the volume of hydrogen is twice that of the volume of oxygen.

The volume of chlorine gas is less than predicted because chlorine dissolves in water.

The products at the electrodes are identified by observations and chemical tests:

Hydrogen gas 'pops' when a lighted splint is placed in the gas.

Oxygen gas relights a glowing splint.

Chlorine bleaches blue litmus paper or UI in the solution.

Bromine turns the solution yellow/orange and iodine will turn it brown.

As well as investigating the products of electrolysis, other factors can be investigated. For example, if you were investigating the electrolysis of sodium chloride solution then you could also investigate the effect of changing the concentration of the sodium chloride solution, and of changing the current passing through the solution.

DO IT!

Describe how the apparatus shown in the Snap It! box is used in the investigation.

SNAP IT!

gas formed at cathode; gas formed at anode; electrolyte; cathode −; anode +

Practical Skills

This practical tests the skills of planning and predicting, carrying out, making observations and analysing the results.

WORKIT!

If an aqueous solution of sodium chloride is electrolysed, what would be the predictions and what would be seen?

Predictions			Observations		
At cathode	At anode	Solution	At cathode	At anode	Solution
Hydrogen formed because sodium is more reactive than hydrogen.	Chloride is a halide ion so chlorine would be formed from the discharge of the chloride ion.	The ions left behind are sodium and hydroxide ions.	The gas pops with a lighted splint which shows hydrogen.	The gas formed bleaches the UI in the solution. This shows chlorine is formed.	The remaining solution turns UI purple around the cathode. This is because the ions remaining are sodium and hydroxide ions which form the alkali sodium hydroxide.

In practicals, make sure you record your observations.

NAILIT!

There are several areas of chemical knowledge that are used in this practical so make sure you are able to answer questions on them.

1 The electrolysis of aqueous solutions.

2 Testing for gases.

3 Formulae of ions.

4 The colour of UI in different types of solution.

✓ CHECKIT!

1 In an investigation, the gas at the cathode popped with a lighted splint and the gas at the anode relit a glowing splint. Name these two gases.

2 Explain why the solution around the anode turns yellowy orange when aqueous potassium bromide is electrolysed.

3 When sodium iodide solution is electrolysed the following reaction takes place:

$H_2O(l) + 2NaI(aq) \rightarrow H_2(g) + I_2(aq) + 2NaOH(aq)$

The iodine turns the solution brown. Describe how you would identify the hydrogen and the sodium hydroxide solution.

Determining reacting volumes by titration

When acids are neutralised by alkalis there are no visible changes.

To see when the neutralisation is complete, an indicator is added to the reaction mixture. The indicator **changes colour** when the correct volumes of acid and alkali have reacted.

Accurate volumes of acid and alkali are measured using a burette and a pipette. A pipette dispenses a known amount of acid or alkali into the conical flask, while the burette dispenses small amounts of solution until there is a reaction. The burette is then used to measure how much has been added.

Volumes are expressed to two decimal places. Two concordant results are required for reliable results. This means that you must have two results within $0.10\,cm^3$ of each other.

As well as using an indicator in the solution and adding an alkali to an acid, you can also add a solid base such as calcium hydroxide to an acid. After adding each sample of the base the pH is monitored by using UI paper or a pH probe and pH meter.

DO IT!

Write or record on an MP3 file a short account of how you can carry out a titration. You should describe how the volumes are measured and the procedure used.

NAIL IT!

The burette can be read to the nearest $0.05\,cm^3$ so the results are expressed to 2 decimal places. Please note that zero is recorded as 0.00 not 0 because the burette reads to $0.05\,cm^3$ so results are recorded to 2 decimal places.

MATHS SKILLS

You may have to read a table of data and use simple mathematical operations such as subtraction and finding the mean of a set of results. Results are expressed to 2 decimal places.

SNAP IT!

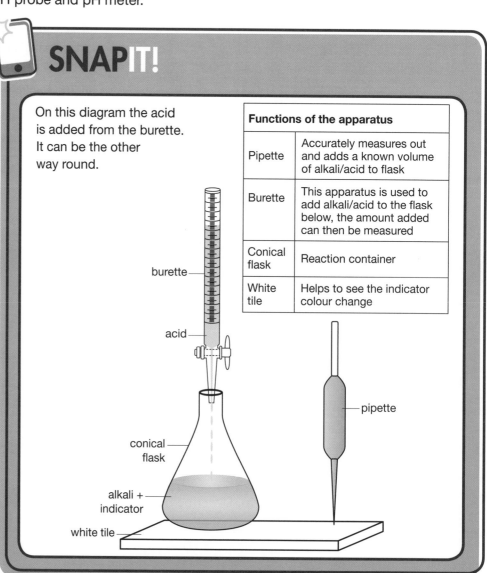

On this diagram the acid is added from the burette. It can be the other way round.

Functions of the apparatus	
Pipette	Accurately measures out and adds a known volume of alkali/acid to flask
Burette	This apparatus is used to add alkali/acid to the flask below, the amount added can then be measured
Conical flask	Reaction container
White tile	Helps to see the indicator colour change

burette

acid

conical flask

alkali + indicator

white tile

pipette

WORKIT!

Given below is a table of results from a titration experiment where an acid is added from the burette to 25.00 cm³ of an alkali.

There are two results that are within 0.10 cm³ of each other and the average of these is used as the reading.

What is the average titration result for this experiment?

Reading	Rough titration	Accurate titration 1	Accurate titration 2	Accurate titration 3
Final reading/cm³	19.00	37.20	18.50	37.10
Initial reading/cm³	0.00	19.00	0.00	18.50
Titre/cm³	19.00	18.20	18.50	18.60

The average accurate titre = (18.50 + 18.60)/2 = 18.55 cm³

Practical Skills

Titration procedure

The point at which the indicator changes colour is the end-point. The volume of acid needed to reach the end-point is called the titre.

For each titration, a known volume of alkali is added to the conical flask using the pipette, followed by a couple of drops of indicator.

The first titration is a rough titration – the acid is added from the burette 1 cm³ at a time until the end-point. This gives an estimate of the volume of acid required in the reaction.

Using the rough titration reading, acid is run into alkali until 1.00 cm³ before the end-point for the rough titration and then add the solution drop-by-drop to give an accurate titre.

This is repeated until you get two results which are within 0.10 cm³ of each other. Your specification may allow results within 0.20 cm³ of each other, check your specification or ask your teacher which is correct for your exams.

After the rough titration, it is good practice to start the next titration where you stopped last time. This means that in the example above we start at 19.00 cm³ and not at 0.00 cm³. This saves time and materials.

Note that the recording of results is a very important part of titrations. You need a column for your rough titration and columns for each accurate titration.

✓ CHECKIT!

1 List the main apparatus used for a titration.

2 Describe a rough titration.

3 Describe the observations that indicate when enough acid has been added to the alkali.

4 In a titration experiment four accurate results were obtained: 24.20 cm³, 24.50 cm³, 24.60 cm³ and 25.80 cm³.

a Which results are rejected?

b What is the average titre for the experiment?

For additional questions,
www.scholastic.co.uk/

1   The five metals aluminium, copper, iron, magnesium and zinc are in the reactivity series.

   a   Put them in order of reactivity from the **least reactive** to **the most reactive**.

   b   Complete the following word equations for each reaction :

   i   zinc(s) + copper(II) sulfate(aq) →

   ii   aluminium(s) + magnesium oxide(s) →

   iii aluminium(s) + iron(III) oxide(s) →

   c   When burning magnesium is lowered into a test tube containing carbon dioxide, the magnesium continues burning.

   At the end of the reaction there are traces of a black solid and a white solid on the sides of the test-tube.

   i   Write the word equation for the reaction including state symbols.

   ii   Write the balanced chemical equation for the reaction including state symbols.

   iii Explain why this is a redox reaction.

   iv   I   Identify the white solid formed.

        II Identify the black solid formed.

2   When hydrochloric acid solution is added to zinc metal, the zinc disappears and the mixture effervesces but when the same acid is added to copper metal there is no reaction.

   a   Explain the effervescence and describe how you can test for the product that causes the effervescence.

   b   Explain why there is no reaction between the acid and copper.

   c   i   Write the ionic equation for the reaction between zinc metal and the acid. Note that the formula for the zinc ion is Zn^{2+}.

   iii Explain why this is a redox reaction.

3   In the electrolysis of aqueous potassium bromide solution, there is a gas produced at the cathode and at the anode the solution turns yellow-orange in colour.

   a   Name the products produced at both electrodes.

   b   What solution remains after the electrolysis?

4   a   A solution of ammonia turns universal indicator blue. What does this tell you about the ammonia solution?

   b   Universal indicator turns yellow in phenol solution. What does this tell you about phenol?

5   A student was given a solution of hydrochloric acid and a solution of sodium hydroxide. They were asked to carry out a titration to find the volume of hydrochloric acid that would exactly react with $25.00\,cm^3$ of the sodium hydroxide solution.

   a   The equation for the reaction is:

   sodium hydroxide(aq) + hydrochloric acid(aq) → sodium chloride(aq) + water(l)

   i   What is the meaning of (aq)?

   ii   Write the balanced chemical equation for the reaction.

   iii Write the ionic equation for the reaction.

   b   In the titration what equipment do they use for the following:

   i   Measuring exactly $25.00\,cm^3$ of the sodium hydroxide solution

   ii   Measuring and adding the acid to the sodium hydroxide solution

   iii The reaction vessel?

   c   Describe the observation(s) which indicate that the titration is complete.

Energy changes

Exothermic and endothermic reactions

An exothermic reaction is one where the reaction gives out heat energy to its surroundings. This results in an increase in the temperature of the surroundings.

Examples of exothermic reactions are the burning of fuels in combustion reactions and most neutralisation and oxidation reactions.

Everyday uses of exothermic reactions are hand warmers and self-heating cans of food.

An endothermic reaction is one where the reaction takes in heat energy from its surroundings. This results in a decrease in the temperature of the surroundings.

Examples of endothermic reactions are thermal decomposition (breaking up a compound using heat) and the reaction of citric acid with sodium hydrogen carbonate.

Sports injury packs use endothermic reactions.

CHECKIT!

1 **a** In a chemical reaction the temperature increased. What type of reaction is this?

   b The table below shows the results from two experiments:

Experiment	Initial temperature/°C	Final temperature/°C	Temperature change
I	20		+25
II	20	15	

   Complete the table and then classify each reaction as either exothermic or endothermic.

2 List some types of reaction that are endothermic reactions.

3 List some uses of exothermic reactions.

Investigation into the variables that affect temperature changes in chemical reactions

DOIT!

When you are carrying out an investigation it is often useful to draw a flow chart of what you are going to do. Discuss it with a practical partner or review it yourself to identify where you might be doing things in the wrong order or points where a piece of apparatus is needed. Practical work is improved by good organisation.

This particular practical places emphasis on you putting forward a hypothesis and making predictions based on it. It also requires the accurate use of appropriate measuring apparatus and the need to make and record a range of measurements. When investigating temperature changes you should know what factors need to be controlled to ensure the results are valid.

Exothermic reactions are accompanied by a temperature rise and **endothermic** reactions give a temperature decrease.

Reactions you could investigate include combustion, neutralisation reactions between acids and alkalis, and acids reacting with either metals or carbonates.

Factors affecting the temperature changes are amount of reactant, surface area (lumps or powder) of solids, concentrations of solutions and the reactivity of different metals with acids.

Relevant pieces of apparatus are thermometers or temperature probes and data loggers; measuring cylinders; spirit burners for combustion experiments – see diagram below; top-pan balance and reaction containers such as beakers and test tubes. The container that is used to measure the heat change for a reaction is called a calorimeter. A polystyrene cup can be used or a lagged container like a beaker. The lagging reduces heat loss through the sides of the container.

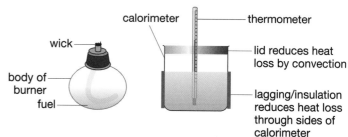

Practical Skills

You could be asked to investigate the variables that affect temperature changes in reacting solutions.

For this practical you should:

- Put forward a hypothesis about what you think would happen based on your knowledge of the chemistry involved.
- Identify variables that could affect the temperature change and explain how you would make the results valid.
- Identify safety factors involved in the experiment.
- Know what measurements you would make.
- Record your results in a suitable form.

STRETCHIT!

Check your specification and tier as you may need to be aware that if you are investigating different substances then equal masses does not mean equal amounts, and masses should be converted to moles using $n = m/M_r$.

WORKIT!

A student was given some magnesium ribbon, magnesium powder and hydrochloric acid. They were asked to investigate the effect of the surface area of the magnesium on the temperature change caused by the reaction. They carried out a fair test and measured the starting temperature for both as 20°C. In the reaction with the magnesium ribbon, the final temperature was 28°C and with the powder it was 42°C.

a List the apparatus she would need and give the use of each piece.

- A polystyrene cup in a small beaker for the reaction container which is very well insulated and a thermometer (or temperature probe and data logger) to measure the temperature changes.
- A measuring cylinder to measure the volume of acid.
- A spatula for adding the powder and a top-pan balance for weighing out the magnesium ribbon and powder.

b Describe how they would make sure all results were valid.

The volume and concentration of the acid should be the same for both experiments and so should the mass of the ribbon and powder. The containers should be identical or use the same one for both experiments.

c Show how they might record their results.

Experiment	Starting temperature/°C	Final temperature/°C	Temperature change/°C
Magnesium powder	20	42	22
Magnesium ribbon	20	28	8

d Make any conclusions possible from their results.

The reaction with the powder gave a greater temperature rise. This is because it had the greater surface area and reacted more quickly. ◄—

You can learn more about the effect of surface area on page 108.

CHECKIT!

NAILIT!

A common error when drawing up a table of results is to forget to put in the units in the column headings.

1 List some factors that could affect the temperature changes in a chemical reaction.

2 A student added measured amounts of magnesium powder to separate calorimeters containing 100 cm³ of 2 mol/dm³ hydrochloric acid and then measured the temperature changes. The results are shown below:

Experiment	1	2	3	4	5	6
Mass of magnesium/g	1.00	2.00	3.00	4.00	5.00	6.00
Temperature change/°C	5.00	10.0	15.0	20.0	24.0	24.0

  a Explain the results obtained for experiments 1 to 4.

  b Suggest an explanation for the results from experiments 5 and 6.

3 List some reactions that could be investigated in terms of temperature changes.

4 Using their reactions with hydrochloric acid, describe how you could place the metals copper, iron, magnesium and zinc in order of reactivity.

Reaction profiles

DOIT!

Draw reaction profiles for:

- a combustion reaction
- a thermal decomposition.

NAILIT!

The arrow for the activation energy must **start at the energy of the reactants and end at the peak of the reaction profile**. The line showing the change in energy of the reaction starts at the energy for the reactants and ends at the energy of the products. It **points downwards for an exothermic reaction** and **upwards for an endothermic reaction.**

A reaction profile shows how the energy changes from reactants to products.

In a reaction profile for an exothermic reaction the products are lower in energy than the reactants because energy is released to the surroundings during the reaction.

In a reaction profile for an endothermic reaction the products are higher in energy than the reactants because energy is taken in from the surroundings during the reaction.

Chemical reactions occur when reacting particles collide with enough energy to react. This energy is called the activation energy (E_a).

The activation energy is the minimum energy required for a reaction to occur. The activation energy is a barrier to reaction.

SNAPIT!

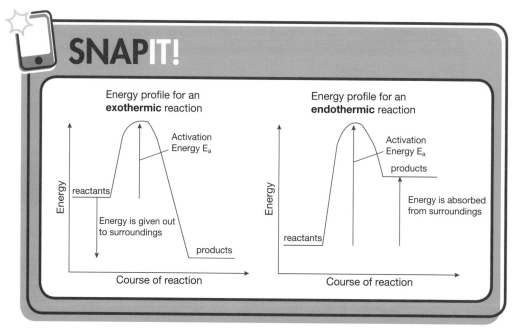

CHECKIT!

1 Draw and label the reaction profile for the combustion of carbon to give carbon dioxide.

2 a i Refer to page 109 and define what is meant by a catalyst.

　　ii Explain how a catalyst speeds up a reaction.

　b i Draw a reaction profile for an endothermic reaction.

　　ii On the same graph, draw the profile you would get for a catalyst for the same endothermic reaction.

The energy changes of reactions

Energy is absorbed when chemical bonds are broken in a chemical reaction. This is an endothermic reaction.

Energy is given out when chemical bonds are formed in a chemical reaction. This is an exothermic reaction.

Bond energies are used to calculate the energy needed to break bonds and the energy given out by making bonds.

The energy given out or taken in during a chemical reaction is measured in kJ/mol.

The energy difference between the energy needed to break the bonds and the energy given out by their formation is the energy change in the reaction.

If the energy needed to break the bonds in the reactants is less than the energy given out by the formation of new bonds in the products, then the reaction is exothermic.

If the energy needed to break the bonds in the reactants is greater than the energy given out by the formation of new bonds in the products, then the reaction is endothermic.

MATHS SKILLS

You will need to read data from a table and carry out simple multiplications, additions and subtractions.

DO IT!

Methane and oxygen react as follows:

$CH_4(g) + 2O_2(g) \rightarrow CO_2(g) + 2H_2O(l)$

For the complete combustion of methane draw a reaction profile and on it show the bonds broken in the reactants and the bonds formed in the products.

To help you, the bonds involved in the burning of propane in oxygen to give water and carbon dioxide are below:

C_3H_8 + $5O_2$ $\longrightarrow$ $3CO_2$ + $4H_2O$

$$
\begin{array}{ccc}
& \text{H} & \text{H} & \text{H} \\
& | & | & | \\
\text{H}-&\text{C}-&\text{C}-&\text{C}-\text{H} + 5\,\text{O}=\text{O} \longrightarrow 3\,\text{O}=\text{C}=\text{O} + 4\,\text{O}\overset{\text{H}}{\underset{\text{H}}{<}} \\
& | & | & | \\
& \text{H} & \text{H} & \text{H}
\end{array}
$$

Bonds broken			Bonds made		
2 C—C		5 O=O	6 C=O		8 O—H
8 C—H					

NAILIT!

It is a common error to miscalculate the number of bonds in a molecule. For example, in the Work It! box there are three carbons in the propane (C_3H_8) molecule and it is tempting to put this as 3 C–C bonds when in fact there are only 2 C–C bonds (C–C–C). Also, remember that in a water molecule there are 2 O–H bonds and in carbon dioxide there are 2 C=O bonds.

WORKIT!

Calculate the energy change for the complete combustion of propane shown in the equation below. The required bond-energies are shown in the table.

$$C_3H_8 \quad + \quad 5O_2 \quad \longrightarrow \quad 3CO_2 \quad + \quad 4H_2O$$

You will be supplied with this information in the exam.

$$H-\overset{\overset{\displaystyle H}{|}}{\underset{\underset{\displaystyle H}{|}}{C}}-\overset{\overset{\displaystyle H}{|}}{\underset{\underset{\displaystyle H}{|}}{C}}-\overset{\overset{\displaystyle H}{|}}{\underset{\underset{\displaystyle H}{|}}{C}}-H + 5\,O=O \longrightarrow 3\,O=C=O + 4\,O{\overset{\displaystyle H}{\underset{\displaystyle H}{<}}}$$

Bond	Bond energy kJ/mol
C–C	350
C–H	415
O=O	500
C=O	800
O–H	465

Bonds broken
2 C—C   5 O=O
8 C—H

Bonds made
6 C=O   8 O—H

Bonds broken: heat energy taken in	Bonds made: heat energy given out
2 C–C bonds need 2 × 350 kJ = 700 kJ of energy to break them	6 C=O bonds give out 6 × 800 kJ of energy when they form = 4800 kJ
8 C–H bonds need 8 × 415 = 3320 kJ of energy to break them	8 O–H bonds give out 8 × 465 kJ of energy when they are formed = 3720 kJ
5 O = O bonds need 5 × 500 = 2500 kJ of energy to break them	
Total energy taken in to break bonds = 700 + 3320 + 2500 kJ = 6520 kJ	Total energy given out when bonds are made = 4800 + 3720 kJ = 8520 kJ

There is more energy given out than taken in so the reaction is exothermic.
The energy of reaction = 8520 − 6520 = 2000 kJ/mol

CHECKIT!

1 When methane reacts with oxygen the following complete combustion reaction takes place:

$$CH_4(g) + 2O_2(g) \rightarrow 2H_2O(l) + CO_2(g)$$

   a Draw the bonds present in the molecules.

   b Use the values in the table above to calculate:

      i   the energy taken in to break bonds

      ii the energy given out when bonds are formed

      iii the energy change for the reaction.

   c Is the reaction exothermic or endothermic? Explain your answer.

Chemical cells and fuel cells

If you place two different metals in an electrolyte (a liquid that conducts electricity) electrons will flow from the more reactive metal to the less reactive metal.

For example, if a zinc plate and a copper plate are placed in sulfuric acid (the electrolyte), the more reactive zinc loses electrons more easily than the copper. If the two plates are connected then these electrons can then flow from the zinc to the copper.

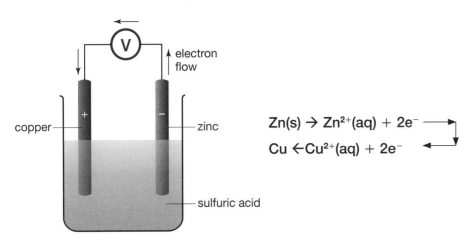

$$Zn(s) \rightarrow Zn^{2+}(aq) + 2e^-$$
$$Cu \leftarrow Cu^{2+}(aq) + 2e^-$$

This electron flow can be used to power an electric circuit.

The greater the difference in reactivity of the two metals the greater the voltage produced by the cell.

Cells contain chemicals that undergo redox reactions to produce electricity.

When two or more cells are connected in series they form a battery and the voltage produced goes up as the number of cells in the battery increases.

There are two types of batteries – rechargeable and non-rechargeable.

In non-rechargeable batteries such as alkaline batteries, the chemical reactions that produce the electricity stop when one of the reactants is used up.

In a hydrogen fuel cell, the reaction between hydrogen and oxygen produces electrical energy rather than heat energy. The only product of the fuel cell reaction is water.

The cell is powered by a constant flow of hydrogen and oxygen and as long as these gases flow the fuel cell will never run out, unlike non-rechargeable cells. Your specification may require you to be able to know the two half equations for the electrode reactions (see Stretch It! box on the next page).

DO IT!

You are given a copper plate, a chromium plate, a magnesium plate, zinc plate, some sulfuric acid, beakers and a voltmeter. Devise an experiment that helps you put the chromium, magnesium and zinc in order of reactivity.

SNAP IT!

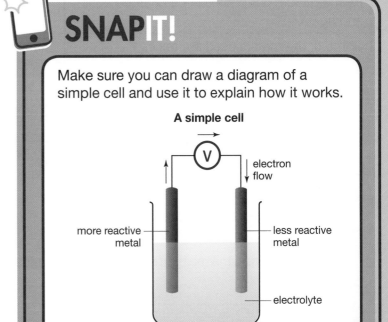

Make sure you can draw a diagram of a simple cell and use it to explain how it works.

A simple cell

Energy changes   Chemical cells and fuel cells

STRETCH IT!

At the negative electrode of the **fuel cell** hydrogen reacts with hydroxide ions to produce water and electrons.

$$2H_2(g) + 4OH^-(aq) \rightarrow 4H_2O(l) + 4e^-$$

This is oxidation because the electrons are lost.

At the positive electrode oxygen gains electrons and reacts with water to produce hydroxide ions.

$$O_2(g) + 2H_2O(l) + 4e^- \rightarrow 4OH^-(aq)$$

This is reduction because electrons are gained.

When the left-hand side and the right-hand side of these two reactions are added together and we cancel out we get:

$$2H_2(g) + 4OH^-(aq) + O_2(g) + 2H_2O(l) + 4e^-$$
$$\rightarrow 4OH^-(aq) + 4H_2O(l) + 4e^-$$

Which becomes $2H_2(g) + O_2(g) \rightarrow 2H_2O(l)$

NAIL IT!

Hydrogen fuels cells are very useful for powering spacecraft as they are compact and lightweight – plus the water produced as waste can be used by the astronauts.

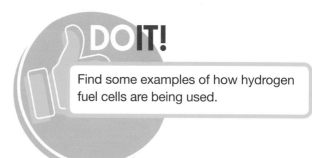

DO IT!

Find some examples of how hydrogen fuel cells are being used.

NAIL IT!

You could be asked about the relative advantages and disadvantages of chemical cells and fuel cells.

Chemical cells	Fuel cells
Can be used anywhere.	Hampered by the need for hydrogen containers.
When non-rechargeable batteries run out, they have to be thrown away and sent to a recycling centre. Rechargeable batteries can be charged again and again.	These will continue to work as long as the hydrogen and oxygen flows. The product of the reaction is water.
Some of the metals used are toxic.	The hydrogen is flammable.

CHECK IT!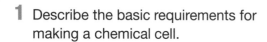

1 Describe the basic requirements for making a chemical cell.

2 State the main product of a hydrogen fuel cell.

3 Explain which of the following two combinations would give the greater voltage:

A cell consisting of magnesium and copper electrodes **or** one consisting of zinc and copper electrodes.

4 State the two half equations for the electrode equations of a fuel cell.

5 a Write the half equations for the reactions taking place in the cell set up by placing magnesium and zinc plates in an electrolyte of sulfuric acid.

b Draw a diagram of this cell and show the direction of the electron flow.

1 Describe how temperature changes during an endothermic reaction.

2 When limestone is heated it undergoes thermal decomposition to give calcium oxide (known as quicklime) and carbon dioxide. The reaction between calcium oxide and water can be used to heat up meals. The relevant equations are shown below:

A $CaCO_3(s) \rightarrow CaO(s) + CO_2(g)$

B $CaO(s) + H_2O(l) \rightarrow Ca(OH)_2(s)$

Classify reactions A and B as either exothermic or endothermic. In each case explain your answer.

3 a List the main differences between a chemical non-rechargeable cell and a hydrogen fuel cell.

b A cell was made from a copper rod and a zinc rod which were placed in an electrolyte. Explain which rod the electrons would flow from if the cell was placed in an electrical circuit.

4 The **incomplete** table below shows the results from an experiment on the reactivity of three metals, X, Y and Z. The same amounts of all three metals were reacted with hydrochloric acid and the temperature change in each reaction was measured.

Metal	Starting temperature	Final temperature	Temperature change
X	22		1
Y	22		19
Z	22	29	

a i Complete the table.

ii Apart from the missing temperature figures what else is missing from the table?

b Describe how you would ensure the results are valid.

c List the apparatus for this experiment.

d Suggest the order of reactivity of the three metals and explain your answer.

5 The diagram opposite shows the reaction profile for a chemical reaction.

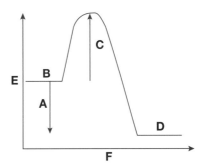

a Write down the correct labels for A to F.

b What type of reaction is represented by the reaction profile above?

c Explain what is meant by the term 'activation energy'.

6 The equation below shows the structures of the reactants and products of the chemical reaction between ethene and chlorine.

$$
\begin{array}{ccccc}
\text{H} & & \text{H} & & \text{H } \text{ H} \\
\diagdown & & \diagup & & | \quad | \\
\text{C} & = & \text{C} & + \text{ Cl} - \text{Cl} \longrightarrow \text{H} - \text{C} - \text{C} - \text{H} \\
\diagup & & \diagdown & & | \quad | \\
\text{H} & & \text{H} & & \text{Cl } \text{ Cl}
\end{array}
$$

ethene   chlorine   dichloroethane

a List the bonds that are broken and calculate the energy required to break all these bonds.

b List the bonds that are made and calculate the energy given out by their formation.

c i Calculate the energy change for the reaction and the units.

ii Explain whether it is exothermic or endothermic.

Table of bond energies

Bond	Bond energy (kJ/mol)
C=C	610
C–H	415
Cl–Cl	245
C–C	350
C–Cl	345

Rates of reaction and equilibrium

Ways to follow a chemical reaction

The main ways of following a chemical reaction to measure its rate are:

- measuring the volume of gas produced over a period of time
- measuring the change in mass of the reactants over a period of time
- measuring how long it takes for a cross to be obscured when a solid is formed in a reaction between two solutions.

When you investigate the factors that affect the rate of a chemical reaction there are several variables that can be changed, measured or controlled. For example, if you were investigating the effect of temperature on the rate of reaction between marble chips and acid, you could measure the volume of gas produced over time. To make sure the results are valid you would keep the concentration of acid and the surface area of the marble chips constant for all the experiments.

The table below summarises facts about variables using this example.

Type of variable	Description	In the example it is...	Where it is plotted on a graph
Independent	The variable whose effect you have chosen to measure	Temperature	On the horizontal or x-axis
Dependent	The variable that you measure to find the effect of changing the independent variable	The volume of gas	Up the vertical or y-axis
Control variables	The variables you keep constant to make results valid	Concentration of acid and surface area of the marble chips	These are not plotted but could be noted in the title of the graph

NAIL IT!

When you are preparing for an experiment make sure you have your results table ready to record your results. The independent variable goes in the first column and is already filled in. The dependent variable will be recorded during the experiment. The control variable does not go in the results table but should be described if you write up the experiment to show your results are valid.

Independent variable Temp (°C)	Dependent variable Volume (cm³)

SNAPIT!

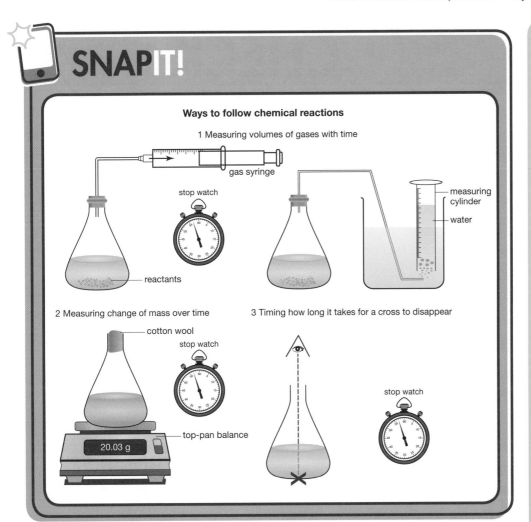

Ways to follow chemical reactions

1 Measuring volumes of gases with time

gas syringe

stop watch

reactants

measuring cylinder

water

2 Measuring change of mass over time

cotton wool

stop watch

top-pan balance

20.03 g

3 Timing how long it takes for a cross to disappear

stop watch

DOIT!

Using the diagrams in the Snap It! box, describe briefly how you would make the measurements in each method and create a suitable results table for each experiment.

NAILIT!

If you are asked to pick an appropriate method for following a chemical reaction to see how quickly it is going, then the equation for that reaction will help you.

You can use the state symbols in the equation to help you decide on the method to use. For example, if you see the (g) state symbol in the products, then you know a gas is produced.

If a gas is given off then measurement of gas volumes using the gas syringe or displacement of water are obvious alternatives. If the gas given off is carbon dioxide then measuring the loss in mass is also a possibility. However, some gases dissolve in water so you should check this when planning the experiment.

When two solutions react to form a solid then the mixture goes cloudy and you can time how long it takes to obscure a cross.

If a solid disappears during a reaction then you can time how long it takes for this to happen.

STRETCHIT!

If you use the disappearing cross technique then you measure how long it takes to obscure the cross so that you cannot see it.

The longer the time taken for this to happen, the slower the reaction is. If you want to have an idea of how quick the reaction is you measure the time, but use 1/time when you plot your results because 1/time tells you how quick the reaction is.

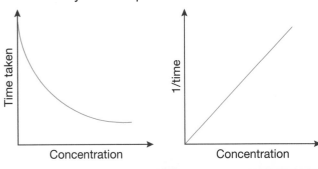

CHECKIT!

1 Suggest which of the three methods shown on page 103 could be used to measure the rate of the following reactions. In some cases more than one method can be used.

a $2HCl(aq) + CaCO_3(s) \rightarrow H_2O(l) + CaCl_2(aq) + CO_2(g)$

b $2HCl(aq) + Mg(s) \rightarrow H_2(g) + MgCl_2(aq)$

2 A student was investigating the effect of concentration on the rate of the reaction between marble chips and hydrochloric acid. They decided to measure the volume of gas over a period of time.

In this investigation state:

a the independent variable

b the dependent variable.

3 The equation below shows the reaction between hydrochloric acid and sodium thiosulfate solution.

$2HCl(aq) + Na_2S_2O_3(aq) \rightarrow SO_2(g) + 2NaCl(aq) + H_2O(l) + S(s)$

The rate of this reaction is usually followed by timing how long it takes to obscure a cross.

a List some problems that might make this method inaccurate.

b i You are given a small electric lamp, a power pack, some black card, a light sensor and a data logger. Using a simple diagram explain how you could measure the rate of the same reaction using this apparatus.

ii Explain how this method would be better than 'obscuring the cross' for measuring the rate.

You can measure the rate of reaction by measuring change in mass over time

Calculating the rate of reaction

The rate of a chemical reaction can be looked at in two different ways. Either using the reactant being used up, in which case the

$$Mean\ rate\ of\ reaction = \frac{Amount\ of\ reactant\ used\ up}{Time\ taken}$$

Or in terms of the product formed in which case the

$$Mean\ rate\ of\ reaction = \frac{Amount\ of\ product\ formed}{Time\ taken}$$

When a graph is plotted to show the change in a product or reactant you will probably get a curve. The rate at any time can be found by drawing a tangent to the curve and measuring its slope.

The steeper the gradient of the tangent the faster the rate of reaction.

When the gradient is zero there is no reaction taking place and the reaction is complete.

DO IT!

Sketch a graph showing the course of a reaction and on it draw a few tangents. Write a brief description about why the tangents show that as time goes on the reaction gets slower.

WORKIT!

In this experiment, the reaction is finished after 63 seconds and the total volume of gas collected is 50 cm³.

This means that the average rate of reaction = 50/63
$$= 0.794\ cm^3/s.$$

At X the tangent's gradient = 20/10 = 2 cm³/s.

At Y the tangent's gradient = 15/20 = 0.750 cm³/s.

At Z the gradient = 0 because the reaction has finished.

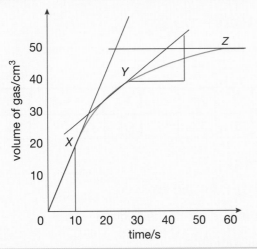

MATHS SKILLS

You will need to:

- Plot a graph or graphs and compare the results.

- Calculate the gradient of a line of best fit. You need at least five data points to draw a line.

- Understand that a tangent is a line that touches a curve at a point but does not cross it anywhere else.

- Draw tangents to a graph, calculate their gradients and use them as a measure of the rate of a reaction.

- Express results to three significant figures.

- Express very small or very large numbers in base form.

- Know that a straight line between concentration and rate shows that the rate is proportional to the concentration.

STRETCHIT!

You may be asked to express the rate in mol per s. Remember for a gas at RTP 1 mol of any gas occupies $24\,000\,cm^3$.

At **X** the rate $= 2\,cm^3/\,s = 2/24\,000\,mol/s$

$$= 8.33 \times 10^{-5}\,mol/s$$

At **Y** the rate $= 0.750\,cm^3/s = 0.750/24\,000\,mol/s = 3.13 \times 10^{-5}\,mol/s$

NAILIT!

For Graph I the reaction giving line A is faster than the reaction responsible for line B, this is shown by the fact the line obtained is steeper at the beginning than the one representing reaction B.

Similarly, for Graph II, reaction C is faster than reaction D and this is why its line is steeper at the beginning than the line for reaction D. The line levels off as the reaction slows down and it is horizontal because the reaction has finished.

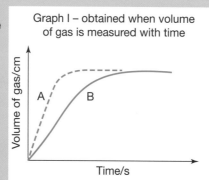

Graph I – obtained when volume of gas is measured with time

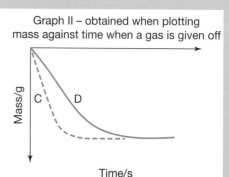

Graph II – obtained when plotting mass against time when a gas is given off

CHECKIT!

1 Describe how you can find the mean rate of a reaction using the amount of product formed in a reaction.

2 Two students carried out an investigation into the reaction between excess calcium carbonate and $100\,cm^3$ of hydrochloric acid.

$$CaCO_3(s) + 2HCl(aq) \rightarrow CaCl_2(aq) + H_2O(l) + CO_2(g)$$

They measured the volume of carbon dioxide produced at various time intervals. The results are shown in the table below.

Time/s	0	5	10	15	20	25	30	40	50	60	70	80
Volume of CO_2/cm³	0	27	41	50	57	62	66	72	77	79	80	80

a Plot these results on a suitable graph.

b i Draw tangents to the graph at 0 s, 10 s and 30 s.

   ii Find the rate of reaction in cm³/s at each of these times.

   iii Explain why the rate decreases with time.

c Explain why the gradient of the tangent drawn at 80 s is zero.

d i Calculate how many moles of carbon dioxide were produced in the reaction.

   ii Calculate the number of moles of hydrochloric acid present.

   iii Calculate the concentration of the hydrochloric acid.

The effect of concentration on reaction rate and the effect of pressure on the rate of gaseous reactions

Particles have to collide in order to react.

When you increase the concentration of a solution in a chemical reaction the rate of the reaction also increases.

This is because when the concentration increases, the reacting particles get more crowded as there are more of them in a given volume, so they collide more frequently and there are more successful collisions.

During a chemical reaction, the concentration of the reactant particles in the solution decreases as they react. This means that they become less crowded and collide less frequently and the reaction slows down.

When a graph is plotted to show how a reaction is progressing, the slope of the tangent to the graph at any time shows us how quickly the reaction is at that time. The quicker the reaction the steeper the slope of the tangent.

As the concentration of the reactant decreases during a reaction, the reaction gets slower and this means that the slope of the graph gets less steep and the graph becomes a curve.

In reactions that involve gases increasing the pressure, it also makes the reactant particles more crowded; they collide more frequently and react more quickly so the rate increases.

NAILIT!

When you talk about collisions saying just 'more collisions' will not get you the marks. There could be more collisions but over a much longer time. Using the word **frequently** is very important.

SNAP**IT!**

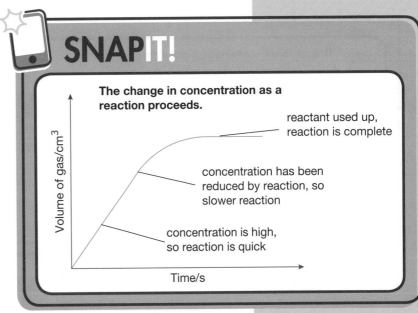

The change in concentration as a reaction proceeds.

reactant used up, reaction is complete

concentration has been reduced by reaction, so slower reaction

concentration is high, so reaction is quick

Volume of gas/cm^3

Time/s

CHECK**IT!**

1 Describe what happens to the rate if the concentration of a reacting solution decreases.

2 Using collision theory, explain why increasing the concentration has an effect on the rate.

3 When calcium carbonate reacts with excess hydrochloric acid, carbon dioxide gas is produced.

   a Sketch a graph of volume of carbon dioxide gas produced over time.

   b On the same scales sketch a graph showing the reaction using the same concentration of acid but only **half the amount** of calcium carbonate.

Rates of reaction – the effect of surface area

If a solid is broken up into smaller pieces its surface area increases.

Smaller pieces have a larger surface area to volume ratio than larger pieces. This means that a powdered solid has a greater surface area than a lump.

If the experiment involves a comparison between the reaction rate given by a powdered reactant and a lump then a line graph cannot be drawn and the results are expressed using bar charts.

A larger surface area means that more solid particles are exposed to collisions with other reactant particles because there are more points of contact.

This means that there are more frequent collisions and the rate of reaction increases.

Therefore, increasing the surface area of a solid reactant increases the rate of reaction.

SNAPIT!

Graphs to show effects of surface area

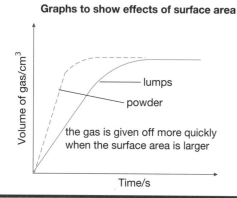

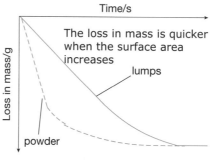

The steepness of the slopes of the graphs show how quickly the reaction is proceeding at any time. For both methods, the initial (starting) slope of the graph is steeper for the powder showing that it is producing a faster reaction. Therefore the greater the surface area the faster the rate.

CHECKIT!

1 State which has the larger surface area – lumps or powder.

2 Explain in terms of collision theory what effect increasing the surface area has on the rate of reaction.

3 A student wanted to find the effect of surface area on the rate of the reaction between calcium carbonate (used as marble chips) and hydrochloric acid.

$$CaCO_3(s) + 2HCl(aq) \rightarrow CaCl_2(aq) + H_2O(l) + CO_2(g)$$

a Explain how they could vary the surface area.

b List two ways they could follow the reaction rate.

c Suggest how they could display the results.

The effects of changing the temperature and adding a catalyst

The activation energy is the **minimum** energy needed for a reaction to take place.

If colliding particles do not have an energy greater than or equal to the activation energy then they will not collide with enough energy to break bonds and react.

When the temperature is raised particles move around more quickly and have more kinetic energy.

This means that there are more **frequent collisions** because they collide more frequently (more collisions per second).

There are more frequent effective collisions because the particles have a greater chance of colliding with an energy greater than the activation energy.

Adding a catalyst to a reaction speeds up the reaction but it is unchanged chemically at the end of the reaction.

A catalyst lowers the activation energy for a reaction by providing an alternative pathway for the reaction which has a lower activation energy.

This means that there will be even more frequent effective collisions and therefore a faster rate of reaction.

Enzymes are biological catalysts and carry out reactions in living organisms. They are also used outside living organisms in commonly used products, for example, washing detergent and baby food.

The formulae for catalysts are not included in chemical equations because they are unchanged chemically by the reaction. They can be written on the arrow between the reactants and products. For example:

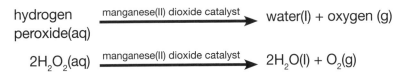

hydrogen peroxide(aq) $\xrightarrow{\text{manganese(II) dioxide catalyst}}$ water(l) + oxygen (g)

$2H_2O_2(aq) \xrightarrow{\text{manganese(II) dioxide catalyst}} 2H_2O(l) + O_2(g)$

NAILIT!

For the variables concentration and surface area, doubling either of them will double the rate. This does not work with temperature. An approximate effect is that the rate for some reactions doubles if the temperature goes up by 10°C.

DOIT!

Manganese(II) dioxide is a catalyst which increases the decomposition of hydrogen peroxide to give water and oxygen gas.

You are given some hydrogen peroxide, manganese(II) dioxide, wooden splints, test tubes and filtration apparatus. Explain how you could show that the manganese dioxide can be reused as a catalyst. Hint: the wooden splints are testing for the presence of a gas.

SNAPIT!

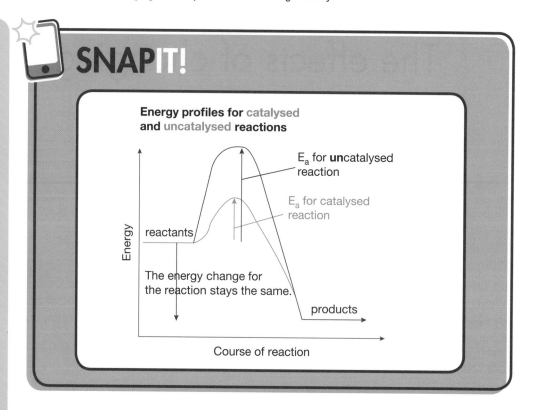

Energy profiles for catalysed and uncatalysed reactions

CHECKIT!

1 Describe the effect of increasing the temperature on the rate of reaction.

2 Using collision theory, explain the effect of raising the temperature on reaction rate.

3 a State what is meant by a catalyst.

b Explain how a catalyst speeds up a chemical reaction.

4 The diagram below shows the energy levels for the reactants and products in an **endothermic** reaction.

Complete the diagram by:

a Drawing the reactions profiles for an **uncatalysed** reaction and a **catalysed** reaction.

b Labelling the two activation energies and the energy of reaction.

An investigation into how changing different factors affects the rate of reaction

This practical places emphasis on you putting forward a hypothesis and making predictions based on it. It also requires the accurate use of appropriate measuring apparatus and the need to make and record a range of measurements including measuring gas volumes or changes in turbidity (cloudiness of solution). When investigating concentration you should know what factors need to be controlled to ensure valid results.

An example of a hypothesis is that increasing the concentration of a reactant in solution increases the rate of reaction. The concentration is your independent variable and is plotted along the horizontal axis (x-axis).

This can be tested by using several different reactions and the practical method requires both the measurement of gas volume with time and either a change in turbidity or colour with time. This is the dependent variable and is plotted up the vertical (y-axis).

A very important part of this practical is the number of control variables you have to keep constant. This is discussed in more detail on the next page.

MATHS SKILLS

Concentration and temperature are both continuous variables. This means that they can have any value and their effects can be shown using a line graph. On the other hand surface area can be large as in powder or small as in large lumps and these are categoric variables and cannot be plotted on a line graph. Their effects must be expressed as bar charts.

You should be able to draw tangents to curves, calculate the slopes of these tangents and express the results in terms cm^3/s or g/s.

You must also remember that the independent variable is plotted on the horizontal axis.

SNAPIT!

Take a picture of the graph below to help you remember how to calculate the rate of reaction from a graph.

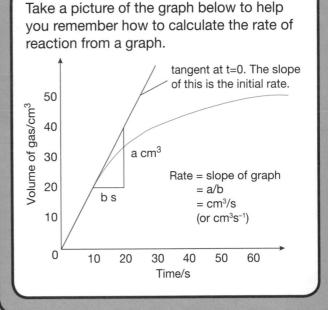

tangent at t=0. The slope of this is the initial rate.

Rate = slope of graph
= a/b
= cm^3/s
(or $cm^3 s^{-1}$)

Practical Skills

The practical skills that you might be tested on are:

1 The variables you would keep constant to ensure valid results. These are the **control variables**.

Independent variable	Control variables (these are kept constant to make results valid)
Concentration (e.g. of acid, sodium thiosulfate etc.)	Temperature, surface area of solid reactant, amount of catalyst if one is used, volume of solution, mass of solid reactant.
Temperature	Concentration of solution, surface area of solid reactant, amount of catalyst if one is used, volume of solution, mass of solid reactant.
Surface area of solid reactant	Concentration of solution, temperature, amount of catalyst if one is used, volume of solution, mass of solid reactant.
Effect of catalyst or amount of catalyst	Concentration of solution, temperature, volume of solution, mass of solid reactant.

2 The apparatus you would use to carry out the experiment.

Apparatus used for measuring gas volumes, loss in mass and turbidity is shown in the Snap It! box on page 103.

A **colorimeter** can be used to follow changes in colour in a reaction, or if the turbidity changes with time, this change can be followed using a **turbidity meter** or a **light meter** held underneath the reaction container while a lamp is held above it. As the solution becomes more cloudy the light detected by the light meter will decrease in intensity.

3 Measuring the rate of reaction.

The simplest way is to measure the volume of gas given off in a measured time for 1 minute or the loss in mass in 1 minute.

Another way is to measure the volume of gas with time or mass with time. Plot the results on a graph and then measure the initial rate. (See Snap It! on the previous page for gas volume as an example.)

Measure how long it takes to give a certain volume of gas or change in mass. If this is used then the time tells you how slow the reaction is. To give a measure of rate you plot 1/time.

If you are investigating the hydrochloric acid/sodium thiosulfate reaction you can either measure how long it takes to obscure a cross **or** monitor the change in turbidity (cloudiness) using a turbidity meter or light meter as outlined above.

CHECKIT!

1 The reaction between sodium thiosulfate solution and hydrochloric acid produces sulfur as a solid and this turns the solution cloudy.

Volume of $Na_2S_2O_3$ solution/cm³	Volume of hydrochloric acid/cm³	Volume of water/cm³	Time taken to obscure cross/s	Reaction Rate/s⁻¹
5	10	35	128	
10	10	30	64	
20	10		32	
30	10		22	
40	10		16	

The rate of reaction is measured by the time it takes to obscure a cross on a piece of paper. The results table below shows the results obtained in one experiment.

a Copy and complete the gaps in the table.

b What variables are kept constant in this experiment?

c Plot a graph of the volume of sodium thiosulfate solution against the rate of reaction and explain what this tells you about the effect of its concentration on the reaction rate. [Hint: The volume of sodium thiosulfate solution is the independent variable.]

Reversible reactions

A reversible reaction is one which can go both ways. This means that as well as reactants forming products, the products can also react under the same conditions to give the reactants.

The reaction where the reactants form the products is called the forward reaction.

The reaction where the products form the reactants is called the reverse reaction.

The symbol used for a reversible reaction is $\rightleftharpoons$.

An example of reversible reactions is the thermal decomposition of ammonium chloride to give ammonia gas and hydrogen chloride gas.

$$NH_4Cl(s) \underset{cool}{\overset{heat}{\rightleftharpoons}} NH_3(g) + HCl(g)$$

If the forward reaction is endothermic then the reverse reaction is exothermic. The opposite is also true.

Example:

$$CuSO_4.5H_2O(s) \underset{exothermic}{\overset{endothermic}{\rightleftharpoons}} CuSO_4(s) + 5H_2O(l)$$

A dynamic equilibrium is when the rate of the forward reaction is equal to the rate of the reverse reaction.

The forward and reverse reactions do not stop, they are going on all the time and that is why it is a dynamic equilibrium.

At the same time the concentrations of the reactants and products remain constant.

DO IT!

Write a short account of the experiments shown in the Snap It! box below. How can you show that they are reversible reactions?

SNAP IT!

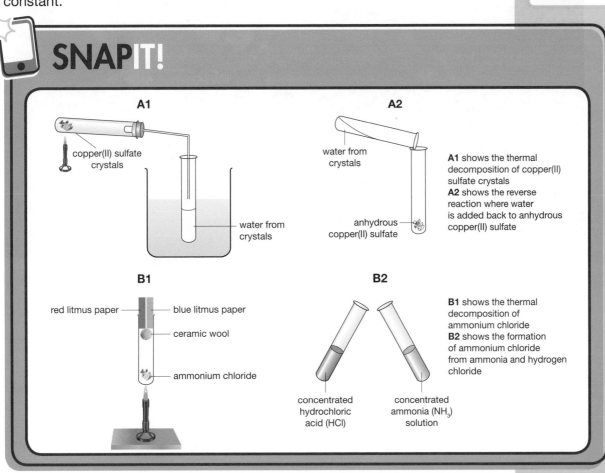

A1
copper(II) sulfate crystals

water from crystals

A2
water from crystals

anhydrous copper(II) sulfate

A1 shows the thermal decomposition of copper(II) sulfate crystals
A2 shows the reverse reaction where water is added back to anhydrous copper(II) sulfate

B1
red litmus paper — blue litmus paper

ceramic wool

ammonium chloride

B2
concentrated hydrochloric acid (HCl)

concentrated ammonia (NH₃) solution

B1 shows the thermal decomposition of ammonium chloride
B2 shows the formation of ammonium chloride from ammonia and hydrogen chloride

CHECKIT! ✓

1 What is the symbol that tells you a reaction is reversible?

2 State what is meant by the term reversible reaction.

3 Two compounds A and B react to form Y and Z in a reversible reaction.

   a Complete the equation for the reaction.

   A + B

   b When A is added to B the temperature goes up. What can you say about the forward and reverse reactions?

   c At the beginning when A is added to B why can't there be any reverse reaction?

   d At **equilibrium** which of the following alternatives is/are correct?

   i Both the forward and reverse reactions stop.

   ii There are equal amounts of reactants and products.

   iii The rate of the forward equals the rate of the reverse reaction.

   iv The concentrations of the reactants and products remain constant.

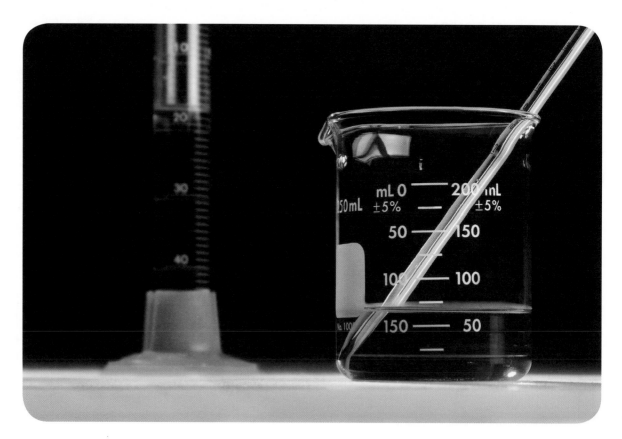

The effect of changing conditions on equilibrium

A chemical system is the reactants and products of a reversible reaction together in a **closed system** (container).

If a chemical system is at equilibrium it means that the rate of the forward reaction equals the rate of the reverse reaction.

There are three conditions that can be changed in a chemical system. These are:

- the **temperature** of the system
- the **pressure** of a system if any of the reactants or products are gases
- the **concentration** of any of the reactants or products.

A change in position of equilibrium means that there is a shift towards either the reactants or products.

If a chemical system is at equilibrium and one or more of the three conditions is changed then the position of equilibrium will **shift** to cancel out the change and we get either more reactants or more products. This is called Le Chatelier's principle.

For example:

- If the temperature is increased, the equilibrium will shift in favour of the reaction which is accompanied by a decrease in temperature. This means that if the reverse reaction is endothermic then more reactants are formed.

- If the **pressure** is increased, the position of equilibrium will shift in favour of the reaction that would lead to a decrease in pressure. This means that the side with **fewer gas molecules** will be favoured. If the numbers of gas molecules on both sides are equal then pressure will have no effect.

- If you increase the **concentration** of one of the products, then the system will try and lower its concentration by forming more reactants.

A catalyst has no effect on the position of equilibrium. It speeds up how quickly equilibrium is reached.

A catalyst speeds up both the **forward** and **reverse** reactions **equally**.

DO IT!

Consider the reversible reaction shown below:

$2C_2H_4(g) + O_2(g) \rightleftharpoons 2CH_3CHO(g)$

CH_3CHO is a substance called ethanal (or acetaldehyde). The forward reaction is exothermic.

Explain to someone the best conditions for getting as much ethanal as possible.

NAIL IT!

Remember these. If the opposite is done then the reverse will happen.

Increasing the concentration of one of the reactants shifts the equilibrium to the right and favours the forward reaction to make more products.

Increasing the pressure means that the equilibrium will shift to lower the pressure, it does this by making fewer gas molecules. Important – pressure has no effect if the number of gas molecules does not change in the reaction.

Increasing the temperature always favours the endothermic reaction. This is because the endothermic reaction lowers the temperature and this counteracts the change.

SNAPIT!

Consider the industrial manufacture of methanol (CH_3OH) from carbon monoxide gas (CO) and hydrogen gas (H_2). A copper catalyst is used in this process.

$$CO(g) + 2H_2(g) \underset{\text{endothermic}}{\overset{\text{exothermic}}{\rightleftharpoons}} CH_3OH(g)$$

Consider the effects of some changes on the position of this equilibrium.

Change	What happens	Explanation
Increase the concentration of CO gas	Equilibrium shifts to right-hand side $\longrightarrow$	The equilibrium moves in order to lower the concentration of CO gas by reacting it with hydrogen to make more methanol.
Increase the pressure	Equilibrium shifts to right-hand side $\longrightarrow$	If you increase the pressure the system tries to lower it by making fewer gas molecules, this means more methanol is produced.
Decrease the temperature	Equilibrium shifts to right-hand side $\longrightarrow$	If you decrease the temperature the system tries to raise it, this favours the exothermic reaction so produces more methanol.

Make your own copy of the table above and take a picture so you can learn on-the-go.

CHECKIT!

1 State what is meant by the term **chemical system**.

2 Describes what the symbol ⇌ means.

3 Describe what is meant by a reverse reaction.

4 State Le Chatelier's principle.

5 When ethene (C_2H_4) gas reacts with steam (H_2O) at 300°C, ethanol (C_2H_5OH) is formed.

$$C_2H_4(g) + H_2O(g) \underset{\text{endothermic}}{\overset{\text{exothermic}}{\rightleftharpoons}} C_2H_5OH(g)$$

   a State and explain the effect on the position of equilibrium when pressure is increased.

   b State and explain the effect on the position of equilibrium when the temperature is increased.

   c State and explain the effect on equilibrium when a catalyst is added.

Rates of reaction and equilibrium — REVIEW IT!

1   When calcium carbonate reacts with dilute hydrochloric acid, the gas carbon dioxide is given off as one of the products.

Suggest two ways you could follow the reaction and measure the rate of this reaction.

2   The curve below shows the line graph obtained when a gas is given off during a reaction.

Graph obtained when volume of gas is measured with time

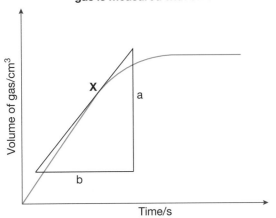

a   Describe how you can calculate the rate of the reaction at any time using the graph.

b   The value of **a** in the graph is 25 cm³ and the value of **b** is 15 s. Calculate the rate of reaction at **X**.

3   The graph below shows two identical reactions but at different temperatures.

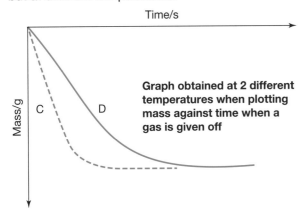

Graph obtained at 2 different temperatures when plotting mass against time when a gas is given off

a   Describe and explain which graph (C or D) has the fastest rate of reaction.

b   Explain which graph is the one given at the higher temperature.

c   Using collision theory explain the effect of temperature on reaction rate.

4   When a catalyst is added to hydrogen peroxide solution the following reaction takes place.

$2H_2O_2(aq) \rightarrow 2H_2O(l) + O_2(g)$

a   A catalyst for this reaction is manganese(IV) oxide.

  i   Define the term catalyst.

  ii If 0.10 g of manganese(IV) oxide is added at the beginning, what is its mass at the end?

b   Draw a reaction profile to show how a catalyst works.

c   Using collision theory explain how a catalyst works.

5   You are asked to investigate the effect of concentration on the rate of reaction.

What variables should be kept constant to ensure valid results?

6   When blue copper(II) sulfate crystals (formula = $CuSO_4.5H_2O$) are heated they form water and a white-grey anhydrous copper(II) sulfate powder (formula = $CuSO_4$) is formed.

The equation for the reaction is:

$CuSO_4.5H_2O(l) \rightleftharpoons CuSO_4(s) + 5H_2O(l)$

a   Explain how you can tell the reaction is reversible.

b   The forward reaction is endothermic. What can you say about the reverse reaction?

c   List **two** observations you would make when the water is added back to the white-grey anhydrous copper(II) sulfate.

7   When ammonium chloride is heated the following reaction takes place:

$NH_4Cl(s) \underset{\text{exothermic}}{\overset{\text{endothermic}}{\rightleftharpoons}} NH_3(g) + HCl(g)$

a   State and explain the effect on the position of equilibrium if temperature is increased.

b   State and explain the effect on equilibrium if pressure is increased.

Organic chemistry

Carbon compounds, hydrocarbons and alkanes

A hydrocarbon is a compound made up of hydrogen and carbon **only**.

Alkanes are hydrocarbons which have the maximum number of hydrogens and no carbon-carbon double bonds. This is why we call them saturated hydrocarbons.

The general formula of the alkanes is C_nH_{2n+2}.

The alkanes are a homologous series (family of chemicals). This means they are a group of compounds with similar chemical properties, the same general formula and differ by a CH_2 each time.

They also show a gradation in physical properties as the molecules get bigger.

Whatever the homologous series, the way each member of the series is named (prefix) is the same.

The start of each name depends on the number of carbons in the molecule.

Number of carbons in chain	Name starts with
1	Meth–
2	Eth–
3	Prop–
4	But–

Most of the hydrocarbons in crude oil are alkanes.

DOIT!

If they are available make ball and stick models of the first four alkanes using the displayed formulae shown in the Snap It! box below.

SNAPIT!

The first four straight chain alkanes are listed below along with their molecular formulae and their displayed formulae.

Name	Molecular formula	Displayed formula
methane	CH_4	H–C–H (with H above and below)
ethane	C_2H_6	H–C–C–H (with H above and below each C)
propane	C_3H_8	H–C–C–C–H (with H above and below each C)
butane	C_4H_{10}	H–C–C–C–C–H (with H above and below each C)

WORKIT!

What are the molecular and displayed formulae for the alkane with 5 carbons?

The molecular formula can be worked out from the general formula — C_nH_{2n+2}

Here $n = 5$ so $2n+2 = 2 \times 5 + 2 = 12$

Therefore the molecular formula $= C_5H_{12}$

When you draw the displayed formula the first thing you do is put the 5 carbons in a row.

$$—C—C—C—C—C—$$

Then give each carbon four bonds.

Now add the hydrogen atoms to each end of the bonds.

Don't forget to write in the hydrogen atoms.

NAILIT!

The simplest way to get displayed formulae correct is to remember that each carbon has got four strong covalent bonds. Also make sure that the lines that represent the covalent bonds go direct from one atom symbol to the other atom symbol.

One of the most common errors is that candidates write down all the carbons and the bonds coming off from them but forget to draw the hydrogens.

Most of the hydrocarbons in crude oil are alkanes

CHECKIT!

1 Explain what is meant by the term **hydrocarbon**.

2 Explain what is meant by the term **homologous series**.

3 State the general formula of the alkanes. Write the molecular formula of the alkane with 6 carbons.

Crude oil, fractionation and petrochemicals

MATHS SKILLS

The only mathematic skill required for this section is the balancing of chemical equations.

Crude oil is a mixture of many hydrocarbons and this means that it can be separated into its components using a physical method.

These hydrocarbons are miscible and have similar boiling points and therefore they can be separated by fractional distillation.

Most of the hydrocarbons are alkanes.

The separation of crude oil into its constituents is called fractionation and the different parts are called fractions.

Before the crude oil enters the fractionating tower it is heated and evaporates to form a vapour.

As it enters the tower the fractions with the higher boiling points condense lower down the tower to form liquids.

The fractions with lower boiling points continue to rise up the tower until the temperature falls below their boiling point and they also condense.

The fractions that are gases at room temperature leave the tower as gases.

See Snap It! box on page 121 for details about fractional distillation of crude oil.

All alkanes have simple molecular structures. The boiling points of the fractions depend on the size of the molecules in that fraction. The larger the molecules the greater the intermolecular forces and the higher the boiling points.

Hydrocarbons are good fuels. They undergo complete combustion in air (oxygen) to give carbon dioxide and water as products and this combustion gives out lots of heat energy in an exothermic reaction.

If there is not enough oxygen then incomplete combustion takes place and poisonous carbon monoxide is produced. (This is covered in more detail in the subtopic, 'Atmospheric pollutants'.)

The apparatus, shown below, is used to test for the products of complete combustion:

DO IT!

Describe how the apparatus shown can be used to identify the products of combustion. Note that cobalt chloride paper changes from blue to pink in the presence of water.

Your description should explain the use of a pump, the upturned filter funnel, the cold water and why the limewater is placed after the cobalt chloride paper.

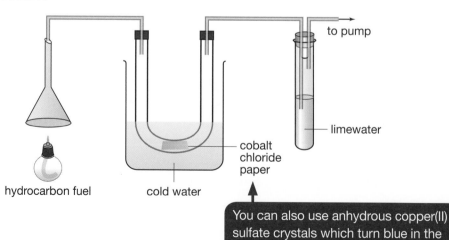

to pump

limewater

cobalt chloride paper

hydrocarbon fuel   cold water

You can also use anhydrous copper(II) sulfate crystals which turn blue in the presence of water.

WORKIT!

Write out a balanced chemical equation for the complete combustion of propane (C_3H_8) in oxygen.

The reactants are C_3H_8 and O_2. The products are H_2O and CO_2.

The best way of balancing these equations is to balance the carbons, then the hydrogens and then count up the number of oxygen atoms needed. For the oxygen you can have $\frac{1}{2}O_2$ if odd numbers are needed.

For propane you have 3 carbons and therefore 3 carbon dioxide molecules; you have 8 hydrogens and therefore 4 water molecules. This means that the total number of oxygen atoms is 10 and this means that we need 5 oxygen molecules on the reactant side.

$$C_3H_8(g) + 5O_2(g) \rightarrow 3CO_2(g) + 4H_2O(l)$$

The combustion of ethane (C_2H_6) illustrates the use of $\frac{1}{2}O_2$ because after going through the procedure we find that 7 oxygen atoms are needed on the reactant side.

$$C_2H_6(g) + 3\frac{1}{2}O_2(g) \rightarrow 2CO_2(g) + 3H_2O(l)$$

SNAPIT!

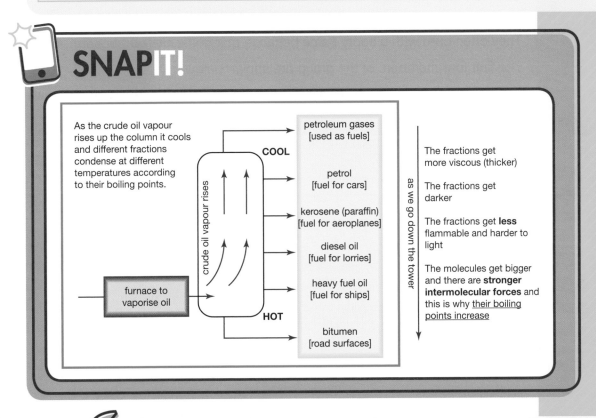

CHECKIT!

1 List the uses of the main fractions coming from the fractionating tower.

2 Explain why it is important to separate crude oil into its fractions.

3 Explain how the boiling points of the fractions change as they go down the column.

4 One fraction X comes off the tower above another fraction Y. Compare the thickness, appearance, ease of lighting and boiling point of X and Y.

5 In the investigation of the products of combustion what are the changes observed in the cobalt chloride paper and the limewater?

6 Complete and balance the following equations for the **complete combustion** of methane (CH_4) and butane (C_4H_{10}).

   a $CH_4(g) + \_\_O_2(g) \rightarrow$ b $C_4H_{10}(g) + \_\_O_2(g) \rightarrow$

The structural formulae and reactions of alkenes

The homologous series of the alkenes are hydrocarbons with the functional group C=C.

Most of the reactions of alkenes depend on the reactions of the C=C group.

Alkenes have the general formula C_nH_{2n}.

They are unsaturated hydrocarbons because they have two hydrogen atoms less than the maximum number.

Like all hydrocarbons, alkenes burn in air to give carbon dioxide and water. They often burn with a sooty flame because of incomplete combustion.

The first four members of the group are shown below:

Name of alkene	Molecular formula	Displayed structural formula
ethene	C_2H_4	
propene	C_3H_6	
butene	C_4H_8	
pentene	C_5H_{10}	

DO IT!

Use ball and stick models to help you to visualise the compounds.

The main type of reaction of alkenes is addition.

In addition reactions the double C=C bond becomes a single C–C bond and the other reactant splits into two. One part of the reactant bonds to one carbon of the C=C bond and the other part bonds to the other carbon. The diagram in the Snap It! box shows this reaction.

The test for alkenes is to add bromine water. Alkenes decolourise the bromine water, which means the bromine water goes from orange to colourless. This is an addition reaction.

SNAP IT!

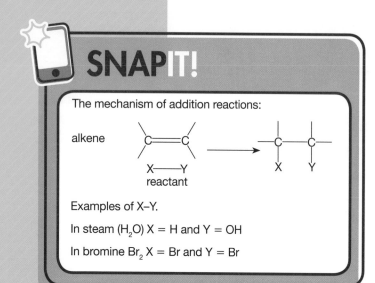

The mechanism of addition reactions:

alkene

reactant

Examples of X–Y.

In steam (H_2O) X = H and Y = OH

In bromine Br_2 X = Br and Y = Br

NAIL IT!

The addition reactions of the alkenes

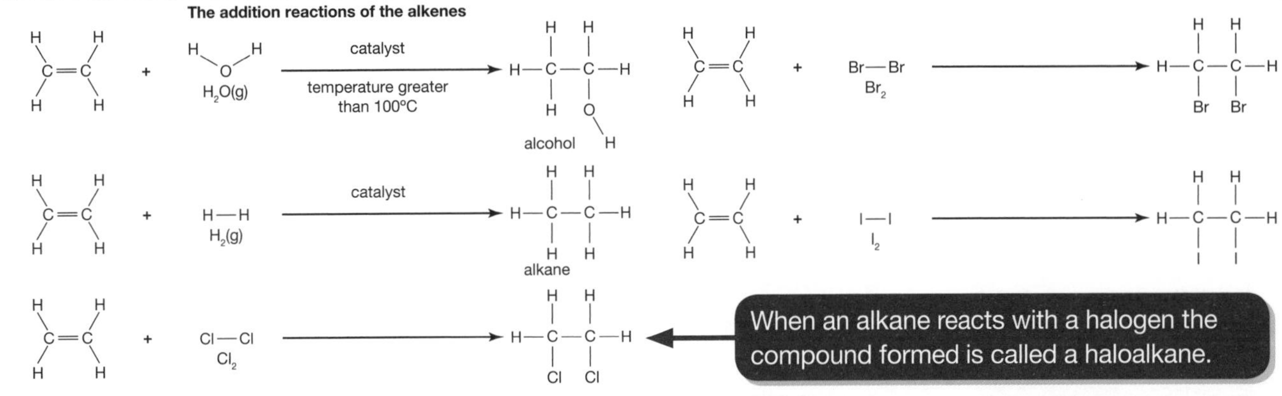

catalyst
temperature greater than 100°C
$H_2O(g)$
alcohol
catalyst
$H_2(g)$
alkane
Cl_2
When an alkane reacts with a halogen the compound formed is called a haloalkane.
Br—Br
Br_2
I_2

WORK IT!

Complete the following reactions using structural formulae. Think of the molecule being added as X—Y. X adds to one carbon and Y to the other.

1 Ethene + bromine

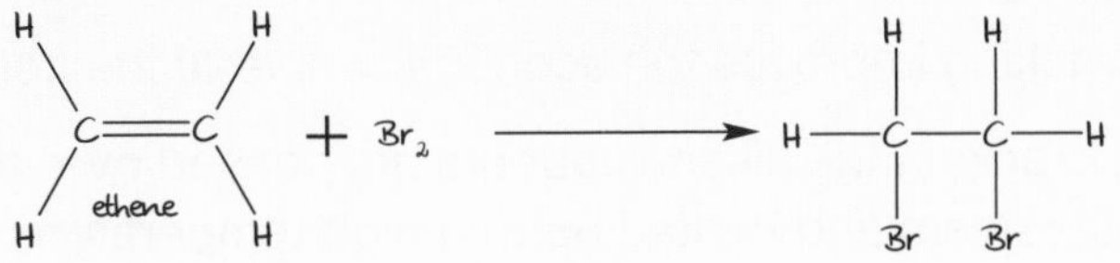

ethene
$+ Br_2$

In Br_2 X = Br; Y = Br

2 Propene + steam

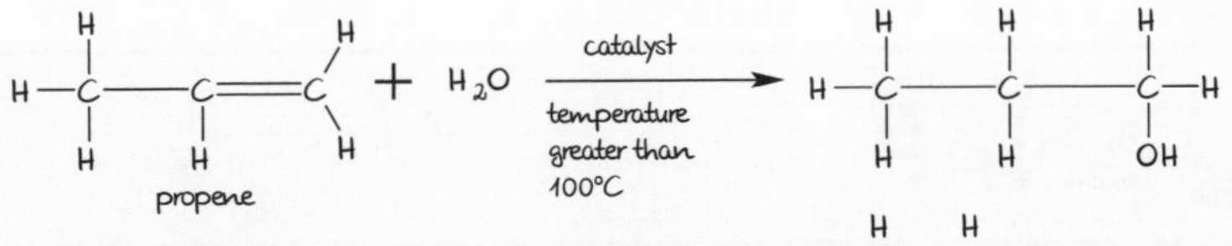

propene
$+ H_2O$
catalyst
temperature greater than 100°C

In H_2O X = H; Y = OH

3 Ethene + hydrogen

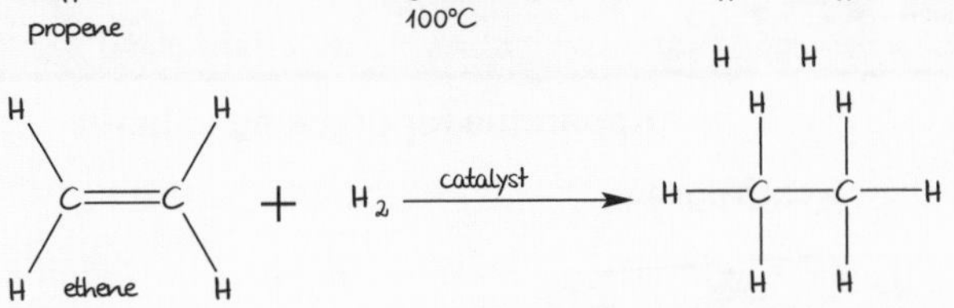

ethene
$+ H_2$
catalyst

In H_2 X = H; Y = H

CHECK IT!

1 State the general formula of the alkenes.

2 a Name the alkene with 4 carbons.

b Explain why methene does not exist.

3 a Explain why alkenes are described as unsaturated hydrocarbons.

b i Give the formula of the alkene with 4 carbons.

ii When the alkene with 4 carbons burns in insufficient oxygen it undergoes **incomplete combustion** to give carbon and water as the products. Write the balanced chemical equation for the reaction.

4 Name the main type of reaction of alkenes.

5 a Draw the structural formula of the product of the reaction of ethene with steam.

b Write the balanced chemical equation for the reaction.

Cracking and alkenes

Cracking is the breaking down of large **alkane** molecules into **smaller** alkanes and **alkenes**.

The smaller alkanes make good fuels, and the alkenes are used to make polymers.

Cracking is an important process for two main reasons:

1. **It converts fractions which have a low demand into higher demand fractions.** For example, after fractional distillation there is not enough of the petrol fraction for use as a fuel, but there is more than required of the kerosene fraction. This means that some of the kerosene can be cracked to give alkanes that make up the petrol fraction.

2. **It makes useful hydrocarbons not naturally found in crude oil.** For example, cracking also gives alkenes which are not found in crude oil but are very important in the manufacture of polymers.

The general formula of alkenes is C_nH_{2n}. Remember the general formula for alkanes is C_nH_{2n+2} and the two fewer hydrogen atoms is because of the C=C double bond in the alkene molecule.

Cracking improves the economic value of the fractions coming off the tower.

In cracking the alkane vapours are passed over a heated catalyst or mixed with steam and heated up to a high temperature.

DOIT!

Refer to your notes and textbook to analyse the results of the experiment in the Snap It! box below.

SNAPIT!

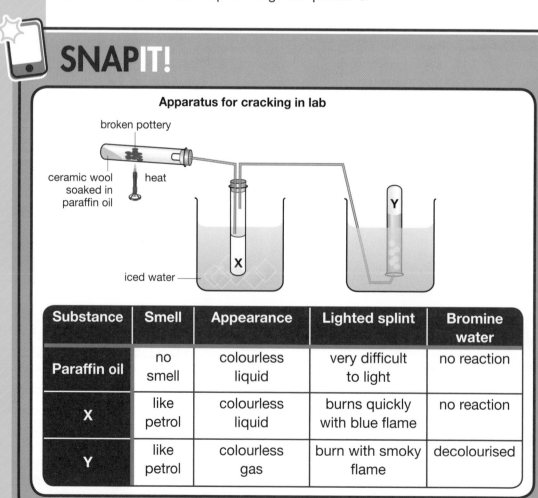

Apparatus for cracking in lab

broken pottery

ceramic wool soaked in paraffin oil

heat

Y

X

iced water

Substance	Smell	Appearance	Lighted splint	Bromine water
Paraffin oil	no smell	colourless liquid	very difficult to light	no reaction
X	like petrol	colourless liquid	burns quickly with blue flame	no reaction
Y	like petrol	colourless gas	burn with smoky flame	decolourised

MATHS SKILLS

Balancing chemical equations: You may have to use general formulae to identify the products in a cracking reaction.

Remember that the general formula of the alkanes is C_nH_{2n+2} and for the alkenes it is C_nH_{2n}.

WORKIT!

In the following reactions identify the alkanes and alkenes:

$$C_8H_{18} \rightarrow C_4H_8 + C_4H_{10}$$
Alkane   Alkene   Alkane

$$C_{10}H_{22} \rightarrow C_2H_4 + C_4H_8 + C_4H_{10}$$
Alkane   Alkene   Alkene   Alkane

An oil refinery

NAILIT!

The important thing about cracking is that it turns chemicals that are not very useful into ones that are very useful and economically important.

The amounts of short chain alkanes which are produced by fractionation of crude oil are not enough to meet demands. Cracking overcomes this shortfall.

CHECKIT!

1 Define cracking.

2 Describe how cracking is carried out in industry.

3 a State the general formula for alkenes.

  b Describe the chemical test for alkenes.

  c Give a use for alkenes.

4 Describe the economic importance of cracking.

5 Complete the following equations and identify the alkanes and alkenes in the reactions.

  a $C_6H_{14} \rightarrow C_2H_6 + \underline{\qquad}$

  b $C_8H_{18} \rightarrow C_2H_4 + C_3H_6 + \underline{\qquad}$

  c $C_{12}H_{26} \rightarrow 3C_2H_4 + \underline{\qquad}$

Alcohols

The alcohols are a homologous series and their functional group is the –OH group.

This means that they have similar chemical properties.

As the number of carbons increase there is a gradual change in physical properties. For example, their boiling points get higher.

Their general formula is $C_nH_{2n+2}O$.

Alcohols have lots of uses as fuels and solvents, and ethanol (CH_3CH_2OH) is used in alcoholic drinks.

Ethanol is the most important alcohol and it can be produced by the fermentation of aqueous sugar solution using yeast.

The process works best at around 40°C. When the ethanol concentration gets to about 15% the yeast is killed and the reaction stops. Oxygen should be excluded from the apparatus because the fermentation process is anaerobic.

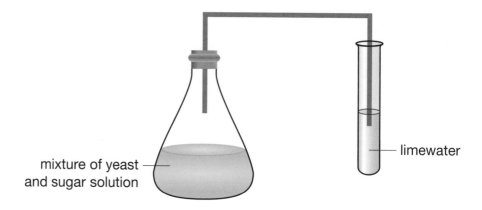

mixture of yeast and sugar solution

limewater

Combustion – alcohols burn in air to give carbon dioxide and water. For example:

$$CH_3CH_2OH(l) + 3O_2(l) \rightarrow 2CO_2(g) + 3H_2O(l)$$

The alcohols tend to burn with a non-luminous (colourless) flame.

Alcohols with less than four carbons are very soluble in water and dissolve to give colourless solutions.

Alcohols can be oxidised to give carboxylic acids. The carboxylic acid formed has the same number of carbons as the alcohol.

If the oxidising agent is purple acidified potassium manganate(VII) then it is decolourised. If it is acidified potassium dichromate(VII) then it changes from orange to green.

When sodium is added to alcohols there is (effervescence) fizzing because hydrogen gas is produced and the sodium disappears to leave a white solid.

DO IT!

Look up your notes on fermentation. You might have biology notes on the topic as well. Use the diagram on this page to help you.

DO IT!

Make sketches of what you see when alcohols react with sodium, burn in air and are oxidised by potassium manganate(VII) or potassium dichromate(VI).

SNAP IT!

Alcohol molecules can be represented in two ways, structural and displayed formula.

Name of alcohol	Structural formula	Displayed formula
methanol	CH_3OH	
ethanol	CH_3CH_2OH	
propanol	$CH_3CH_2CH_2OH$	
butanol	$CH_3CH_2CH_2CH_2OH$	

NAIL IT!

The only balanced chemical equations you need to do for the alcohols is the equation for combustion. One of the common errors is that it is easy to forget that there is already one oxygen atom in the alcohol molecule. ½O_2 molecules are allowed. Start with carbon, then hydrogen and then oxygen.

CHECK IT!

1 Name the alcohol with 3 carbons.

2 State the functional group in alcohols.

3 Draw the structural and displayed formulae for the alcohol which has the molecular formula C_2H_6O.

4 Write the balanced chemical equation for the combustion of:

  a $CH_3CH_2CH_2CH_2OH$

  b CH_3OH.

5 Draw and explain the apparatus you would use in the laboratory to carry out the fermentation of glucose.

6 a If ethanol is oxidised what carboxylic acid is formed?

  b Describe the observations when the oxidising agent used is:

    i acidified potassium manganate(VII)

    ii acidified potassium dichromate(VI).

Carboxylic acids

The carboxylic acids are a homologous series with the functional group —COOH.

Their general formula is $C_nH_{2n}O_2$.

An acid is a substance that produces hydrogen ions when dissolved in water.

The carboxylic acid (–COOH) group gives hydrogen ions when the acid dissolves in water.

But in aqueous solution only a small proportion of carboxylic acid molecules ionise to give hydrogen ions.

For this reason they are weak acids and in reactions they react more slowly than strong acids such as hydrochloric acid.

Solutions of carboxylic acids always have higher pH values than those of strong acids that have the same concentration.

As acids, they react with carbonates to form a salt, carbon dioxide and water. As carbon dioxide gas is produced the reaction gives effervescence (fizzing).

Carboxylic acids react with alcohols to produce esters. For example, ethanol and ethanoic acid react to form ethyl ethanoate and water. This reaction needs a strong acid as a catalyst.

If the carboxylic acid is heated with an alcohol and a strong acid catalyst like sulfuric acid, an ester is formed and can be detected by its fruity smell.

DO IT!

Get a piece of A4 or A3 paper and draw up a summary sheet for 'Organic chemistry'. You will need to have columns for functional group, general formula, names of first four in group and main reactions.

SNAP IT!

Name of carboxylic acid	Structural formula	Displayed formula
methanoic acid	HCOOH	
ethanoic acid	CH_3COOH	
propanoic acid	CH_3CH_2COOH	
butanoic acid	$CH_3CH_2CH_2COOH$	

NAILIT!

It is the hydrogen ions that are responsible for the reactions of acids, so carboxylic acids will react more slowly than strong acids like hydrochloric acid.

STRETCHIT!

Carboxylic acids are weak acids because they are only partially ionised in water. For example, in a solution of ethanoic acid only 4 out of every 1000 molecules produce hydrogen ions. A solution of the same concentration of hydrochloric acid, which is a strong acid, is fully ionised.

CHECKIT!

1 State the functional group of carboxylic acids.

2 Draw the structural and displayed formulae for the carboxylic acid with 2 carbons.

3 When calcium carbonate is added to an aqueous solution of ethanoic acid there is **fizzing** and **the reaction is slow.** Explain these observations.

Addition polymerisation

DOIT!

Search online for 'polymerisation animation'. Any short video you choose will give you some idea of how the process takes place.

In addition polymerisation small alkene molecules called monomers join together to make very large molecules called polymers.

In addition polymerisation there is only one product.

In an addition polymer there is a repeating unit and this has the same atoms as the monomer.

A polymer is named by simply placing 'poly' in front of the name of the monomer. For example, the polymer formed from propene is called **polypropene**.

SNAPIT!

The general equation for addition polymerisation is shown below. W, X, Y and Z can be any non-metal atom or group of atoms:

$$n \begin{array}{c} W \quad X \\ | \quad | \\ C=C \\ | \quad | \\ Y \quad Z \end{array} \longrightarrow \left[\begin{array}{c} W \quad X \\ | \quad | \\ C-C \\ | \quad | \\ Y \quad Z \end{array} \right]_n$$

monomer   polymer repeat unit

Four important things about the formula of the polymer repeat unit:

1 The n shows there are many repeat units.
2 The atoms or groups on the double bond are in the correct order.
3 The double bond is now a single bond.
4 Do not forget the bonds on each side that show the unit is attached to others on both sides.

NAILIT!

In the product, W, X, Y and Z are unchanged and in the same positions. The C=C has become C—C and the spare bonds at each end show that the unit carries on bonding to other units on either side. The lower case 'n' is a large number.

If you are asked to draw the alkene monomer from the repeat unit, the reverse procedure applies. The C—C becomes C=C and the W, X, Y and Z stay in the same positions. Do not forget to remove the bonds at each end.

Plastics are examples of polymers used in everyday life

WORKIT!

1 Show the repeat units for the polymers formed from the following monomers:

a) ethene

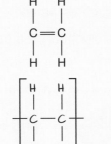

b) chloroethene

2 Draw the monomers used to make the following polymers:

CHECKIT!

1 Define the term monomer.

2 Draw the repeating unit for the polymer formed from the alkene dichlorethene (see below).

3 Draw the alkene responsible for making the following polymer.

4 Name the polymer formed from butene.

Condensation polymerisation

A condensation reaction takes place when two molecules react to form a larger molecule and a small molecule such as water.

An example is the reaction between an alcohol and a carboxylic acid to form an ester and water.

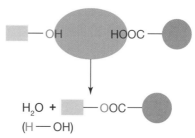

ester (the larger molecule)

If the alcohol has two —OH groups on it and the carboxylic acid has two —COOH groups on it then the condensation reaction can carry on and on to form a polyester.

The general polymers HO —▬— OH and HOOC —●— COOH react as shown below

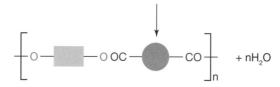

Each alcohol bonds to 2 carboxylic acids and each carboxylic acid bonds to 2 alcohols. This happens many many times to form a condensation polymer

$$\left[O-\blacksquare-O\ OC-\bullet-CO \right]_n + nH_2O$$

A polyester is a condensation polymer.

The alcohol and the carboxylic acid molecules are the monomers.

Examples of monomers for condensation polymerisation are $HOCH_2CH_2OH$ and $HOOCCH_2CH_2CH_2CH_2COOH$.

Nylon rope is an example of a polymer formed by condensation polymerisation

DO IT!

Write a short description of the main features of addition polymerisation and condensation polymerisation.

SNAPIT!

The formation of a condensation polymer such as a polyester is shown below:

Formation of a polyester

$$nHOCH_2CH_2OH + nHOOCCH_2CH_2CH_2CH_2COOH$$

elimination
of n H$_2$O

$$\left[\begin{array}{c} OCH_2CH_2OOCCH_2CH_2CH_2CO \end{array}\right]_n$$

WORKIT!

If the alcohol is HOCH$_2$CH$_2$OH and the carboxylic acid is HOOCCH$_2$CH$_2$COOH then the structure of the condensation polymer is:

$-[OCH_2CH_2OOCCH_2CH_2CO]_n-$

What are the two monomers that would form the polymer

$-[OCH_2CH_2CH_2OOCCH_2CH_2CH_2CH_2CO]_n- ?$

The two monomers are HOCH$_2$CH$_2$CH$_2$OH (the alcohol) and HOOCCH$_2$CH$_2$CH$_2$CH$_2$COOH (carboxylic acid).

NAILIT!

The link between two monomers in a polyester is the ester link or –OOC– group of atoms. So if you have two monomers, an alcohol and a carboxylic acid, then the OOC links together the alcohol and the carboxylic acid. As each ester link is formed one water molecule is eliminated. If n polymer repeat units are formed then 2n links are formed and 2n water molecules are eliminated. The final condensation polymer has the following general structure:

$-[O\text{-alcohol chain-}OOC\text{-carboxylic acid chain-}CO]_n-$

Reversing the procedure you can examine the structure of the polymer and draw the structures of the monomers HO–alcohol chain–OH and HOOC–carboxylic acid chain–COOH

✓ CHECKIT!

1 a i Explain what is meant by the term **condensation reaction**.

   ii Name the simple molecule eliminated when a polyester is formed.

   b Describe the main differences between addition polymerisation and condensation polymerisation.

2 What is the condensation polymer formed from these two monomers?

   HOOC-COOH and HOCH$_2$CH$_2$OH

3 Draw the monomers responsible for forming this polymer.

   $-[OCH_2OOCCO]_n-$

Amino acids and DNA

Amino acids have at least two functional groups in their molecules.

Amino acids are the monomers that form condensation polymers called polypeptides or proteins. The small molecule eliminated each time is water.

There are 20 different naturally occurring amino acids and these can be linked in different sequences giving different proteins.

DNA (deoxyribonucleic acid) gives genetic instructions from which the essential proteins in our body are made.

DNA is a large molecule which consists of two polymer chains which together form a double helix.

Each DNA chain is a condensation polymer of four different monomers called nucleotides. All the large molecules found in organisms are condensation polymers. Examples are starch and cellulose which are polymers of the monomer glucose.

DOIT!

Look at your biology notes about DNA and proteins, and add any additional notes that help your understanding of these polymers.

SNAPIT!

The amino acid glycine H_2NCH_2COOH forms the condensation polymer $-(NHCH_2CO)_n-$

A protein contains different amino acids in a condensation polymer. The amino acids are linked by the peptide bond:

$-NHCO-$

CHECKIT! ✓

1 State the small molecule that is always eliminated in condensation polymerisation.

2 Polysaccharides are polymers of sugars. Examples are starch and cellulose. The diagram below is a simplified version of monomer sugar rings. Draw the condensation polymer formed from these monomers.

3 Give a brief description of DNA as a polymer.

4 Draw the repeating unit found in polyglycine.

Organic chemistry

REVIEW IT!

1 a Determine the molecular formulae of the compounds A to D shown below.

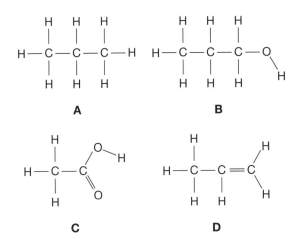

A

B

C

D

b Which of the compounds A to D is or are:

i a hydrocarbon

ii an alkene

iii a carboxylic acid

iv an alcohol

v an alkane?

c Name all four compounds.

2 a Identify the functional group in an alkene.

b Why are the alkenes considered a homologous series?

c Describe the chemical test for alkenes.

d Complete the following reactions:

i

$$\underset{H}{\overset{H}{>}}C=C\underset{H}{\overset{H}{<}} + Br_2 \longrightarrow$$

ii

$$\underset{H}{\overset{H}{>}}C=C\underset{H}{\overset{H}{<}} + H_2 \xrightarrow{catalyst}$$

iii

$$\underset{H}{\overset{H}{>}}C=C\underset{H}{\overset{H}{<}} + H_2O \xrightarrow[300°C]{catalyst}$$

3 a State the physical property which allows us to separate crude oil into its fractions using fractional distillation.

b As we go up the fractionating tower what happens to the following properties:

i viscosity

ii boiling point

iii ease of lighting?

c Explain the trend in boiling point as you go up the tower.

4 Alkanes are the main components of crude oil.

a What is the general formula of the alkanes?

b Complete and balance the following equations for the complete combustion of the two hydrocarbons methane and ethane:

i $CH_4(g) + O_2(g) \rightarrow$

ii $C_2H_6(l) + O_2(g) \rightarrow$

c The diagram below shows the apparatus used to investigate what is formed when an alkane burns in air.

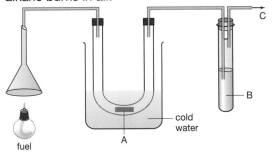

C

cold water

A

fuel

B

i Give the correct labels for A, B and C.

ii Describe what happens to A. What does the change show?

iii Describe what happens to the liquid in B. What does the change show?

5 a Why is it necessary to carry out cracking on alkanes which have large molecules?

b Complete the following equations:

i $C_{10}H_{22} \rightarrow C_4H_8 +$

ii $\rightarrow C_3H_6 + C_6H_{14}$

Chemical analysis

Testing for gases

Several chemical reactions produce a gas or gases. In solutions this produces effervescence (fizzing).

Hydrogen is a flammable gas. The test for hydrogen is a burning splint which is extinguished (put out) with a 'pop'.

The equation for this combustion reaction is: $2H_2(g) + O_2(g) \rightarrow 2H_2O(l)$

Oxygen (O_2) is required for combustion. The test for oxygen is a glowing splint which relights in oxygen.

Carbon dioxide reacts with a solution of limewater (calcium hydroxide solution) to give solid calcium carbonate. When carbon dioxide is passed into limewater the limewater turns cloudy/milky.

The equation for this reaction is:

$CO_2(g) + Ca(OH)_2(aq) \rightarrow CaCO_3(s) + H_2O(l)$

colourless liquid   white solid

Chlorine (Cl_2) bleaches blue litmus paper (or UI paper). This is used as the test for chlorine.

SNAPIT!

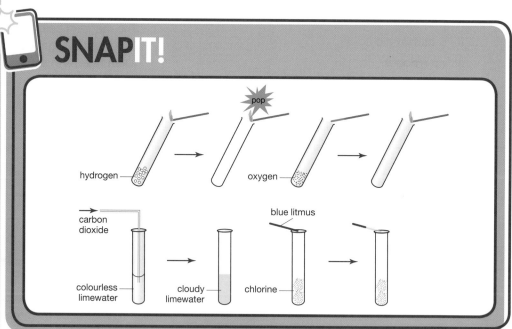

hydrogen   pop   oxygen

carbon dioxide

blue litmus

colourless limewater   cloudy limewater   chlorine

CHECKIT!

1 Describe how you would test for the gases produced in the following reactions.

    a $2H_2O_2(aq) \rightarrow 2H_2O(l) + O_2(g)$

    b $CaCO_3(s) + 2HCl(aq) \rightarrow CaCl_2(aq) + CO_2(g) + H_2O(l)$

    c $Mg(s) + 2HCl(aq) \rightarrow MgCl_2(aq) + H_2(g)$

    d $2NaCl(aq) + 2H_2O(l) \rightarrow 2NaOH(aq) + H_2(g) + Cl_2(g)$

Identifying metal ions using flame tests and flame emission spectroscopy

Positive metal ions are often referred to as cations because they move towards the cathode (the negative electrode) in electrolysis.

When the salts of some metals are heated in a blue or roaring Bunsen burner flame they give a distinctive characteristic colour that can be used to identify the metal ion present. This is called a flame test.

When carrying out the flame test a very hot (roaring blue) Bunsen flame must be used.

If the flame test is used to identify the metals in a mixture some flame colours are masked by others. For example, the lilac flame given by potassium ions is easily masked by the stronger yellow colour of sodium ions.

SNAPIT!

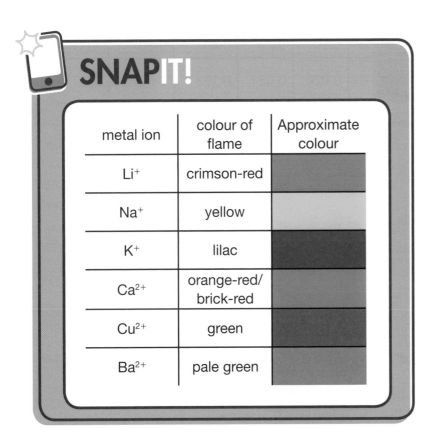

metal ion	colour of flame	Approximate colour
Li⁺	crimson-red	
Na⁺	yellow	
K⁺	lilac	
Ca²⁺	orange-red/ brick-red	
Cu²⁺	green	
Ba²⁺	pale green	

DOIT!

Devise a method or make a short MP3 recording of how you would do a flame test.

NAILIT!

Learn the colours of the flames. There could well be a question on identifying salts and the flame colours would form part of the answer.

NAILIT!

When performing flame tests make sure you follow all of the safety instructions – a roaring blue flame is very hot!

Flame emission spectroscopy uses the same principles as the flame test but uses instrumentation to do it. Atomic absorption spectroscopy works by atoms absorbing radiation, which has the same energy as the colours it produces in the flame test. These absorptions appear as dark lines in the spectrum. The advantages are the same as those for emission spectroscopy.

A small sample is put into a flame and the light given out is passed through a spectroscope. A series of coloured lines called a line spectrum is obtained and one of these lines is the one that is used to analyse the sample.

The intensity of the line gives a measure of the concentration of the ion.

The advantages of flame emission spectroscopy over the simple flame test are:

- It is more sensitive.

- It can be used to measure the concentration of the ion in the sample.

- It can look at distinctive areas of the colour spectrum emitted by a heated element and not by others. This overcomes the problem of some colours being masked by others.

- This means that it can be used to analyse the composition of mixtures which cannot be done using the flame test.

MATHS SKILLS

One possible question about instrumentation could involve figures for a calibration graph, and using them to find an unknown concentration.

WORKIT!

On the graph paper provided, draw a calibration line for the following readings from a flame emission spectroscope.

Conc.mg/cm³	0	0.10	0.20	0.40	0.80	1.00
Line intensity/ arbitrary units	0	0.026	0.051	0.103	0.207	0.25

A solution X gave a reading of 0.078. What is its concentration?

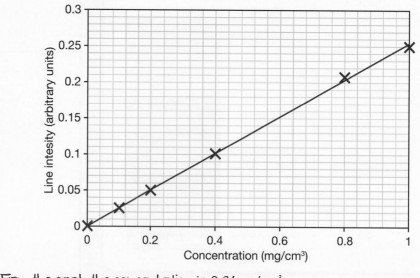

From the graph the concentration is 0.31 mg/cm³.

CHECKIT!

1 State the colours of Ca^{2+} and K^+ ions in the flame test.

2 List some advantages of instrumentation when detecting ions in the flame test.

Identifying metal ions using sodium hydroxide solution

When aqueous sodium hydroxide solution is added to the solutions of some metals, precipitates (solids) are formed and the colours of these precipitates can be used to identify the metal ion present.

If the formula of the metal ion is M^{n+} then the formula of the precipitate is $M(OH)_n$.

The colours of these precipitates are summarised below:

Name and formula of ion	Colour of precipitate	Extra comments
Magnesium Mg^{2+}	White	Same as calcium but gives no colour in flame test
Calcium Ca^{2+}	White	Gives an orange-red colour in flame test
Aluminium Al^{3+}	White	The white precipitate dissolves when excess (extra) sodium hydroxide solution is added
Copper(II) Cu^{2+}	Blue	
Iron(II) Fe^{2+}	Green	
Iron(III) Fe^{3+}	Brown	

SNAPIT!

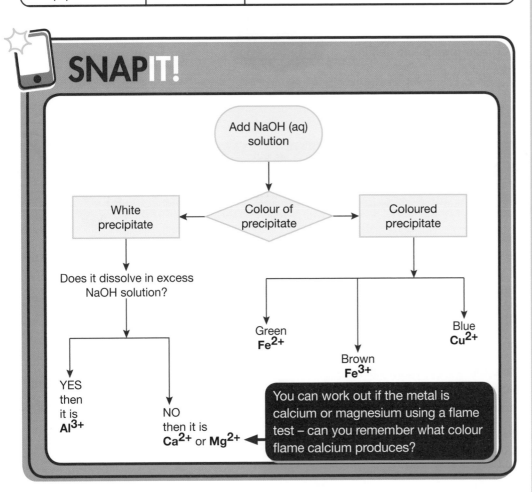

Add NaOH (aq) solution

Colour of precipitate

White precipitate

Coloured precipitate

Does it dissolve in excess NaOH solution?

Green
Fe^{2+}

Brown
Fe^{3+}

Blue
Cu^{2+}

YES then it is Al^{3+}

NO then it is Ca^{2+} or Mg^{2+}

You can work out if the metal is calcium or magnesium using a flame test – can you remember what colour flame calcium produces?

DOIT!

The flowchart in the Snap It! box does not have to be the one you use. See if you can make up your own.

Copy or print out the flowchart in the Snap It! box. Add colour to it. Also add in the other cations that give coloured flames in the flame test.

STRETCHIT!

If you are asked to write the ionic equation for a precipitation reaction then only the metal ion and hydroxide ions are involved. The anion in the metal salt and the sodium ions in the sodium hydroxide are spectator ions because they do not take part in the reaction.

Ionic equations were covered in displacement reactions of the halogens and in the reactivity series.

For example:

$Mg^{2+}(aq) + 2OH^-(aq) \rightarrow Mg(OH)_2(s)$

$Fe^{3+}(aq) + 3OH^-(aq) \rightarrow Fe(OH)_3(s)$

NAILIT!

When you write the chemical equations for these reactions you should know that the metal and the hydroxide are always listed together. State symbols are also important here. The precipitate, which is the hydroxide, is the solid (s) and all the other substances are in solution (aq).

For example:

$2NaOH(aq) + MgSO_4(aq) \rightarrow Mg(OH)_2(s) + Na_2SO_4(aq)$

A green precipitate settling in solution

CHECKIT!

1 Describe the colour of the precipitate you would get if you added sodium hydroxide solution to the following solutions:

   a $CaCl_2(aq)$ b Iron(III) nitrate

   c $CuSO_4(aq)$

2 Describe how you would distinguish between two solutions which contain magnesium and aluminium ions.

3 Write the word and balanced chemical equations for the reaction of copper(II) sulfate ($CuSO_4$) solution with sodium hydroxide (NaOH) solution.

4 Write the ionic equation for the reaction of sodium hydroxide solution with $CuSO_4$ solution.

5 When a solution containing green Fe^{2+} ions is left overnight the solution gradually turns brown in colour.

   a State the name of the chemical in the new solution.

   b Explain why this is an oxidation reaction.

Testing for negative ions (anions) in salts

Negative ions can also be called anions because they move towards the anode (positive electrode) in electrolysis.

The five ions that are tested for are the three halide ions (Cl^-, Br^- and I^-), sulfate ions (SO_4^{2-}) and carbonate ions (CO_3^{2-}).

The tests for the halide ions and sulfate ions require you to add an acid before the testing solution. This is to remove any carbonate ions that would also react with the testing solution and produce a white precipitate. This would interfere with the interpretation of the colour of precipitate produced by the salt.

The acid used contains the same negative ion as the testing solution. This means that nitric acid is added before silver nitrate and hydrochloric acid is added before barium chloride solution.

The tests are shown below:

Ion tested for	Testing reagents	Results of positive test
Chloride (Cl^-)	Add nitric acid followed by silver nitrate solution	White precipitate (of silver chloride)
Bromide (Br^-)	Add nitric acid followed by silver nitrate solution	Cream precipitate (of silver bromide)
Iodide (I^-)	Add nitric acid followed by silver nitrate solution	Yellow precipitate (of silver iodide)
Sulfate (SO_4^{2-})	Add hydrochloric acid followed by barium chloride solution	White precipitate (of barium sulfate)
Carbonate (CO_3^{2-})	Add hydrochloric acid then pass gas formed through limewater	Effervescence (fizzing) and gas produced turns limewater cloudy/milky

DO IT!

It's a good idea to review previous topics before you revise this one. For example, the formulae of the halide ions were covered in the topic on ions, and the test for carbonate ions was previously looked at when you studied the reactions of acids in chemical changes.

NAIL IT!

If you are asked to write the chemical equations for the reactions of halides and sulfate you must remember that the negative ion combines with the metal in the test reagent to form a solid.

For example, if you were writing the equation for the reaction between sodium chloride solution and silver nitrate solution the equation is as follows.

$AgNO_3(aq) + NaCl(aq) \rightarrow NaNO_3(aq) + AgCl(s)$

STRETCH IT!

Depending on your specification and the tier you are following, you may need to write the ionic equations for these reactions.

For all three sets of ions remember that the negative ion (anion) you are testing for will react with the positive ion (cation) in the test reagent.

Ion being tested for	Testing reagent and positive ion	Ionic equation
Cl^-	Silver nitrate solution (Ag^+)	$Ag^+(aq) + Cl^-(aq) \rightarrow AgCl(s)$
Br^-	Silver nitrate solution (Ag^+)	$Ag^+(aq) + Br^-(aq) \rightarrow AgBr(s)$
I^-	Silver nitrate solution (Ag^+)	$Ag^+(aq) + I^-(aq) \rightarrow AgI(s)$
SO_4^{2-}	Barium chloride solution (Ba^{2+})	$Ba^{2+}(aq) + SO_4^{2-}(aq) \rightarrow BaSO_4(s)$
CO_3^{2-}	Hydrochloric acid (H^+)	$2H^+(aq) + CO_3^{2-}(s) \rightarrow CO_2(g) + H_2O(l)$

SNAPIT!

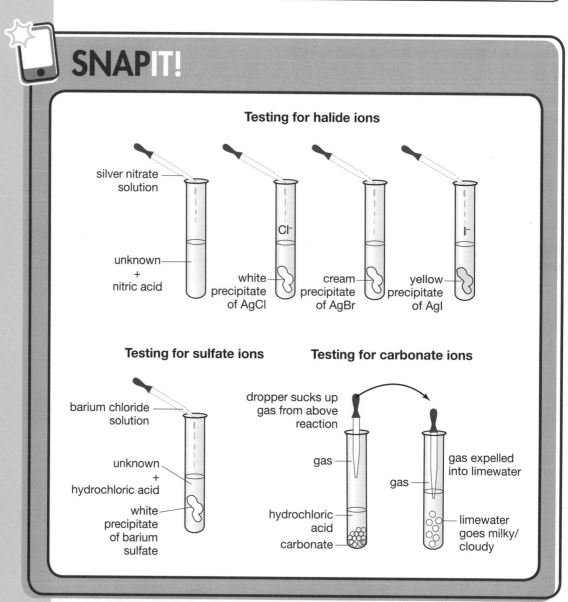

Testing for halide ions

silver nitrate solution

unknown + nitric acid

Cl^-

I^-

white precipitate of AgCl

cream precipitate of AgBr

yellow precipitate of AgI

Testing for sulfate ions

barium chloride solution

unknown + hydrochloric acid

white precipitate of barium sulfate

Testing for carbonate ions

dropper sucks up gas from above reaction

gas

gas

gas expelled into limewater

hydrochloric acid

carbonate

limewater goes milky/cloudy

CHECKIT!

1 State the reagents used to test for the following ions:

   a chloride ions   b sulfate ions   c carbonate ions.

2 A solution was known to contain two negative ions. When it was tested with silver nitrate solution and nitric acid it gave a cream precipitate. The same solution also gave a white precipitate with hydrochloric acid and barium chloride solution.

Name the two ions present.

Identifying ions in an ionic compound

This is one of the practicals you could be questioned on in the exam. The practical emphasises that you carry out a practical safely and accurately, carry out chemical tests and make conclusions based on the results.

Identifying the ions in an ionic compound requires knowledge of how to test for positive and negative ions (cations and anions).

DOIT!

Make up a flowchart that will help you identify the cation (positive ion) and the anion (negative ion) in an ionic compound.

SNAP**IT!**

When testing for the halide and sulfate anions, the testing chemical is always added along with the corresponding acid. This removes any carbonate ions that would interfere with the result. For example, you always add nitric acid before adding silver nitrate solution and hydrochloric acid before adding barium chloride solution.

Stage	Test	Apparatus	Procedure
1	Flame test	Bunsen burner, tripod, gauze, heat-resistant pads, watch glass, nichrome wire, tongs, hydrochloric acid, distilled water	Solid in watch glass, add HCl to solid. Dip clean nichrome wire in the sample and place in roaring blue flame.
2	Sodium hydroxide/ precipitation test	Test tubes, test-tube rack, wash bottle, dropping pipettes, sodium hydroxide solution	Make up solution in distilled water. Add NaOH solution drop by drop. Observe the colour of any precipitate formed.
3	Negative ion tests	Test tubes, test-tube rack, wash bottle, distilled water, droppers, barium chloride solution, hydrochloric acid, silver nitrate solution, nitric acid, limewater	Add HCl to solid and if there is effervescence pass gas through limewater. If the next test is for sulfate ion then dissolve the unknown in dilute HCl and then add barium chloride solution. If it is for halide ion then dissolve in nitric acid and then add silver nitrate solution.

NAILIT!

In the exams you are likely to get a table of test results and be asked to identify the cations (positive ions) and anions (negative ions) present using these results. You will need to identify both ions to name the compound.

WORKIT!

Using the results below, identify the ions present in the three compounds X, Y and Z and give the name of each compound along with its formula.

Substance	Flame test	Sodium hydroxide	Barium chloride solution	Silver nitrate solution	Hydrochloric acid
X	Crimson flame	No reaction	No reaction	No reaction	Effervescence and gas turned limewater milky
Y	No colour	White precipitate that dissolved in excess NaOH	White precipitate	No reaction	No reaction
Z	Brick-red flame	White precipitate	No reaction	Cream precipitate	No reaction

X contains the lithium cation, Li^+ and the carbonate anion, CO_3^{2-}. The compound is lithium carbonate, Li_2CO_3.

Y contains the aluminium cation, Al^{3+} and the sulfate anion, SO_4^{2-}. The name of the compound is aluminium sulfate, $Al_2(SO_4)_3$.

Z contains the calcium cation, Ca^{2+} and the bromide anion, Br^-. The name of the compound is calcium bromide, $CaBr_2$.

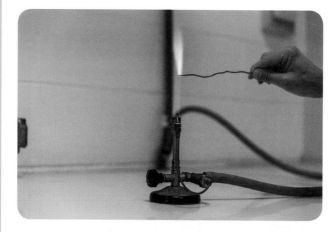

Performing a flame test

CHECKIT!

1 Identify the negative ions present in A, B and C.

Substance	Barium chloride solution	Silver nitrate solution	Hydrochloric acid
A	No reaction	Yellow precipitate	No reaction
B	White precipitate	No reaction	Effervescence
C	No reaction	White precipitate	No reaction

2 Describe the tests you would use to identify the anions and cations present in the following compounds:

    a Magnesium sulfate   **b** Sodium carbonate

    c Iron(II) chloride   **d** Potassium iodide.

Chemical analysis

REVIEW IT!

1 a Explain how you would carry out a flame test. Your answer should name the apparatus you would use and describe the procedure you would follow.

b State the colour of the flames seen with the following compounds:

i sodium chloride

ii copper sulfate

iii $CaCl_2$

iv KBr.

2 Describe your observations when the following actions are carried out.

a Hydrochloric acid is added to solid calcium carbonate.

b Nitric acid and silver nitrate solution is added to:

i sodium iodide solution

ii potassium chloride solution

iii potassium bromide solution

iv sodium chloride solution.

c Hydrochloric acid and barium chloride solution are added to:

i sodium sulfate solution

ii sodium chloride solution.

d Sodium hydroxide solution is added to:

i magnesium sulfate solution

ii aluminium sulfate solution

iii iron(II) chloride solution.

3 Identify the compounds that give the results in the table below:

Substance	Flame test	Sodium hydroxide	Barium chloride solution	Silver nitrate solution
X	No colour	White precipitate	White precipitate	No reaction
Y	Yellow flame	No reaction	No reaction	Cream precipitate
Z	Lilac flame	No reaction	No reaction	White precipitate

Chemistry of the atmosphere

The composition and evolution of the Earth's atmosphere

MATHS SKILLS

The composition of the atmosphere is usually expressed in percentages and the percentage of a gas can be found using the equation

$$\text{Proportion of gas} = \frac{\text{volume of gas}}{\text{total volume}} \times 100$$

The present composition of the Earth's atmosphere (dry air) is 78% (about four-fifths) nitrogen, 21% (about one-fifth) oxygen and 1% of other gases like argon and the other noble gases, carbon dioxide, and water vapour.

This composition has evolved over billions of years.

In the early days of the Earth's existence there was a lot of volcanic activity and this gave rise to an atmosphere containing lots of water vapour and carbon dioxide along with methane, nitrogen and ammonia.

As the Earth cooled, the water vapour condensed and formed the oceans, rivers and lakes.

At some stage in the Earth's history, life began and algae and photosynthetic bacteria carried out photosynthesis.

In photosynthesis, glucose is made from the reaction between carbon dioxide and water. Oxygen is a by-product of this reaction.

carbon dioxide(g) + water(l) $\xrightarrow{\text{light}}$ glucose(s) + oxygen(g)

$6CO_2(g) + 6H_2O(l) \xrightarrow{\text{light}} C_6H_{12}O_6(s) + 6O_2(g)$

As the oxygen in the atmosphere increased because of photosynthesis, animals evolved.

As the oxygen increased, the amount of carbon dioxide was reduced by various processes. These processes were: dissolving in water; limestone formation; photosynthesis; crude oil and natural gas formation; coal formation.

Once nitrogen was formed it remained in the atmosphere because it is very unreactive. This explains its high concentration in the atmosphere.

DO IT!

Look at the apparatus in the Snap It! box. Use your notes or textbook to find out how it works.

SNAPIT!

The apparatus below is used to find the composition of air.

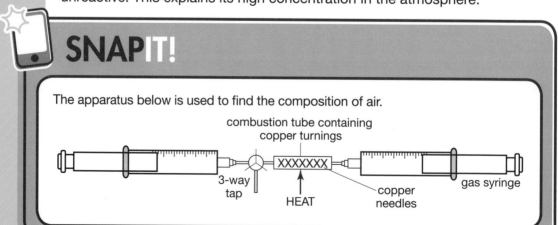

combustion tube containing copper turnings

3-way tap

HEAT

copper needles

gas syringe

Removal process	Result
As the oceans formed carbon dioxide dissolved in the water to form insoluble solid metal carbonates.	These carbonates formed sediments so the carbon dioxide was locked in solids.
Photosynthesis uses carbon dioxide and water to make sugars such as glucose.	Carbon dioxide removed from the air.
The carbon dioxide in the oceans was converted into calcium carbonate by plankton and other marine organisms.	Their remains were compressed to form limestone.
Sometimes these dead marine organisms were covered with mud and compressed by other layers in anaerobic conditions.	These remains formed crude oil and natural gas.
A similar process happened with dead land plants.	These remains formed coal as a sedimentary rock.

NAILIT!

This table shows the ways that carbon dioxide has been removed during the lifetime of the Earth.

WORKIT!

In an experiment to work out the composition of air, the apparatus was the same as that shown in the Snap It! box on page 146.

$100 \, cm^3$ of air was drawn into the apparatus through the 3-way tap. After heating, the volume of gas present was reduced to $79 \, cm^3$.

a What is the percentage of oxygen in air?

The volume of gas has gone down because the oxygen reacted with the copper needles.

This means that the percentage of oxygen $= \dfrac{\text{volume of oxygen}}{\text{Total volume}} \times 100\%$

$= \dfrac{21}{100} \times 100\% = 21\%$

b What is the equation for the reaction taking place in the apparatus?

$2Cu + O_2 \longrightarrow 2CuO$

✓ CHECKIT!

1 List the main gases found in the early atmosphere of the Earth.

2 State four ways that carbon dioxide has been removed from the atmosphere during the Earth's lifetime.

3 Write the word and balanced chemical equations for photosynthesis.

Climate change

A key thing to remember in this topic is that all evidence collected by scientists has to be peer reviewed. This means that research has to be examined and tested by other scientists in the same field.

The media are also important because the interpretation they put on scientific evidence can influence public opinion and behaviour.

Most of the solar radiation reaching the Earth is shortwave UV and visible light. The energy reflected back by the Earth is longer wavelength infrared radiation.

This infrared radiation is absorbed by gases in the atmosphere which then re-emit this energy in all directions but a lot goes back to the Earth which then warms it up. This natural increase in temperature is known as the greenhouse effect.

The two main greenhouse gases are carbon dioxide (CO_2) and methane (CH_4). Scientists have discovered a correlation between the rise and fall of carbon dioxide in the atmosphere and the average global temperature.

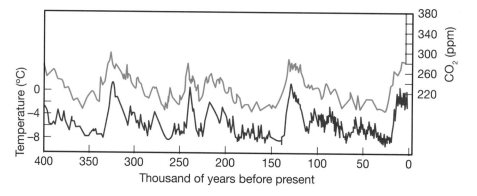

The rapid rise in carbon dioxide concentration has been linked to the burning of fossil fuels such as crude oil and coal to generate energy.

Deforestation may also have an effect on carbon dioxide in the atmosphere. Deforestation's effect is twofold because it reduces the number of trees that take up carbon dioxide by photosynthesis and carbon dioxide is then emitted as the felled trees are burned to clear the land.

Two big sources of methane are:

• livestock farming (from animal digestion and waste decomposition)

• rubbish decay in landfill sites.

To stop the rise in carbon dioxide concentration humans need to consider how to decrease the burning of fossil fuels.

This has proved difficult for various reasons:

• a lack of affordable alternative energy sources

• economic growth relies on cheap energy

• objections to the idea that global warming is caused by human activity

• lack of international co-operation.

SNAPIT!

Potential consequences of climate change

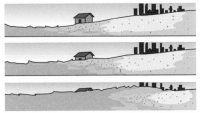

rising sea levels as ice caps melt

more frequent and violent storms

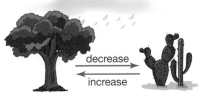

increased or decreased rainfall

reduction in crops

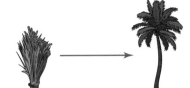

change in crops grown

change in distribution of wildlife

DOIT!

Research one of the **possible consequences** shown in the Snap It! box, to see if climate change is actually taking place. What evidence is there?

NAILIT!

One question that you might have to answer is 'Why have some countries been slow to reduce their burning of fossil fuels?' Possible answers are as follows:

- Some people think that climate change is just one part of a natural cycle.
- Some people believe that the evidence is still not 100% reliable.
- There is a difficulty with predicting the possible effects of climate change because different scientific models have different limitations and therefore make different predictions.
- In the short term, the alternatives to burning fossil fuels are more expensive.
- Lobbying by the petroleum and coal industries.
- Governments are slow to replace fossil fuels with other forms of energy.
- Inability of international bodies like the UN to get all nations to agree to reduce their use of fossil fuels.

CHECKIT!

1 State the two main greenhouse gases.

2 Explain why the rise in carbon dioxide in the atmosphere is often blamed for global warming.

3 State the type of radiation absorbed and re-emitted by greenhouse gases.

4 Explain the causes of the rise in carbon dioxide concentration in the atmosphere.

Reducing the carbon footprint

The carbon footprint of a product or activity is the total amount of carbon dioxide and greenhouse gases emitted over the lifetime of that product or activity.

There are a number of ways to remove or reduce the carbon footprint.

- Increase the use of alternative energy supplies. For example, solar cells, wind power and wave power.
- Energy conservation involves reducing the amount of energy used by using energy-saving measures such as house insulation or using devices that use less energy.
- In Carbon Capture and Storage (CCS) the carbon dioxide given out by power stations can be removed by reacting it with other chemicals and then storing it deep under the sea in porous sedimentary rocks, especially those that used to be part of oilfields.
- Carbon taxes and licences. Penalising companies and individuals who use too much energy by increasing their taxes.
- By removing carbon dioxide from the air using natural biological processes, especially photosynthesis. This is done by planting trees or trying to increase marine algae by adding chemicals to the sea. This is called carbon offsetting.
- Using plants as biofuels, because plants take in carbon dioxide, when they are burned they only release the same amount of carbon dioxide, which is zero net release. This makes them carbon-neutral.

NAILIT!

You may be asked why people, companies or countries do not reduce their carbon footprints. Possible answers are as follows:

- People are reluctant to change their lifestyle. For example, still using large cars instead of smaller more fuel-efficient ones.
- Even energy-saving devices have a carbon footprint because of the processes used in the extraction of materials to make them and the energy used in their manufacture and in their disposal.
- Countries and companies still find it more economic to use lots of energy.
- Countries may not co-operate with each other.
- There is still disagreement that climate change is man-made and about its causes.
- People are still not sure of the facts and do not know about the possible consequences of climate change.

SNAPIT!

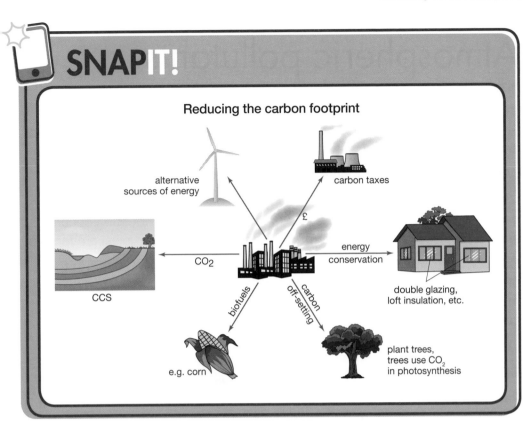

Reducing the carbon footprint

alternative sources of energy

carbon taxes

CO₂

CCS

£

energy conservation

double glazing, loft insulation, etc.

biofuels

carbon off-setting

plant trees, trees use CO₂ in photosynthesis

e.g. corn

DOIT!

Look at your notes on aluminium extraction by electrolysis. Why does this process have a large carbon footprint?

CHECKIT!

1 Describe what is meant by the term carbon footprint.

2 Explain the following terms:

   a carbon offsetting

   b carbon capture and storage.

3 List two reasons why people are not reducing their carbon footprint.

4 Photovoltaic cells and other alternative sources of energy reduce the need for burning fossil fuels but they do have a carbon footprint. Explain why.

5 The data below shows the savings in carbon dioxide emissions by two different methods of home insulation when a **detached house** is insulated.

Method	Reduction in carbon dioxide emissions/kg
Loft insulation	990
Cavity wall insulation	1100

   a State which of these reductions would be less for a terraced house. Explain your answer.

   b Calculate how many moles of carbon dioxide would have been emitted without insulating the loft of the detached house. ($M_r(CO_2) = 44$)

   c Calculate the volume of carbon dioxide that would have been emitted.

151

Atmospheric pollutants

An atmospheric pollutant is something that is introduced into the atmosphere and has undesired or unwanted effects.

When hydrocarbons undergo complete combustion in air they produce carbon dioxide and water as well as energy.

If there is insufficient (not enough) air then incomplete combustion occurs and carbon monoxide (CO) and particulates (small soot particles) are formed.

Carbon monoxide (CO) is a toxic gas. It combines with haemoglobin in the blood and reduces the capacity of the red blood cells to carry oxygen. This means the the cells around the body do not receive sufficient oxygen. This can cause death.

The reaction is a reversible one:

$CO(g) + HbO_2 \rightleftharpoons O_2(g) + HbCO$ ◄──── Hb = haemoglobin

Particulates cause global dimming (reflect sunlight back out to space before it reaches the atmosphere) so that less sunlight gets through to the Earth's surface. They are also irritants and cause damage to the lungs.

At the high temperatures caused by combustion in car engines, nitrogen and oxygen can combine to form oxides of nitrogen. These cause respiratory problems. Eventually these oxides dissolve in water to form acid rain. Acid rain causes weathering of buildings and damages plants and aquatic life.

Fossil fuels contain sulfur and when this burns in air it forms sulfur dioxide (SO_2). This is a very acidic gas and when it dissolves in clouds of water vapour it causes acid rain. It also causes respiratory problems.

To reduce the formation of sulfur dioxide many petrochemicals are desulfurised.

NAIL IT!

Particulates from incomplete combustion are mostly made of carbon.

DO IT!

Construct a mind map based on climate change, greenhouse gases and pollution.

STRETCH IT!

The equations for the formation of carbon monoxide and particulates follow the same rules as for the balancing of any other equation. Remember that you are allowed to use ½ molecules of oxygen in these equations and water is always formed as the other product.

The burning of methane is the simplest example of the combustion of a hydrocarbon. Just for comparison, the equation for the complete combustion of methane is as follows:

$CH_4(g) + 2O_2(g) \rightarrow CO_2(g) + 2H_2O(l)$

The equation for carbon monoxide formation is:

$CH_4(g) + 1\tfrac{1}{2}O_2(g) \rightarrow CO(g) + 2H_2O(l)$

For particulates (which are carbon):

$CH_4(g) + O_2(g) \rightarrow C(g) + 2H_2O(l)$

Notice for both of these less oxygen is used up and the methane undergoes incomplete combustion.

NAIL IT!

As a rule, the oxides of all non-metals (except hydrogen) are acidic.

Make sure you are able to write the balanced chemical equations for forming sulfur dioxide and oxides of nitrogen.

For sulfur dioxide:

$S(s) + O_2(g) \rightarrow SO_2(g)$

For oxides of nitrogen, the first oxide is nitrogen monoxide (NO):

$N_2(g) + O_2(g) \rightarrow 2NO(g)$

Another oxide of nitrogen is nitrogen dioxide (NO_2). This is very dangerous as it damages the lungs and produces acid rain:

$N_2(g) + 2O_2(g) \rightarrow 2NO_2(g)$

Smoke from burning fuel can combine with chemicals in the air and form smog. This can be seen as a thick haze or fog over cities and can cause breathing problems. In 1952 a thick layer of smog over London was responsible for several thousand deaths.

SNAP IT!

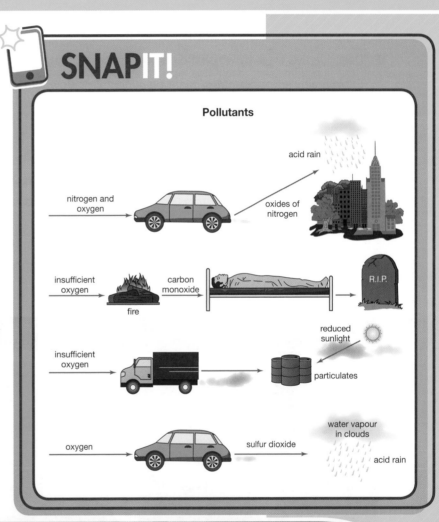

Pollutants

✓ CHECK IT!

1 List the four pollutants formed by burning fossil fuels and for each one give its effects.

2 Explain why a coal or wood fire should always be in a well-ventilated room.

3 a i Write the balanced chemical equation for the complete combustion of methane to give carbon dioxide.

   ii Write the balanced chemical equation for the incomplete combustion of methane to give carbon monoxide.

Chemistry of the atmosphere

1   State the main gases in the atmosphere of the early Earth.

2   List five ways by which the amount of carbon dioxide in the atmosphere has been reduced.

3   Describe the composition of the present atmosphere of the Earth.

4   Name two greenhouse gases and explain how they cause the greenhouse effect.

5   Describe the evidence that rising levels of carbon dioxide are causing global warming.

6   Explain why some areas of the Earth might expect flooding as a result of climate change.

7   Explain what is meant by the term 'carbon footprint'.

8   Describe five ways by which the carbon footprint of an organisation or individual person can be reduced.

9   Explain why some countries might be reluctant or slow to reduce their carbon footprint.

10 Explain the term atmospheric pollutant.

11 Carbon monoxide is a pollutant.

    a i   State the molecular formula of carbon monoxide.

       ii Explain how carbon monoxide can form as an atmospheric pollutant.

       iii Explain why carbon monoxide is considered toxic to humans.

    b Oxides of nitrogen are pollutants.

       i   Explain how oxides of nitrogen are formed as atmospheric pollutants.

       ii Explain why nitrogen monoxide is considered an atmospheric pollutant.

12 Explain why sulfur should be removed from petrol.

Using resources

Finite and renewable resources, sustainable development

The natural resources used by chemists to make new materials can be divided into two categories – finite and renewable. Finite resources will eventually run out as they are used faster than the Earth can make them. Examples are fossil fuels and various metals even though we are able to get some valuable materials from places like the oceans.

Renewable resources are ones that can be replaced at the same rate as they are used up or faster. They are derived from plant materials. An example is ethanol, which can be made from sugar from fermentation. Ethanol can be mixed with petrol to create a new fuel for cars (biofuel) instead of pure petrol which is extracted from the finite resource, crude oil.

Many of the Earth's natural resources are running out and if they are used at the current high rates they will be depleted (used up) very soon. In order to increase the lifetime of these finite resources, the industry has to develop processes that increase the lifetime of natural resources.

Sustainable development meets the needs of present development without depleting natural resources. In a sustainable process:

* there is a high yield

* there are few waste products

* there is very little impact on the environment and the products should not harm the environment.

DO IT!

The list below shows different methods of waste management.

Put them in order from 'worst' to 'best' method in terms of increasing the sustainability of a product.

A Burning product to produce energy

B Reuse the product

C Placing in landfill

D Design product differently to prevent waste

E Recycle or compost the product

SNAPIT!

Sustainable processes should do the following:

* have reactions with high atom economy

* use renewable resources

* have as few steps as possible to reduce transfer loss

* use catalysts.

MATHS SKILLS

One of the main concerns related to sustainability is the number of years left before certain finite resources are exhausted.

The remaining reserves are usually in very large amounts and they are usually expressed in millions (10^6), billions (10^9) and trillions (10^{12}).

In order to answer these questions you should be able to manipulate numbers by expressing them in standard form.

WORKIT!

In 2013, the known USA reserves of natural gas were 646 trillion m³.

At the present rate, the consumption is 765 billion m³ per annum.

Calculate how many years the USA has left before its natural gas is depleted.

The reserves $= 646 \times 10^{12}\,m^3 = 6.46 \times 10^{14}\,m^3$

The consumption per annum $= 765 \times 10^9\,m^3 = 7.65 \times 10^{11}\,m^3$

Therefore the number of years left $=$ reserves/consumption per annum

$$= 6.46 \times 10^{14} / 7.65 \times 10^{11}$$

$$= 844 \text{ years}$$

An oil pump in a field of rapeseed

CHECKIT! ✓

1 State what is meant by the following terms:

   a finite resource

   b renewable resource

   c sustainable development.

2 Describe four characteristics of a sustainable process and for each one explain why it increases the sustainability of the process.

3 The USA has 17.7 billion metric tonnes of coal reserves remaining. The annual consumption of coal in the USA is 175 million metric tonnes per annum. How long will it be before the USA runs out of its own coal? Suggest what could be done to extend this time.

Life cycle assessments (LCAs)

DO IT!

Draw a table that summarises the advantages and disadvantages to the environment of using paper and plastic bags.

A life cycle assessment is an analysis of the environmental impact of a product at each stage of its lifetime, from its production all the way to its disposal.

The stages in a life cycle assessment are as follows:

- The extraction/production of raw materials.
- The production process – making the product, the packaging and any labelling.
- How the product is used and how many times it is used.
- The end of the life of the product – how is it disposed of at the end of its lifetime? Is it recycled?

The diagram in the Snap It! box below shows a typical life cycle assessment.

The use of energy, resources and waste production can be calculated or measured reasonably accurately.

On the other hand, pollution effects are more difficult to measure or calculate.

LCAs can be used by companies to avoid unnecessary generation of waste and lead them to rethink their procedures.

SNAP IT!

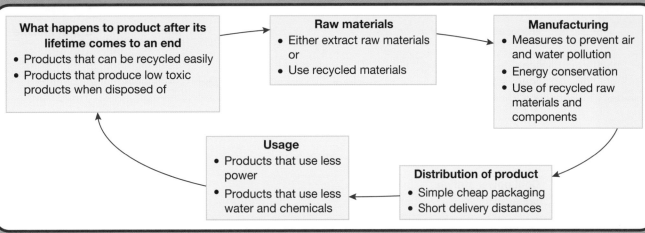

WORK IT!

What is a more sustainable product – a paper bag or a plastic bag?

Paper bags come from trees - a renewable resource. Plastic (polyethylene) bags are made from ethene which is produced during cracking of petrochemicals - a finite resource.

During the production stage paper has a greater impact on the environment than plastic bags. Paper bag production consumes much <u>more water</u>, produces <u>more acidic greenhouse gases</u> and has a greater global warming effect.

Paper bags are damaged by water and <u>less easily reused</u>.

Paper bags are heavier and after use generate 5 times <u>more solid waste</u> than plastic bags.

These results show that plastic bag production has fewer unwanted effects than for paper bags.

CHECKIT!

1 Explain what is meant by a life cycle assessment.

2 State the four stages/parts of a life cycle assessment.

3 The table below shows the greenhouse emissions in grams of greenhouse gas per kilowatt hour of power produced for four ways of producing electricity. The measurements are made over the lifetime of the generating device.

Method of electricity generation	Greenhouse gas emissions (in g/kWh) over the lifetime of the device
Silicon photovoltaic cell	45
Coal power station	900
Natural gas power station	420
Nuclear power station	30

a Describe and explain the values for greenhouse emissions of the coal and natural gas power stations.

b Describe and explain the values for the photovoltaic cell and the nuclear power station.

4 The flowcharts below show the greenhouse emissions as a percentage of the total for stages in the lifetimes of a photovoltaic cell and a coal power station.

Solar photovoltaic

Manufacture/construction	Operation	End of lifetime
• Raw materials extraction • Materials production • Manufacture • Installation • Construction	• Power generation • Operation of cell and maintenance	• Decommissioning • Disposal
65%	**25%**	**10%**

Coal power station

Manufacture/construction	Operation	End of lifetime
• Raw materials extraction • Construction materials manufacture • Manufacture • Power plant construction	• Coal mining • Coal refining • Coal transport • Coal burning • Power plant operation and maintenance	• Decommissioning • Waste disposal • Reclaiming of land
less than 1%	**more than 98%**	**less than 1%**

a Explain why the bulk of the emissions for the photovoltaic cell come at the beginning.

b For the coal power station only 1% of the greenhouse emissions come at the beginning of its lifetime and only 1% comes at the end of its lifetime. Explain these relatively small numbers.

Alternative methods of copper extraction

Copper is extracted from copper-rich ores by smelting and electrolysis.

In smelting, use is made of the fact that copper is less reactive than carbon so the ore is roasted with carbon. For example, malachite, an ore which is mostly copper(II) carbonate, is first decomposed to copper(II) oxide.

$CuCO_3(s) \rightarrow CuO(s) + CO_2(g)$

The copper(II) oxide is then reduced to copper by the carbon.

$2CuO(s) + C(s) \rightarrow Cu(s) + CO_2(g)$

If the ore contains mainly copper(II) sulfide (CuS) then reaction with oxygen produces impure copper and sulfur dioxide.

$CuS(s) + O_2(g) \rightarrow Cu(s) + SO_2(g)$

Some of the copper(II) sulfide produces copper(II) oxide which can then be reduced using carbon as shown above.

The other method is electrolysis. In this method sulfuric acid is added to give copper(II) sulfate solution. Electrolysis gives pure copper at the cathode.

If the copper produced by smelting is impure then this impure copper is made the anode in electrolysis. It dissolves to give copper(II) ions which are then deposited on the cathode as pure copper.

copper anode $\xrightarrow{\text{loses 2 electrons}}$ copper(II) ions in solution $\xrightarrow{\text{gains 2 electrons}}$ copper on cathode

- If the copper ores are low-grade ores (low in copper) then it is uneconomical to extract copper from them using the usual methods so alternatives are used. Bioleaching is a process where bacteria use copper sulfide as a source of energy and separate out the copper, which can be filtered off from the liquid produced. Bioleaching is slow but uses only about 30 to 40% of the energy used by copper smelting.

- Phytoextraction takes advantage of plants that take up copper from slag heaps that contain low-grade copper ores. The copper concentrates in the plant and is left in the ash when the plants are burned. Sulfuric acid is added to the ash to give copper(II) sulfate solution.

Phytoextraction is an environmentally friendly but slow method of extraction.

Copper can be extracted from this copper(II) sulfate solution by adding scrap iron. The iron displaces pure copper from the solution.

$Fe(s) + CuSO_4(aq) \rightarrow Cu(s) + FeSO_4(aq)$

DOIT!

Record an MP3 describing the extraction of copper by smelting, bioleaching and phytoextraction. Alternatively explain the processes to a revision partner.

NAILIT!

Phytoextraction is also called phytomining, check your specification to see which term you should use.

NAILIT!

The electrolysis of copper sulfate can use different electrodes. If inert electrodes (electrodes that do not take part) are used then copper ions from the solution are discharged at the cathode as copper.

If a copper anode is used then the copper at the anode dissolves to give copper(II) ions (Cu^{2+}). These copper(II) ions gain electrons as they are discharged at the cathode to give pure copper. This means that copper can be purified by making impure copper the anode in electrolysis.

159

SNAPIT!

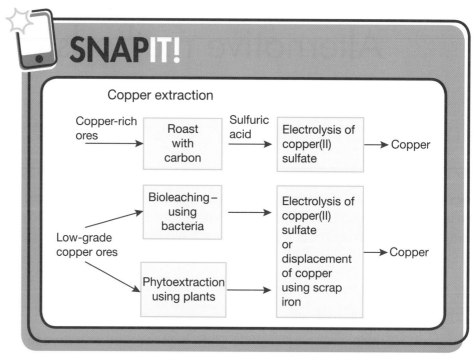

Copper extraction

STRETCHIT!

The half equations for the electrolysis of copper using copper electrodes are as follows:

At anode $Cu(s) \rightarrow Cu^{2+}(aq) + 2e^-$

At cathode $Cu^{2+}(aq) + 2e^- \rightarrow Cu(s)$

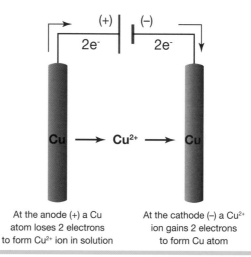

At the anode (+) a Cu atom loses 2 electrons to form Cu^{2+} ion in solution

At the cathode (−) a Cu^{2+} ion gains 2 electrons to form Cu atom

CHECKIT! ✓

1   a   Describe what is meant by a low-grade copper ore.

    b   i   A low-grade ore of copper contains 0.5% copper. Calculate the mass of copper in 1 tonne (10^6 g) of this copper ore.

        ii Calculate how many moles of copper are present in this mass of copper. [A_r(Cu) = 63.5]

2   a   Explain why carbon is used in copper smelting.

    b   Describe the two stages in the extraction of copper from copper(II) carbonate using carbon. Give the balanced chemical equations for each step.

3   a   State the organisms used in bioleaching.

    b   List the advantages and disadvantages of bioleaching.

4   Describe how impure copper is purified using electrolysis.

Making potable water and waste water treatment

Potable water is water that is safe to drink.

This type of water does not have to be pure. It usually contains small concentrations of salts and no microbes. It can also have chemicals added. For example, fluoride can be added to reduce dental decay in children. In areas where water is plentiful, the impure water goes through a series of processes to make it potable (see Snap It! box below).

In arid countries, sea water is made potable by distillation or reverse osmosis. Israel, for example, gets very little rain and uses reverse osmosis to get about 70% of its water. These methods use a lot of energy.

NAILIT!

This topic is closely aligned with that of subtopics, 'Mixtures and compounds' and 'Identifying ions in an ionic compound'. You should revise these together as the purity of water is an important concept. You should know how to test whether your water is pure or impure.

SNAPIT!

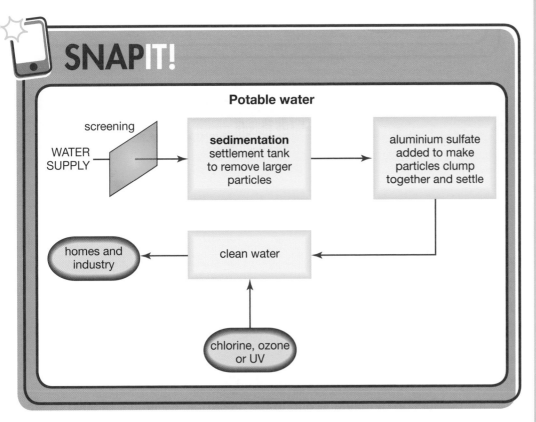

Potable water

screening

WATER SUPPLY

sedimentation settlement tank to remove larger particles

aluminium sulfate added to make particles clump together and settle

homes and industry

clean water

chlorine, ozone or UV

DOIT!

Write the different steps for water purification on cards. Jumble or shuffle them and put them in the correct order. Compare with the diagrams in the Snap It! boxes.

Repeat for the treatment of waste.

Large amounts of waste water are produced by industry and domestic consumers.

Before it is returned to the environment this water is treated using a number of processes including filtration/screening, sedimentation or settling.

Large pieces of grit and soil are separated by screening or filtration and the remaining liquid is passed into settling tanks.

After sedimentation the sludge obtained is treated using anaerobic digestion (carried out in the absence of oxygen). This produces methane which can be used as a fuel to run the sewage plant and a solid that can be used as a fertiliser or as a fuel. The liquid, or effluent, is then treated using aerobic digestion (in the presence of oxygen) and then returned to the environment.

SNAPIT!

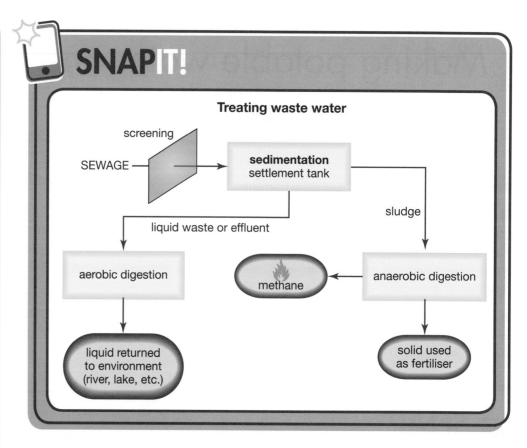

Treating waste water

CHECKIT!

1 **a** What is meant by potable water?

   b Describe how you can show that potable water contained:

      i dissolved solids   **ii** chloride ions.

   c **i** Describe a chemical test for pure water.

      ii Describe a test for pure water based on a physical property.

2 State the chemical technique that screening most resembles.

3 What do you understand by the following terms:

   a anaerobic   **b** aerobic   **c** sedimentation?

4 **a** Explain how the production of methane during the anaerobic treatment of solid waste increases the sustainability of water treatment processes.

   b List any other ways that the process is made more sustainable.

5 Some water can be extracted from underground rocks such as limestone. Justify which stage in the purification process may be unnecessary if this is the source of water.

6 A sample of water was thought to contain **chloride and bromide** ions. The water would not pass for human consumption if bromide ions were present. Two students were given the task of showing that bromide ions were present.

   Student 1 suggested adding silver nitrate solution along with nitric acid.

   Student 2 suggested passing chlorine gas through the water.

   a Explain why the process suggested by student 1 would not give a clear-cut result.

   b Explain why the method suggested by student 2 would work. Describe the observation that would confirm the presence of bromide ions.

Ways of reducing the use of resources

If we do not reduce our use of different materials then the sources of these materials will run out.

Extraction of metals from their ores requires lots of energy and therefore will also further deplete the reserves of fossil fuels still available.

Extraction also leads to the creation of more waste and mining the metal ores has bad impacts on the environment.

- Glass bottles can be reused or the glass can be crushed and melted to be reformed. This saves energy and conserves resources that are used to make the glass.

- Aluminium extraction requires lots of electrical and heat energy and the ore of aluminium (bauxite) is running out. Bauxite mining and concentration has a bad environmental impact. Recycling aluminium saves 95% of the energy used in extraction and produces 95% less greenhouse gases.

- Separating iron from other metals is relatively easy because it is magnetic. Recycling iron and steel saves a lot of energy (and because of this a lot of fossil fuels) and reduces the emission of greenhouse gases and pollutants. Scrap iron is also used to help in the production of steel.

- Plastics can be sorted and then recycled or incinerated. They can also be cracked to give hydrocarbon fuels and alkenes.

DO IT!

Choose a material and sketch out a poster to persuade people to recycle the material.

SNAP IT!

Reusing and recycling reduces:

- use of fossil fuels
- greenhouse gas emissions
- mining of ores
- negative impact on environment.

NAIL IT!

Revise the extraction of aluminium at the same time as you revise this topic – the savings made by recycling aluminium will make more sense.

✓ CHECK IT!

1 List at least **three** advantages of recycling metals and glass.

2 **a** Explain why so much aluminium is recycled.

   b Suggest how aluminium could be separated from iron in a recycling plant.

3 Sometimes waste plastics can be cracked to give alkenes as one of the products. Justify how this can be thought of as a way of recycling.

Rusting

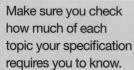

Corrosion occurs when a metal reacts with substances in the environment.
This leads to weakening of the metal.

Aluminium does not corrode because it has a protective layer of aluminium
oxide that does not flake off.

The corrosion of iron is called rusting.

Rust is a form of hydrated iron(III) oxide ($Fe_2O_3.nH_2O$). This is why both water
and air are required for rusting to take place.

Iron(s) + oxygen(g) + water(l) → hydrated iron(III) oxide(s)

When hydrated iron(III) oxide (Fe_2O_3) forms it flakes off, exposing iron
underneath to more rusting.

This generator is covered in rust

As iron is so widely used, rusting is very costly.

There are two ways to stop rusting taking place:

1. Barrier methods. These stop air and water getting to the iron. Examples
    are painting, greasing/oiling and coating with tin or plastic (for food cans).

2. Using sacrificial metals. These are metals more reactive than iron and
    they react instead of the iron. Coating with zinc is called galvanising. If
    the zinc is scratched the iron will still not rust because the zinc reacts
    instead of the iron.

Sacrificial metals are used to stop rusting on ships. Cleaning and repainting is
costly so blocks of the sacrificial metal, magnesium, are placed on the side of
the ship and when they are finished, they are simply replaced.

SNAPIT!

Experiments on rusting

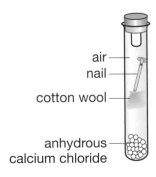

air
nail
cotton wool
anhydrous
calcium chloride

oil
boiled
water

air
water

A - anhydrous calcium chloride removes water so only air is present

B - boiling water removes dissolved air and the oil stops the air getting back into the water

C - air and water are present

Result: no rusting

Result: no rusting

Result: rusting takes place

Rust can cause damage to ships

DOIT!

Sketch out a plan for an experiment that tests what effect less reactive metals have on the speed of rusting.

✓ CHECKIT!

1 Define the term corrosion.

2 State the substances required for rusting of iron to occur.

3 The formula of rust can be written as $Fe_2O_3.nH_2O$. Complete the equation below to show its formation.

   __Fe(s) + __O$_2$(g) + nH$_2$O (l) → __Fe$_2$O$_3$.nH$_2$O(s)

4 Explain how painting stops rusting taking place.

5 Explain how attaching a magnesium alloy bar to the hull of a ship prevents rusting.

Alloys as useful materials

Pure metals are usually soft because the layers of metal ions can easily slide over each other without disrupting the structure. Mixing a metal with other metals stops the layers sliding over each other and the metal is made harder.

Alloys are mixtures of mainly metals. Steels are mixtures of iron with different amounts of carbon and other metals.

In steel the amount of carbon with the iron affects the properties of the steel.

Steels are harder if the amount of carbon is increased.

- Mild steel which is used for car bodies and pipes has a low percentage of carbon because the steel needs to shaped and bent.

- High-carbon steel is very hard and this makes it ideal for use in hammers and drills. Even though this is high carbon it is only about 1–1.5%.

The other metals added to steel depend on the properties required.

If you want steel that is hard and does not corrode then chromium and nickel are added. This type of steel is called stainless steel and used to make cooking utensils, knives and forks, etc.

Gold is a very soft metal and to make it more hardwearing for objects like rings it is alloyed with metals like copper, silver and zinc.

Pure gold is 24 carat. A 12 carat gold object is 50% gold and a 9 carat gold object is about 37.5% gold.

Aluminium alloys are used for aeroplane bodies because they have a high strength to weight ratio. The metals added to the aluminium are magnesium and copper.

Copper is very soft. Brass is an alloy of copper and zinc which is harder than copper but still malleable. Brass is used for bathroom fittings and musical instruments.

Bronze is an alloy of copper and tin and is used to make statues.

DO IT!

Sketch diagrams of the metal particles in a pure metal and an alloy. Use these diagrams to explain why steels get harder as the percentage of carbon increases.

We use moles to work out the percentages because this gives a measure of the ratio of metal atoms in the alloy.

WORKIT!

A sample of brass contained 25.4 g of copper and 6.5 g of zinc.

What is the percentage composition of the brass in terms of moles?

A_r of copper = 63.5 and A_r of zinc = 65.

Number of moles of copper = $mass/A_r$ = 25.4/63.5 = 0.400 mol;
Number of moles of zinc = 6.5/65 = 0.100 mol.

Percentage of copper = $\dfrac{\text{no. of moles of copper}}{\text{total no. of moles}} \times 100\%$ = $\dfrac{0.400}{0.500} \times 100$ = 80%;
Percentage of zinc = 20%.

SNAPIT!

Some common alloys and their uses

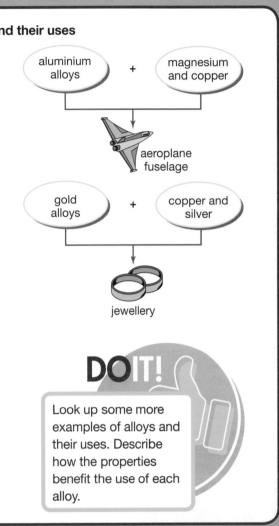

car
body work

low-carbon
steel

Steels

stainless
steel

kitchen knives

medium-
carbon steel

girders

high-carbon
steel

drills

tin

+

bronze statues

copper
alloys

+

zinc

brass instruments

aluminium
alloys + magnesium
and copper

aeroplane
fuselage

gold
alloys + copper and
silver

jewellery

DOIT!

Look up some more
examples of alloys and
their uses. Describe
how the properties
benefit the use of each
alloy.

✓ CHECKIT!

MATHS SKILLS

When working out
molar amounts and
percentages in alloys
remember that
$n = m/A_r$.

1 Define the term alloy.

2 Describe the effect of decreasing the amount of carbon in steel.

3 State the metals in the following alloys:

   a brass

   b bronze

   c stainless steel.

4 A sample of bronze was found to contain 14.3 g of tin and 55.9 g of copper. Calculate the
percentage composition of the bronze in terms of moles. [A_r(Cu) =63.5 and A_r(Sn) = 119]

Ceramics, polymers and composites

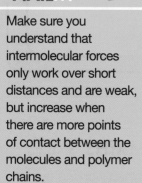

DO IT!

Look up other examples of composites. If you have a squash or tennis racquet then what is the matrix and what is the reinforcement?

NAIL IT!

Make sure you understand that intermolecular forces only work over short distances and are weak, but increase when there are more points of contact between the molecules and polymer chains.

In LDPE the branching stops the chains getting close together so very few intermolecular forces are able to form between the chains. This means that the polymer has a low density and the low attractions between the chains means that they can slide over each other and so the polymer is very flexible and stretches easily.

Glass is formed when sand (silicon dioxide) is melted and then rapidly cooled.

Adding other compounds to the sand when forming the glass gives different types of the material.

Soda-lime glass is used for making windows and is made from sand, sodium carbonate and limestone.

Borosilicate glass is made from sand and boron trioxide. It has a higher melting point than soda-lime glass and it is used for glass objects that can be heated, for example, test tubes, flasks, and so on.

The structure of glass is disordered and resembles the structure of a liquid. Ceramics, such as pottery, consist of metal ions and covalent structures arranged in layers.

Ceramics are hard, brittle and electrical insulators.

If substances like clay are mixed with water these layers slide over each other. After heating the water is removed and strong bonds are formed between the layers.

The properties of polymers depend on the monomers from which they are made and the conditions during production.

There are several types of polyethylene (PE). **L**ow-**D**ensity **P**oly**E**thylene (LDPE) is formed at high pressure and high temperature. The biggest use of LDPE is plastic bags.

High-**D**ensity **P**oly**E**thylene (HDPE) is made using special catalysts and uses lower temperatures and pressures. Examples of uses are corrosion-resistant pipes, milk jugs and plastic wood substitutes.

Thermosoftening polymers are made of individual polymer chains. When heated these chains are easily separated and the polymer melts.

Thermosetting polymers have chains that are linked by covalent bonds. When these polymers are heated they do not melt.

Composites are materials made from two or more materials that have different properties and when combined produce a material with different properties from the constituent materials.

Many composites consist of a material that provides strength or reinforcement and another that provides the supporting matrix.

Examples of composites are:

- Reinforced concrete – the matrix is the cement and the reinforcement is gravel and steel wires.

- Fibre glass – strands of glass fibre provide the reinforcement and a plastic resin provides the matrix.

SNAPIT!

Types of plastic

LDPE

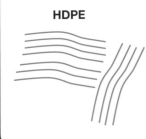

LDPE – chains are not close and there are few intermolecular forces between the chains giving LDPE a low melting point and making the plastic flexible.

HDPE

HDPE – chains are close and aligned so that intermolecular forces are maximised, increasing the melting point and making the plastic more rigid because the chains do not slide over each other so easily.

Thermosoftening

Weak – inter-molecular forces between chains are easily broken so the plastic melts.

Thermosetting

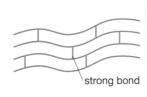

strong bond

Strong – chains joined by strong bonds cannot be separated so plastic does not melt.

WORKIT!

The table below shows the physical properties of an alloy, stainless steel, and a ceramic, silicon carbide.

Property	What does the property tell you?	Silicon carbide (SiC)	Stainless steel
Hardness/GPa	Resistance to wear and can withstand impact better	22	5
Toughness/MPa per m²	Resistance to fracturing and chipping	4	220
Specific gravity	Density compared with water	3.2	7

Why is stainless steel better for knives and scissors than silicon carbide?

Stainless steel has a much higher toughness so it will not chip easily when used.

✓ CHECKIT!

1 List the substances used to make borosilicate glass.

2 Explain why the structure of glass is similar to that of a liquid.

3 a State what the letters LDPE and HDPE stand for.

b Describe the packing of the chains in HDPE.

c Explain why this makes HDPE a more rigid material than LDPE.

4 a Explain what is meant by a composite material.

b Explain how reinforced concrete works as a composite material.

5 Explain why thermosetting plastics do not melt.

6 Using the table of properties shown above in the worked example explain why:

a Silicon carbide is better for grinding tools.

b Silicon carbide is used rather than stainless steel in body armour.

The Haber process

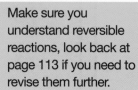
Ammonia has the formula NH_3. It is an important starting material for the production of nitric acid and fertilisers.

The Haber process is used to manufacture ammonia from the elements nitrogen and hydrogen.

The equation for the reaction is:

$N_2(g) + 3H_2(g) \rightleftharpoons 2NH_3(g)$

The reaction is reversible and the forward reaction is exothermic. This means that the reverse reaction is endothermic.

In the industrial process the nitrogen comes from the fractional distillation of liquid air and the hydrogen comes from natural gas.

The conditions used are a temperature of 450°C, a pressure of 200–250 atmospheres and an iron catalyst.

In the industrial process the conversion to ammonia is about 20–25%. The ammonia that is formed is cooled, condenses and is then run off as a liquid.

Unreacted nitrogen and hydrogen is recycled.

As it is exothermic, the forward reaction would be favoured by a lowering the temperature and produces more ammonia if the temperature is low.

The problem is that a low temperature would make the reaction slow. To overcome this problem a compromise is arrived at and a temperature of 450°C is used. This gives a reasonable rate of reaction and a passable yield.

The formation of ammonia means that the number of gas molecules goes down from four to two. If the pressure is raised the chemical system will try and lower it by making fewer gas molecules and this means that formation of ammonia is favoured by a high pressure.

The pressure used is about 200 to 250 atmospheres. Higher pressures would give a better yield but are expensive.

STRETCHIT!

The Contact Process is used to produce sulfur trioxide (SO_3) from sulfur dioxide (SO_2) and oxygen (O_2).

$$2SO_2(g) + O_2(g) \xrightleftharpoons[450°C]{\text{vanadium pentoxide catalyst}} 2SO_3(g)$$

As there are fewer gas molecules on the right-hand side of the equation it follows that the forward reaction is favoured by increased pressure. But the equilibrium lies towards the product, so to save money only a small pressure of about 10 atmospheres is used to push the gases through.

The forward reaction is exothermic and would be favoured by a low temperature. 450°C is a compromise because it speeds up the reaction but does not affect the equilibrium too much.

The vanadium pentoxide catalyst speeds up the reaction.

In the process 96% conversion of sulfur dioxide to sulfur trioxide is possible.

An iron catalyst is used to speed up the rate of reaction. A catalyst will not affect the position of equilibrium.

In the industrial process the amounts of nitrogen and hydrogen are in the ratio 1 nitrogen to 3 hydrogens as in the equation.

SNAP IT!

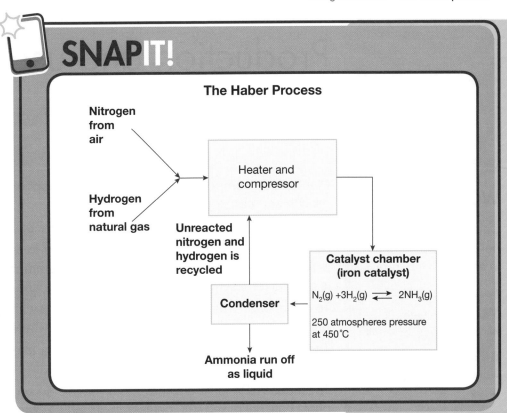

The Haber Process

Nitrogen from air

Hydrogen from natural gas

Heater and compressor

Unreacted nitrogen and hydrogen is recycled

Catalyst chamber (iron catalyst)

$N_2(g) + 3H_2(g) \rightleftharpoons 2NH_3(g)$

250 atmospheres pressure at 450°C

Condenser

Ammonia run off as liquid

WORKIT!

What is the percentage conversion to ammonia at 500°C and 300 atmospheres pressure?

There are four lines so use the correct one.

The answer is 20%.

MATHS SKILLS

You need to be able to read data from graphs.

In questions like this make sure you use a ruler so your answer is accurate.

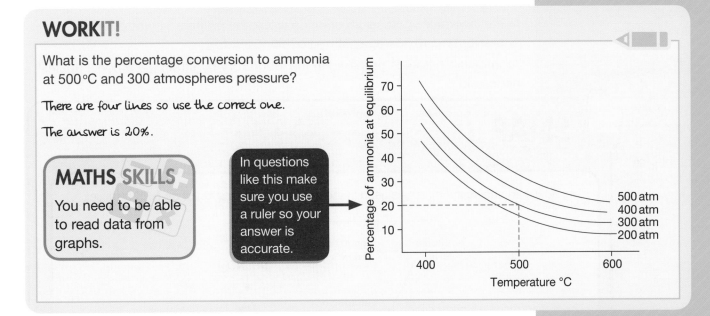

CHECK IT!

1 Explain why a high pressure is used in the Haber process.

2 The production of ammonia is favoured by a low temperature. Explain why a temperature of 450°C is used.

3 Explain the effect of an iron catalyst on the yield of ammonia.

4 The conversion rate to ammonia is around 20%. Describe what happens to the unreacted gases.

5 Calculate the volume of nitrogen used if 3000 dm³ of hydrogen are passed into the reaction chamber.

Production and uses of NPK fertilisers

WORKIT!

Calculate the percentage of nitrogen in ammonium nitrate.

Ammonium nitrate is NH_4NO_3. The mass of nitrogen is $2 \times 14 = 28$

The relative formula mass $= 14 + 4 + 14 + 48 = 80$

The percentage of nitrogen $= 28/80 \times 100 = 35\%$

Plants need compounds of nitrogen (N), phosphorus (P) and potassium (K) for growth and carrying out photosynthesis.

Fertilisers containing these three elements are called NPK fertilisers.

Ammonia from the Haber process is oxidised to form nitric acid (HNO_3) which is then reacted with ammonia (NH_3) to give ammonium nitrate (NH_4NO_3). This is a good fertiliser because it is water-soluble and contains lots of nitrogen.

To get phosphorus, phosphate rock is treated with nitric acid to form phosphoric acid (H_3PO_4) and calcium nitrate ($Ca(NO_3)_2$).

The phosphoric acid is reacted with ammonia to give ammonium hydrogen phosphate (($(NH_4)_2HPO_4$) which is soluble.

To produce NPK fertilisers, the ammonium nitrate and ammonium hydrogen phosphate are mixed with potassium chloride. Potassium chloride is obtained by mining.

In the laboratory potassium chloride would be prepared by titration of potassium hydroxide against hydrochloric acid.

Ammonium nitrate is prepared in the laboratory by titrating ammonia against nitric acid.

SNAPIT!

The flowchart shows the materials used in the **industrial preparation of an NPK fertiliser.**

```
ammonia          nitric acid        ammonium
(NH3)     ----→  (HNO3)      ----→   nitrate
                                     (NH4NO3)

phosphate rock   phosphoric   ammonium     NPK        potassium
+ nitric acid -→ acid      -→ phosphate -→ fertiliser ← chloride KCl
                             (NH4)2HPO4
```

CHECKIT!

1 Define NPK fertiliser.

2 Explain why ammonium nitrate is a good fertiliser.

3 Justify why fertiliser production happens on the same site as the Haber process.

4 State the equation for the formation of ammonium hydrogen phosphate from ammonia and phosphoric acid.

5 Calculate the percentage of phosphorus in ammonium hydrogen phosphate.

Analysis and purification of a water sample

This practical emphasises that you carry out a practical safely and accurately and safely use a range of equipment to purify and/or separate chemical mixtures including evaporation and distillation.

Practical Skills

Questions you should be able to answer:

- What apparatus can I use?
- How can you test the water sample for purity?
- What chemical test should be used?

NAILIT!

Questions you could ask yourself:

- How can you show that there is a dissolved solid in the solution you are given? What apparatus would you use?
- What tests would you use to identify any dissolved solids?
- How do the pieces of apparatus shown in the diagrams work to purify the water?
- How would you show that the purified water was indeed pure?

SNAPIT!

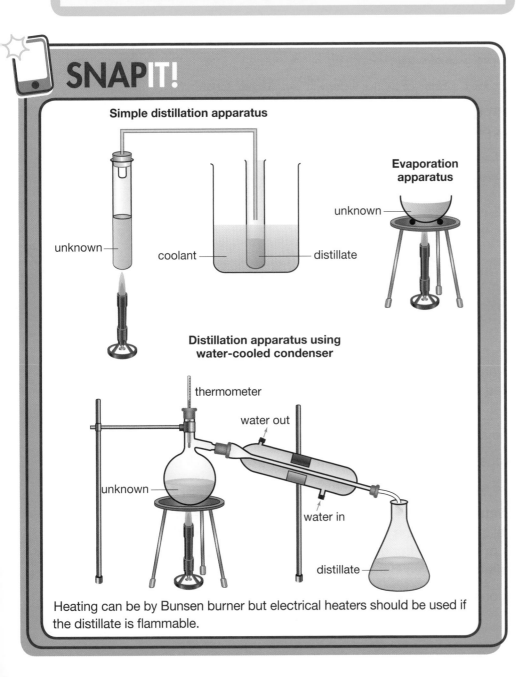

Simple distillation apparatus

unknown — coolant — distillate

Evaporation apparatus

unknown

Distillation apparatus using water-cooled condenser

thermometer

water out

unknown

water in

distillate

Heating can be by Bunsen burner but electrical heaters should be used if the distillate is flammable.

WORKIT!

A sample of water was evaporated to dryness and a residue was obtained which was white in colour.

When the residue was tested using the flame test no colour was obtained.

Samples of the water were added to separate test tubes and the following results were obtained:

1 On addition of sodium hydroxide the solution gave a white precipitate.

2 A separate sample gave no precipitate with silver nitrate solution but did give a dense white precipitate with barium chloride solution.

3 After using a simple distillation apparatus to purify the water, the distillate gave very faint white precipitates with both sodium hydroxide and separately with barium chloride solution.

4 When a condenser and flask were used to purify the water, the distillate gave no precipitates with the sodium hydroxide solution or barium chloride solution.

What do these results show?

The white residue showed that the water was impure and did contain a dissolved solid.

The white colour of the residue indicates that the original solution did not contain a transition metal, otherwise it would have been coloured.

The result with sodium hydroxide solution shows that the original solution contained magnesium ions.

The result with silver nitrate solution showed that no halide ions were present but the result with barium chloride solution did show the presence of sulfate ions.

These results show that the dissolved substance in the water was magnesium sulfate.

After using the simple distillation apparatus the fainter precipitates show that less of the dissolved solid was present but that the purification process was not completely successful.

After distillation using the condenser no precipitate with either sodium hydroxide or barium chloride solution showed there wasn't any dissolved substance in the water. This showed that purification was successful.

CHECKIT!

1 A sample of water turned universal indicator paper red. It gave no residue when it was evaporated to dryness. When tested with silver nitrate solution it gave a white precipitate.

   a i State the apparatus you could use instead of the UI paper.

      ii Explain the advantage of using this apparatus over the UI paper.

   b Suggest the substance dissolved in the water.

2 A sample of water gave a white residue when it was evaporated to dryness. The water also gave a yellow flame in the flame test and when tested with silver nitrate solution gave a yellow precipitate. After distillation no coloured flame was given in the flame test and no precipitate was given in the silver nitrate test.

   What conclusions can you draw from these results?

additional questions, visit:
v.scholastic.co.uk/gcse

1 a Explain the difference between a finite and a renewable resource.

   b Ethanol can be obtained from sugar by fermentation and from the reaction between ethene and steam. Explain which of these two processes is more sustainable.

2 The diagram below shows the main steps in the treatment of water to give potable water.

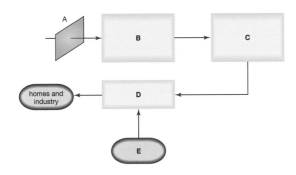

   a i Describe what is happening at A.

      ii State what is added at C and explain why it is added.

      iii Explain why the water at D is not fit to drink.

      iv Describe the process taking place at E and explain why it is important.

   b List two ways by which potable water is obtained from seawater.

   c Potable water is not pure water.

      i Outline how you could show that potable water contains dissolved impurities.

      ii Describe a physical test which could be used to show pure water has been made.

   d When waste water is treated the sludge formed after settlement is digested anaerobically.

      a Define the term anaerobic.

      b List two useful products from anaerobic digestion.

3 a Explain what is meant by the following three terms when applied to the extraction of copper:

      i smelting   ii phytomining

      iii bioleaching.

   b You are given a solution of copper(II) sulfate. Give two ways you would obtain pure copper from the solution.

4 a Explain the term life cycle assessment.

   b List the four stages in the product's lifetime that are analysed for their impact on the environment.

5 The diagram to the right shows the arrangement of polymer chains in a thermosetting polymer.

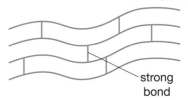
strong bond

   a Explain why this type of polymer does not melt.

   b Explain why this type of polymer is a good choice for making electrical plugs.

6 a Write the chemical equation for the formation of ammonia in the Haber process.

   b What are the conditions used in the Haber process?

   c Explain why a high pressure is used in the Haber process.

   d List three compounds that would be found in an NPK fertiliser.

Glossary/Index

Concentration The amount in moles or grams of a substance that is dissolved in 1 dm^3 of solution. **60–63, 80, 102, 107, 111, 115**

Condensation polymerisation Chemical reaction in which monomer molecules are joined together to form a long polymer chain. Each time a bond is formed in the chain a small molecule, usually water is also formed. Examples of condensation polymers are polyesters and nylon. **132–3**

Corrosion This occurs when a metal reacts with substances in the environment. **164–5**

Covalent bond The bond formed between two atoms by sharing a pair of electrons, one electron coming from each atom. **42–46**

Crude oil A thick liquid found in the Earth's crust. It is a mixture of hydrocarbons, mainly alkanes. **118–125, 146–8**

Crystallisation A separation method used to obtain a soluble solid from a solution. **11–12, 76**

D

Delocalised electrons Electrons that are free to move. **47–8**

Desulfurisation The removal of sulfur from fossil fuels to reduce the amount of sulfur dioxide formed when they burn in air. **152**

Diamond A form of carbon in a giant covalent structure. Each carbon atom is joined to four others by strong covalent bonds. **44–5**

Diatomic molecules Molecules which contain two atoms. The molecules of hydrogen, oxygen, nitrogen and the molecules of the halogens are all diatomic. **53, 86**

Discharged An ion is discharged when it either gains or loses electrons at an electrode during electrolysis. **81–87, 159**

Displacement reactions A reaction that takes place when a more reactive element takes the place of a less reactive element in a compound. **30–31, 32–3, 68, 78**

Displayed formula This formula shows all the atoms and bonds present in a compound. **118, 122, 127–8**

DNA A natural condensation polymer consisting of two polymer chains which form a double helix. The monomers in DNA are called nucleotides. **134**

Ductile A substance is ductile if it can be drawn into a wire. **27, 34, 47–8**

E

Effective collisions An effective collision is one which results in a chemical reaction. **109**

Electrical conductivity The ability of a substance to allow electricity to pass through it. **27, 41, 48, 84**

Electronic structure or configuration The number of electrons in each electron shell of an atom. **25–6, 38–43**

Empirical formula The simplest ratio of atoms in a compound. **10, 38**

Endothermic A reaction or change that takes in energy from the surroundings and is accompanied by a decrease in temperature of the surroundings. **93–8, 113–6**

Exothermic A reaction or change that transfers energy to the surroundings. It is accompanied by an increase in temperature of the surroundings. **93–8, 113–6**

F

Fermentation The conversion of glucose to carbon dioxide and ethanol in the absence of oxygen. **126, 155**

Filtration A separation method used to separate an insoluble solid from a liquid. **12**

Finite resources Resources that will eventually run out. **155–6**

Flame emission spectroscopy A method of chemical analysis that uses the intensity of light *emitted* from a flame at a particular wavelength. The intensity is used to determine the quantity of an element in a sample. **137–8, 143–4**

Formulation A mixture which has components added that are designed to improve the properties or effectiveness of one of the components. **14–15**

Forward reaction The reaction taking place when reactants form products. **113–15**

Fractional distillation A separation method used to separate two or more miscible liquids with similar boiling points. **12, 23, 120, 124, 170**

Fractionation The splitting up of crude oil into its constituents or fractions by using fractional distillation. **120, 125**

Fractions Different parts of crude oil. Each fraction is a mixture of several compounds with similar boiling points. **120, 125**

Frequency of collisions How many collisions that take place per second. It is the frequency of collisions that is a measure of the rate of a reaction rather than how many collisions take place. **107–9**

Fuel A substance which burns to give thermal energy or reacts to give electrical energy. **72, 99–100, 125, 148, 153**

Fuel cell This produces electrical energy by the oxidation of the fuel such as hydrogen or methane. **99–100**

Fullerenes These can be in the form of spheres or elliptical tubes. An example is the spherical Buckminster fullerene with the molecular formula C_{60}. **46**

Functional group A group of atoms in a carbon compound that give the compound its distinctive properties. All the compounds in a homologous series have the same functional group. **122–134**

G

General formula A general formula shows the ratio of carbon to other atoms in a homologous series and represents the composition of the whole series. **118, 122, 124, 126, 128**

Giant covalent structure A giant structure held together in three dimensions by strong covalent bonds. **44**

Giant ionic structure A giant three-dimensional lattice of ions held together by strong ionic bonds. **40**

Graphene A single layer of carbon atoms, one atom thick from a graphite structure. **44–5**

Graphite A form of carbon having a giant covalent structure. The carbon atoms are arranged in layers of hexagonal rings. Each carbon atom is joined to 3 others in the structure by strong covalent bonds. **44–5**

Group A vertical column of elements with similar properties. The elements have the same number of electrons in their outer shell. **23–34**

H

Haber process Industrial process used to make ammonia. **34, 170–171**

Halide ion Negative ion with a charge of -1 formed when the atom of a halogen gains one electron. **30–33, 85, 141–43**

Halogens Group 7 of the periodic table - the elements fluorine down to astatine. They have similar properties because they all have seven electrons in their outer shell. **30–33, 85, 141–3**

Hexagonal rings In graphite and graphene the atoms are arranged in six-membered hexagonal rings of carbon atoms. **44**

Homologous series A series of compounds with the same general formula, similar chemical properties and same functional group. They show a gradation in physical properties as the number of carbons increases and each member differs from the next one by $-CH_2-$. **118, 122, 124, 126, 128**

Hydrocarbon A compound of carbon and hydrogen **only**. **118–125**

Protein A condensation polymer formed from amino acids which are the monomers. **134**

Proton A subatomic particle found in the nucleus of the atom. A proton has a positive charge equal to the negative charge of an electron, and a relative mass of one equal to the relative mass of a neutron. A hydrogen ion is sometimes called a proton. **18–22**

Pure A pure substance can be either a single element on its own or a single compound on its own. **14–15**

R

Rate of reaction How quickly a reaction takes place. It is measured either by how quickly reactants *disappear* or by how quickly products *appear*. **102–112**

Reactants The substances taking part in a chemical reaction. Written on the left-hand side of a chemical equation. **51–59**

Reaction profile This shows how the energy changes during the course of a reaction when reactants react to form products. **108**

Reactivity series The order of reactivity of metals. It is usually quoted from potassium as the most reactive down to gold as the least reactive. **68–9**

Rechargeable cells Cells that can be recharged when they run out of reactants. **99–100**

Recycling A way of making new materials from products which have come to the end of their lifetime. **157**

Reduced A substance is reduced when it either loses oxygen or gains electrons. **68, 71, 78, 81, 83**

Reduction The loss of oxygen or the gain of electrons in a reaction. **68, 71, 78, 81, 83**

Relative atomic mass The mass of an atom compared to 1/12 the mass of an atom of carbon-12. The relative atomic mass of an element also takes into account the relative abundances of its naturally-occurring isotopes. **21–4, 53**

Relative charges and masses Because the charge on an electron and a proton are so small it is easier to compare them and use relative charges. Similarly is easier to use the relative masses of the neutron and proton. **19**

Relative formula mass The sum of the relative atomic masses in the formula of a substance. **53–4**

Renewable resources Resources, usually from plants, that can be replaced very quickly. **155–6, 163**

Reverse reaction Reaction taking place when products react to form the reactants. **113–16**

Reversible reaction A reaction that can proceed in both directions. Reactants can form products in the forward reaction and products can form reactants in the reverse reaction. **113–16**

Room temperature and pressure 20°C and 1 atm. pressure. 1 mol of a gas occupies $24dm^3$ ($24\,000cm^3$) at room temperature and pressure. **36, 64**

Rough titration A titration where liquid is added from the burette, 1 cm³ at a time. This is used when an approximate volume is required. **90–91**

Rusting The corrosion of iron. It requires oxygen and water. **164–5**

S

Sacrificial metal A metal such as zinc or magnesium which is more reactive than iron. The metal is bolted to or covers the iron and reacts instead of the iron. **164–5**

Saturated hydrocarbon A hydrocarbon which has the maximum number of hydrogen atoms present in its structure. **118–19**

Simple distillation A separation method used to separate a liquid from a soluble solid. **12, 174**

Smelting Extraction of a metal by roasting with carbon. The metal is less reactive than carbon. **159**

Soda lime glass Glass made from sodium carbonate and sand. **168**

Solute The solid that dissolves in a liquid to form a solution. **60**

Solvent The liquid that dissolves a solid to form a solution. **12, 16–17, 60, 126**

Spectroscope A device used to analyse the light emitted by a substance when it is heated strongly. **138**

Standard solution A solution with a known concentration. **62**

Stationary phase The stationary phase in paper chromatography is paper. In thin-layer chromatography it is the silica on the plate. **16–17**

Steels Mixtures of carbon and iron. Other metals can be added according to requirements. **163, 166, 168**

Strong acid An acid which is completely ionised in water. An example is hydrochloric acid. **62, 79–80, 128**

Sub-atomic particles The particles that make up an atom. These are the electrons, neutrons and the protons. **18–26**

Sulfur dioxide Formed when sulfur burns in air. It causes respiratory problems and when dissolved in water it forms acid rain. **152**

Surface area The area of a solid that is in contact with other reactants, either in solution or in the gas phase. Powders have a larger surface area than lumps. The smaller the particle the larger the surface area. **49, 94, 108, 111–12**

Sustainable development This meets the needs of present development without depleting natural resources. **155–6**

Chemical equation A way to represent the substances reacting and those being formed in a chemical reaction using chemical formulae. Both sides of the equation are joined by an arrow on which can be written the conditions used. **29, 52, 57**

T

Tangent This is a straight line drawn to touch a reaction curve at a certain point. The slope or gradient of the tangent is a measure of the rate of reaction corresponding to that point. **105–7**

Thermal conductivity The ability of a substance to allow heat energy to pass through it. **34, 47**

Thermal decomposition The breaking up of a compound using heat. Reactions which are thermal decompositions are endothermic processes. **93, 113**

Thermosetting plastics These plastics are rigid and do not melt when heated. **168–9**

Thermosoftening plastics These plastics are flexible and soften when heated. **168–9**

Titration An analytical technique used to find the exact volume of a solution that reacts with a known volume of another solution of known concentration. **62, 90–1**

Transition metals The metals in the middle block of the periodic table. **34**

U

Unsaturated hydrocarbon A hydrocarbon which has less than the maximum number of hydrogen atoms present in its structure. Examples are the alkenes. Unsaturated compounds decolourise bromine water. **118–9**

W

Weak acid An acid which is only partially ionised in water. An example is ethanoic acid. Ethanoic acid is only 0.4% ionised in aqueous solution. **79–80, 128**

Answers

Atomic structure and the periodic table
Review it!

1 a $2Na(s) + Cl_2(g) \rightarrow 2NaCl(s)$

b i Both have only 1 chemical symbol and therefore only 1 type of atom.

ii Na is a shiny silver white solid; Cl is a pale green gas.

iii Ions

c The sodium chloride is not chemically combined with the water and they can be easily separated by physical means.

2 The group is a vertical column of elements and a period is a horizontal row.

3 Each element can only have one atomic number and that number is unique to that element. If it had an atomic number of 12 it would not be sodium.

4 Group 6, period 3

5 a X is found in the middle of the periodic table in the transition elements.

b Shiny; good electrical conductor; good thermal conductor; malleable; ductile; denser than the group 1 elements.

6 a −1

b When they react the Group 7 elements gain one electron to form a stable outer shell, their reactivity depends on their ability to gain this extra electron. As the group descends, the outer shell is further from the positively charged nucleus and is shielded from the nucleus by an increasing number of electrons. This means that as you go down the group the attractive force on an electron being gained gets less and it gets harder to capture the extra electron.

7 a It has 12 protons and 12 electrons.

b These are isotopes. Each isotope has the same number of protons but a different number of neutrons.

c Let there be 100 atoms of gallium. 60 atoms have a mass number 69 with a total mass of 4140 atomic mass units. 40 atoms have a mass number of 71 the total mass of 2840 atomic mass units.

Therefore 100 atoms have a total mass of 4140 + 2840 atomic mass units = 6980 atomic mass units. The relative atomic mass is the average mass of each atom $= \frac{6980}{100} = 69.8$ atomic mass units

8 Elements with similar properties were placed in vertical columns and ordered by their relative atomic masses. Where the known elements did not fit the pattern he left spaces for elements which had not yet been discovered.

9 Group 1 elements lose their outer electron when they react. As the group is descended, this outer electron is further from the attractive force of the nucleus and there are more shielding electrons between the nucleus and the outer electron. This means that the outer electron feels less of an attractive force and is more easily lost therefore making the lower elements more reactive.

10 The noble gases have stable full outer electron shells. This means they do not have to gain or lose electrons to become stable.

11 a Mendeleev's periodic table was organised in groups of elements with similar properties. If argon had very distinct properties then it had to fit into its own group and therefore they had to be a group of elements with similar properties.

b It did not react with any other elements.

12 a As the group is descended the elements get darker in appearance. Iodine is a dark grey solid; astatine is below iodine and would be darker in colour which suggests that it is black.

b At_2

c NaAt

d -1. The ion is At^-.

Bonding, structure and the properties of matter
Review it!

1 The lithium atom loses its outer electron to form the Li^+ ion. The ion has a stable full outer electron shell.

2 a 1 nm to 100 nm (1 nm = 1×10^{-9} m)

b (Titanium dioxide nanoparticles in) sunscreens; (Silver nanoparticles are used in) antibacterial preparations; (Fullerenes are used to) deliver drugs and as lubricants.

3 a

b $MgCl_2$

c The ionic bonds between the magnesium and chloride ions are very strong and because it is a giant structure all the bonds have to be broken. This requires lots of energy and a high melting point.

d In solids the ions are not free to move, therefore they cannot carry the current and do not conduct electricity.

4 a
```
      H
      • x
  H x C x H
      • x
      H
```

b Methane is a neutral molecule and the intermolecular forces between methane molecules are weak and require a small amount of energy to break them. Therefore methane has low melting and boiling points making it a gas at room temperature.

5 a Giant covalent structure

b The bonds between the carbon atoms in both diamond and graphite are strong covalent bonds, all these bonds have to be broken. This requires lots of energy, so the melting point is high.

c The bonds in the layers of graphite are strong covalent bonds but between the layers the intermolecular forces are weak and easily broken allowing the layers to slide over each other easily.

d In graphite each carbon is bonded to other carbons leaving a spare electron. These spare electrons are delocalised in the layer and can carry an electric current making graphite a good electrical conductor. In diamond there are no spare electrons or charged particles making it a poor conductor.

6 A – Simple molecular   B – Giant ionic

C – Giant metallic   D – Giant covalent

7 a Methane has a simple molecular structure with weak intermolecular forces so it has low melting and boiling points. Potassium chloride has a giant ionic structure with strong ionic bonds between the ions. All these bonds need lots of energy to break them and therefore it has high melting and boiling points.

b The ions in magnesium oxide are Mg^{2+} and O^{2-}. In potassium chloride they are K^+ and Cl^-. The larger charges on the Mg^{2+} and O^{2-} means that their ionic bonds are stronger than those between the K^+ and Cl^- ions, these need more energy to break and therefore magnesium oxide has higher melting point.

c Zinc ions are larger than copper ions in the giant metallic lattice, this means that the layers of ions cannot slide over each other as easily, making the alloy a harder material.

d Sodium has a giant metallic structure in which there are delocalised electrons in both the solid and liquid states and these delocalised electrons can carry an electric current. This means that sodium is a good electrical conductor in both the solid and liquid states. Sodium chloride has a giant ionic structure. In the solid state the ions are not free to move and cannot carry an electric current so as a solid sodium chloride is a poor conductor. In the liquid state they can move and carry the current making sodium chloride a good electrical conductor.

antitative chemistry

view it!

a   i 8.33×10^{-2};   ii 2.23×10^5
    iii 8.561×10^2 iv 4.53×10^{-5}

b   i   4.00   ii 6.57×10^{-2}
    iii 4.55×10^{-2}
    iv 4.39×10^{-4} v 5.68×10^5

a   i $H_2(g) + Cl_2(g) \rightarrow 2HCl(g)$

    ii $2Na(s) + Br_2(l) \rightarrow 2NaBr(s)$

    iii $6K(s) + N_2(g) \rightarrow 2K_3N(s)$

    iv $Mg(s) + 2AgNO_3(aq) \rightarrow$
        $Mg(NO_3)_2(aq) + 2Ag(s)$

    v $4Na(s) + O_2(g) \rightarrow 2Na_2O(s)$

b   The law of conservation of mass states that the mass of the reactants = mass of products; this means that the number and type of atoms on left-hand side of the equation must be the same as those on the right-hand side.

a   96   b   74   c   148   d   61

e   174   f   134.5   g   60

a   0.1

b $0.1 \times 6.02 \times 10^{23} = 6.02 \times 10^{22}$

c $0.1 \times 24dm^3 = 2.4dm^3$

a   Atom economy method I $= \frac{44}{173}$
    $\times 100\% = 25.4\%$

    Atom economy method II $= \frac{44}{44} \times$
    $10\% = 100\%$

b   Reduces waste

$HCl(aq) + NaOH(aq) \rightarrow NaCl(aq) + H_2O(l)$

Volume of NaOH $= \frac{30}{1000} = 0.03$ dm³ Vol of HCl $= 0.02$ dm³

No. of moles of NaOH $= C \times V = 1 \times 0.03$ mol $= 0.03$ mol

No. of mol of HCl = no. of mol of NaOH$=0.03$ mol

Concentration of HCl $= \frac{n}{V} = \frac{0.03}{0.02} = 1.5$ mol/dm³

a $\frac{6}{24} = 0.25$ mol

b   No. of mol of HCl $= C \times V = 1 \times \frac{200}{1000}$ $= 0.2$ mol

c   From the equation 1 mol of magnesium reacts with 2 mol of HCl. Therefore 0.25 mol of magnesium react with 0.5 mol of HCl. There are only 0.2 mol of HCl and this is the limiting reactant.

Chemical changes

Review it!

1   a   copper, iron, zinc, aluminium, magnesium

    b   i $\rightarrow$ zinc sulfate(aq) + copper(s)

        ii $\rightarrow$ NO REACTION

        iii $\rightarrow$ aluminium oxide(s) + iron

    c   i   magnesium(s) + carbon dioxide(g) $\rightarrow$ magnesium oxide(s) + carbon(s)

        ii $2Mg(s) + CO_2(g) \rightarrow MgO(s) + C(s)$

        iii   The magnesium gains oxygen – oxidation and the carbon dioxide loses oxygen – reduction

        iv   I magnesium oxide II carbon

2   a   The gas, hydrogen, is produced which can be tested for using a lighted splint. The gas pops.

    b   The copper is less reactive than hydrogen and will not displace it from the acid.

    c   i $Zn(s) + 2H^+ (aq) \rightarrow H_2(g) + Zn^{2+}$ (aq)

        ii   The zinc loses electrons when going from the neutral Zn to the positive Zn^{2+} ion. This is oxidation. The H^+ ions gain electrons when forming H_2 and this is reduction.

3   a   Hydrogen at cathode; bromine at anode.

    b   A solution of potassium hydroxide

4   a   Its solution is a weak alkali

    b   Phenol solution is a very weak acid

5   a   i   Dissolved in water – an aqueous solution

        ii $NaOH(aq) + HCl(aq) \rightarrow NaCl(aq) + H_2O(l)$

        iii $H^+ (aq) + OH^-(aq) \rightarrow H_2O(l)$

    b   i   pipette   ii   burette   iii   conical flask

    c   The indicator changes colour.

Energy changes

Review it!

1   It decreases.

2   A is an endothermic reaction because it is a thermal decomposition reaction.

    B is an exothermic reaction because it gives out heat to warm up the food.

3   a   The non-rechargeable cell will eventually stop producing a voltage because the chemicals will run out. The hydrogen fuel cell will keep on going as long as the hydrogen and oxygen are allowed to flow into the cell. Chemical cells can be used anywhere whilst the hydrogen fuel cell is hampered by the need for a supply of hydrogen to be available.

    b   The zinc is more reactive than the copper and therefore loses its electrons to form zinc ions more easily than the

copper. This means that electrons would flow from the zinc to the copper making the zinc the negative electrode.

4   a   i   23; 41; 7

        ii   The units for temperature /°C.

    b   Use the same amount of acid (same volume/same concentration), the metals should have the same surface area (e.g. all 3 are powders), use either the same calorimeter/reaction vessel or identical ones.

    c   Thermometer or temperature datalogger, top-pan balance, well insulated calorimeter, spatula.

    d   Least reactive X, Z, Y Most reactive. X gives the lowest temperature rise then Z than Y which gives the greatest temperature rise.

5   a   A Heat of reaction or energy change for reaction   B reactants

        C Activation energy   D Products

        E Energy   F Course of reaction

    b   Exothermic

    c   The energy required for the reaction to take place.

6   a $4C-H, 1C \mathbin{=\!\!=} C, 1 Cl-Cl \rightarrow 4C-H, 1C-C, 2C-Cl$

        The 4 C–H bonds are unchanged and can be omitted from the calculation.

        1×610 1×245 1×350
        2×345

        The energy taken in to break bonds $= 610 + 245 = 855$ kJ

    b   The energy given out when forming bonds $= 350 + 690 = 1040$ kJ

    c   i   185 kJ/mol

        ii   The energy given out is greater than the energy taken in, therefore the reaction is exothermic.

Rates of reaction and equilibrium

Review it!

1   Measure the volume of carbon dioxide produced with time. Measure the loss in mass as time progresses.

2   a   Measure the gradient of the tangent to the graph at any point.

    b   Rate $= \frac{25}{15}$ cm³/s $= 1.67$ cm³/s

3   a   C because it has the steeper gradient at the beginning.

    b   C because increasing the temperature increases the rate.

    c   As the temperature increases the particles collide more frequently and with greater force, so the frequency of effective collisions increases and so does the rate.

4   a   i   A catalyst speeds up a chemical reaction and is unchanged chemically at the end of the reaction.

        ii   0.10 g

181

b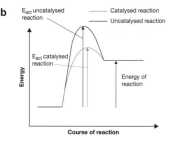

c A catalyst lowers the activation energy and this means that more particles have enough energy to react so that when they collide the collision is more likely to produce a reaction.

5 Temperature and surface area of a solid if one is involved. If two or more solutions are involved, then one concentration can

b **i** A and D **ii** D **iii** C **iv** B **v** A

c A = propane B = propanol
C = ethanoic acid D = propene

2 **a** The C=C group

b They have the same functional group and they have similar chemical properties.

c Add bromine water. The bromine water is decolourised.

d **i**

$$H-\underset{\underset{Br}{|}}{\overset{\overset{H}{|}}{C}}-\underset{\underset{Br}{|}}{\overset{\overset{H}{|}}{C}}-H$$

ii

$$H-\underset{\underset{H}{|}}{\overset{\overset{H}{|}}{C}}-\underset{\underset{H}{|}}{\overset{\overset{H}{|}}{C}}-H$$

iii

$$H-\underset{\underset{H}{|}}{\overset{\overset{H}{|}}{C}}-\underset{\underset{OH}{|}}{\overset{\overset{H}{|}}{C}}-H$$

3 **a** Crude oil is composed of a mixture of miscible liquids with similar boiling points.

b **i** The fractions become less viscous.

ii The boiling points decrease.

iii The fractions become easier to light.

c The fractions contain smaller molecules and this means that there are weaker intermolecular forces, therefore the molecules are more easily separated to become gases.

4 **a** C_nH_{2n+2}

b **i** $CH_4(g) + 2O_2(g) \rightarrow CO_2(g) + 2H_2O(l)$

ii $C_2H_6(g) + 3\frac{1}{2}O_2(g) \rightarrow 2CO_2(g) + 3H_2O(l)$

c **i** A = cobalt chloride paper;
B = limewater; C = to pump

ii The cobalt chloride paper changes form blue to pink. This shows that water is formed.

iii The limewater goes cloudy showing that carbon dioxide is formed.

5 **a** The amounts produced of the fractions with large molecules are more than required. At the same time the amounts of the fractions with smaller molecules are less than required. Cracking converts the larger molecules into smaller ones.

---

be varied (the independent variable) whilst the others are kept constant.

6 **a** The ⇌ sign shows that the reaction can proceed both ways

b It is exothermic

c It turns blue and there is heat given out

7 **a** The equilibrium will shift to the right.

b An increase in pressure favours the side with fewer gas molecules and this is the left-hand side.

Organic chemistry
Review it!

1 **a** $A = C_3H_8$ $B = C_3H_8O$ $C = C_2H_4O_2$
$D = C_3H_6$

b **i** C_6H_{14} **ii** C_9H_{20}

Chemical analysis
Review it!

1 **a** You need a nichrome wire, a Bunsen burner, a heat-proof mat, a watch glass and tongs. Place the solid being tested in the watch glass, add hydrochloric acid and then dip the nichrome wire into the solution/mixture. Hold the wire in a roaring blue Bunsen flame and note the colour formed.

b **i** Yellow **ii** Green

iii Orange-red **iv** Lilac

2 **a** Effervescence/fizzing

b **i** Yellow precipitate
ii White precipitate
iii Cream precipitate
iv White precipitate

c **i** White precipitate
ii No change/no reaction

d **i** White precipitate
ii White precipitate that re-dissolves on adding excess sodium hydroxide solution.
iii Green precipitate

3 X = magnesium sulfate

Y = sodium bromide

Z = potassium chloride

Chemistry of the atmosphere
Review it!

1 Carbon dioxide, water vapour, methane, nitrogen and ammonia

2 Dissolving in the water forming the oceans. Uptake by plankton in the sea which then form their shells; they are compressed by sediments and form limestone. Photosynthesis by plants. Plankton covered by sediments in the absence of oxygen form oil. Plants covered by sediment then compressed form coal

---

3 78% nitrogen; 21% oxygen; the remaini 1% consists of noble gases and approximately 0.04% of carbon dioxide

4 Carbon dioxide and methane absorb infrared radiation and then are re-radiate back to Earth, warming up the atmosph

5 The recent rises in carbon dioxide level are mirrored by increased temperature the atmosphere.

6 The increased global temperature cause the ice caps to melt, thus increasing the water in the oceans and the water levels rise given rise to floods. Also severe storms lead to greater rainfall and flood

7 The total amount of carbon dioxide emit over the lifetime of an activity or produc

8 • Energy conservation will reduce the amount of carbon dioxide produce by burning fossil fuels.

• The use of alternative energy resources will also reduce the amo of carbon dioxide produced by burning fossil fuels.

• In carbon capture and storage carbo dioxide produced in power stations i pumped into deep underground por rocks at the sites of exhausted oil we

• Carbon taxes penalised people/ companies/organisations that use too much energy and this will inhib people from overuse of energy.

• Carbon offsetting is when plants ar planted which taking carbon dioxi through photosynthesis thus reduc the amount of carbon dioxide in the atmosphere.

9 • People are reluctant to change their lifestyle. For example, they still use large cars which consume more ene

• Countries do not cooperate with ea other.

• Some countries still believe that glo warming is a natural phenomenon a is not caused by humans.

• People are still unsure of the facts a the consequences of global warmir

• Countries still find it economical to use fossil fuels

10 An atmospheric pollutant is something that is introduced into the atmosphere and has undesired or unwanted effects

11 **a** **i** CO

ii By the incomplete combustion carbon-containing fuels.

iii It is toxic because it reduces th amount of oxygen getting to the brain.

b **i** Oxides of nitrogen are formed by the reaction between nitrog and oxygen at high temperatur

ii For example, in car engines an exhausts and in thunderstorms

12 Sulfur dioxide is formed by the reaction of sulfur and oxygen. It dissolves in water to form acid rain and it causes respiratory problems.

Using resources

Review it!

1 a A finite resource will run out but a renewable one can be replaced.

b The fermentation of sugar is the sustainable process because the sugar can be regrown again whilst the ethene comes from the cracking of crude oil which is a finite resource.

2 a i Large objects are screened out of the water

ii Aluminium sulfate is added to make small particles clump together and settle to the bottom of the tank

iii It contains bacteria

iv Chlorine is added OR the water is treated with UV light to kill bacteria

b Distillation or reverse osmosis

c i Evaporate off the water

ii The boiling point

d i In the absence of oxygen

ii Methane and fertilisers

3 a i Roasting with carbon

ii Plants which absorb copper are planted on sites where there are low-grade copper ores. After they have grown they are harvested and burned to leave copper deposits in the ashes.

iii Bacteria use low grade copper sulfide ore in heaps for an energy source and they oxidise the ores. The liquids leaching from the heaps contain copper ions.

b Electrolysis and displacement of the copper by adding a more reactive metal such as iron.

4 a A life cycle assessment is an analysis of the environmental impact of a product at each stage of its lifetime from its production all the way to its disposal.

b The extraction/production of raw materials. The production process – making the product, including packaging and labelling. How the product is used and how many times it is used. The end of the life of the product – how is it disposed of at the end of its lifetime. Is it recycled?

5 a The chains cannot slide over each other because they are joined by strong covalent bonds.

b It will not melt if the plug gets hot and it does not conduct electricity and is therefore safe to handle.

6 a $N_2(g) + 3H_2(g) \rightarrow 2NH_3(g)$

b A temperature of 450°C; a pressure of 200-250 atmospheres and an iron catalyst.

c The formation of ammonia means that the number of gas molecules goes down from 4 to 2. If the pressure is raised the chemical system will try and lower it by making fewer gas molecules and this means that formation of ammonia is favoured by a high pressure.

d Ammonium nitrate, ammonium hydrogen phosphate and potassium chloride.

Atoms, elements and compounds

① **This question is about atoms, elements and compounds.**

a Draw one line from each word to its correct description. (4 marks, ★★)

| Atom | A substance that contains two or more elements chemically combined. |

| Element | A substance that contains two or more elements not chemically combined. |

| Compound | A substance made of only one type of atom. |

| Mixture | The smallest part of an element that can exist. |

b Which of the following substances are elements? Tick two boxes. (2 marks, ★★)

Br_2	☐
Na_2CO_3	☐
Ar	☐
H_2O	☐

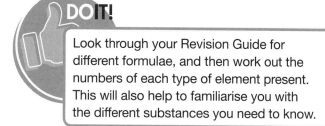

DO IT!

Look through your Revision Guide for different formulae, and then work out the numbers of each type of element present. This will also help to familiarise you with the different substances you need to know.

c Which of the following represents a compound? Tick one box. (1 mark, ★★)

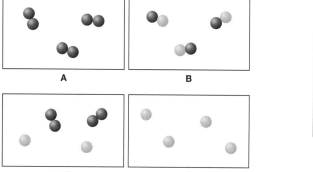

A

B

C

D

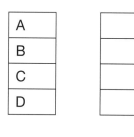

A	☐
B	☐
C	☐
D	☐

d How many atoms are there in a molecule of magnesium nitrate, $Mg(NO_3)_2$? (1 mark, ★★★)

....

e How many different elements are there in a molecule of sulfuric acid, H_2SO_4?
(1 mark, ★★★)

....

② **Use your periodic table to help you to answer the following questions.**

a Name two elements that are found in group 7. (2 marks, ★)

....

b Give the symbols of two elements that are found in group 1. (2 marks, ★) ....

Mixtures and compounds

(1) **Place each substance under the correct heading in the table below.** (3 marks, ★)

air	salty water	oxygen
hydrogen	water	sodium hydroxide

Element	Compound	Mixture

> **NAILIT!**
>
> In this section you need to be aware of the differences between mixtures and compounds, and how mixtures can be separated. These methods are also covered in other topics (e.g. fractional distillation and the production of soluble salts).

(2) **A student prepares a soluble salt by reacting copper(II) oxide with hydrochloric acid. He ends up with a solution of copper(II) chloride. Describe how a dry sample of copper(II) chloride could be obtained from this mixture.** (2 marks, ★★)

....

....

(3) **A mixture of salt and water can be separated by simple distillation.**

a **Name the piece of apparatus labelled A.**
(1 mark, ★)

....

b **Explain how a sample of pure water can be collected using this apparatus.**
(3 marks, ★★★)

....

....

....

....

....

....

....

(4) **Rock salt is a naturally occurring mineral that consists of a mixture of sodium chloride and sand. Sodium chloride is soluble in water and sand is insoluble in water. Describe how both the sodium chloride and sand could be separately extracted from the rock salt.**
(4 marks, ★★★)

....

....

....

....

....

....

Pure substances and formulations

1. **Explain what is meant by the term pure.** (1 mark, ★)

   ....

   ....

2. **Milk is sometimes described as pure.**

   a **Explain why milk is not scientifically pure.** (2 marks, ★★)

   ....

   b **Outline how you could show this in an experiment.** (3 marks, ★★★)

   ....

   ....

3. **Pure aspirin melts at 136°C. A sample of an aspirin tablet starts to melt at 125°C. What does this tell you about the aspirin tablet?** (1 mark, ★★★)

   ....

   ....

4. **One way to make pure water is from salt water, using a process known as distillation, shown in the diagram below.**

....

....

Heat

....

   a **Label the diagram to show (i) salt water, (ii) pure water vapour (iii) pure water.** (3 marks, ★★)

   b **Explain how distillation allows pure water to be produced from salt water.** (3 marks, ★★★)

   ....

   ....

(5) A paracetamol tablet has a mass of 2g. It contains 500 mg of paracetamol ($C_8H_9NO_2$), 1.25 g of starch ($C_6H_{10}O_5$) a bulking agent, and 0.25 g of magnesium stearate ($Mg(C_{18}H_{35}O_2)_2$) a lubricant to prevent the tablet sticking to the packaging.

a Explain why the paracetamol tablet is an example of a formulation. (1 mark, ★)

....

b Calculate the percentage composition of paracetamol in the tablet, in terms of mass. (2 marks, ★★★)

....

....

c Calculate the number of moles of each compound in the tablet. (6 marks, ★★★★)

i Paracetamol

....

....

ii Starch

....

....

iii Magnesium stearate

....

....

d Calculate the percentage composition of paracetamol in the tablet, in terms of moles. (2 marks, ★★★★)

MATHSSKILLS

The formulae you will need for formulation calculations are:

$$\text{Percentage} = \frac{\text{mass of component}}{\text{total mass}} \times 100\%$$

$$\text{Number of moles} = \frac{\text{mass}}{M_r}$$

....

....

....

....

....

Chromatography

① **Tick two statements that are correct.** (2 marks, ★)

Chromatography is a technique that can be used to separate mixtures into their components.	
Chromatography works because different compounds have different levels of attraction for the paper and the solvent.	
Chromatography involves three phases – a mobile phase, a stationary phase and a dynamic phase.	
Chromatography is a technique that can be used to create mixtures from their components.	
Chromatography gives you information about the quantity of the components in a mixture.	

NAILIT!

Remember that water isn't the only solvent that can be used for the mobile phase. Often, scientists will try different solvents until there is a good separation between the spots. Commonly used solvents include: ethanol, dichloromethane and ethyl ethanoate.

② **A student wanted to identify the inks used in a black pen. She set up the equipment as shown below.**

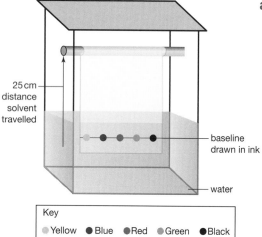

25 cm distance solvent travelled

baseline drawn in ink

water

Key
Yellow ● Blue ●Red Green ●Black

a **Suggest two errors in the way the student has set up the experiment. Explain the problems each of these errors would cause.** (4 marks, ★★)

....

....

....

....

....

b **The R_f value for the yellow ink is 0.88. The R_f value for the green ink is 0.84. Dot C has travelled 22 cm. Calculate the R_f of dot C and identify its colour.** (3 marks, ★★★)

....

....

MATHSKILLS

In the exam, you may need to rearrange the formula:

$$R_f = \frac{\text{Distance moved by spot}}{\text{distance moved by solvent}}$$

Distance moved by the spot = R_f × distance moved by the solvent

Distance moved by the solvent = R_f × distance moved by the spot

NAILIT!

Sometimes, solutes can have an elongated (stretched) spot, which can make it difficult to identify unknown substances. One of the skills involved choosing a mobile phase is choosing one which gives good, clear results for the substances you're looking at.

Scientific models of the atom

(1) How did scientists describe the structure of the atom before electrons were discovered? (2 marks, ★★)

....

....

(2) The plum pudding model was then suggested after the discovery of the electron. The image to the right shows a diagram of this model. Describe what the plum pudding model shows. (2 marks, ★★)

....

....

....

(3) Further experiments by Rutherford tested the plum pudding model by firing alpha particles at gold foil. Instead of them all passing through the foil, some of them were deflected.

a What is the charge on an alpha particle? (1 mark, ★)

....

b Why did most of them pass through the gold foil? (1 mark, ★★)

....

c Why were some of the alpha particles deflected? (1 mark, ★★)

....

d What was the overall conclusion from this experiment? (2 marks, ★★★)

....

....

e Which sub-atomic particle did Chadwick prove existed in the nucleus? (1 mark, ★★)

....

NAILIT!

The main fact that you need to know about the development of the atomic model is how Rutherford's scattering experiment changed scientists' ideas about the plum pudding model.

Atomic structure, isotopes and relative atomic mass

(1) **Complete the table of the relative charges and masses of the sub-atomic particles.** (3 marks, ★★)

Sub-atomic particle	Relative charge	Relative mass
	+1	
		Very small
Neutron		

NAILIT!

Learn the names of the sub-atomic particles, along with their relative masses and charges; this is often assessed in exam questions.

(2) **Explain why the overall charge of a magnesium atom is neutral.** (2 marks, ★★)

....

....

(3) **Element Z has a mass number of 184 and an atomic number of 74.**

a **Calculate the number of protons, electrons and neutrons in an atom of Z.** (2 marks, ★★)

....

....

DOIT!

You could be asked questions about any element in the periodic table. Pick random elements and calculate the number of protons, electrons and neutrons in each. This will also help to familiarise you with the periodic table.

b **Use the periodic table to identify the name of element Z.** (1 mark, ★★)

....

(4) **Use the words in the box below to complete the following passage about isotopes. You will not need to use all of the words, and some words may be used more than once.**

Isotopes of an element have the same .... number but a different .... number. This means that atoms of the same element have the same number of .... but different numbers of .... Two isotopes of carbon are C-12 and C-13. Both of these isotopes have .... protons; however, C-12 has .... neutrons and C-13 has .... neutrons. (3 marks, ★★)

12	atomic	7	neutrons	electrons	6	mass	13	protons

(5) **There are two naturally occurring isotopes of bromine, Br-79 and Br-81.**

Describe the similarities and differences between these two isotopes, referring to the number of sub-atomic particles in your answer. (3 marks, ★★★★)

....

....

....

(6) **The relative atomic mass of chlorine is 35.5. Chlorine exists as two isotopes, one of which is Cl-35. This makes up 75% of naturally occurring chlorine. Use this information to calculate the mass number of the other isotope of chlorine.** (3 marks, ★★★★★)

....

....

The development of the periodic table and the noble gases

(1) Use your periodic table to answer the following questions. (4 marks, ★★)

DO IT!

> Early versions of the periodic table show the elements that had been discovered placed in order of increasing atomic weight. Why?

a Carbon is in group .... of the periodic table.

b Potassium is in period .... of the periodic table.

c Why are phosphorous and nitrogen placed in the same group?

....

d Why are sulfur and silicon placed in the same period?

....

(2) Mendeleev decided to arrange the elements according to their properties. The table below shows an early version of his periodic table.

Row	Group I	Group II	Group III	Group IV	Group V	Group VI	Group VII	Group VIII
1	H							
2	Li	Be	B	C	N	O	F	
3	Na	Mg	Al	Si	P	S	Cl	
4	K	Ca		Ti	V	Cr	Mn	Fe, Co, Ni, Cu

a What is the correct name for the horizontal rows in the periodic table? (1 mark, ★)

....

b Why did Mendeleev leave gaps? (1 mark, ★★)

....

c How are the elements arranged in the modern version of the periodic table? (1 mark, ★★)

....

d Suggest why it took a long time for the noble gases to be discovered. (1 mark, ★★)

....

(3) The noble gases are found in group 0 of the periodic table, their boiling points are shown in the table below.

a What is the trend in boiling points?
(1 mark, ★★)

....

b Predict the boiling point of krypton.
(1 mark, ★★)

....

Noble gas	Boiling point/°C
He	−269
Ne	−246
Ar	−186
Kr	
Xe	−108
Rn	−62

Electronic structure

(1) **The diagram represents an element from the periodic table.**

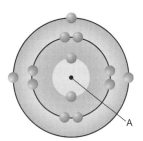

a **What is the name of the part labelled A?** (1 mark, ★★)

....

b **What are the names of the sub-atomic particles found in A?** (2 marks, ★★)

....

....

The mass number of this element is 27.

c **Name the element represented by this diagram.** (1 mark, ★★)

....

d **How many neutrons does this element have?** (1 mark, ★★)

....

(2) **The electronic structures of six elements, A, B, C, D, E and F, are shown below.**

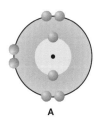

2, 8, 8, 1

B

A

2,8

D

C

E

F

Use the correct letter or letters to answer each question.

a **Which atom represents an element in group 3?** (1 mark, ★) ....

b **Which element has the symbol O?** (1 mark, ★★) ....

c **Which two elements are in the same group?** (2 marks, ★★) ....

d **Which two elements are in period 4?** (2 marks, ★★) ....

e **Which element is a noble gas?** (1 mark, ★★) ....

f **Which element forms a 2⁻ ion?** (1 mark, ★★★) ....

Metals and non-metals

(1) **Match up these words with their correct meanings.** (3 marks, ★)

Malleable	Makes a ringing sound when hit.
Ductile	Can be hammered into shape.
Sonorous	Can be drawn into wires.

(2) **Some elements in the periodic table are highlighted below.**

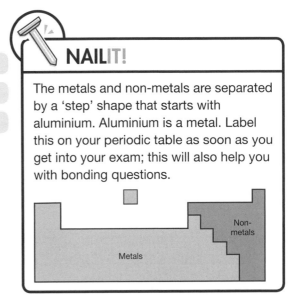

NAIL IT!

The metals and non-metals are separated by a 'step' shape that starts with aluminium. Aluminium is a metal. Label this on your periodic table as soon as you get into your exam; this will also help you with bonding questions.

Choose the correct element to answer each question. (1 mark each)

a Which element is in group 1? (★) ....

b Which element is used in jewellery? (★) ....

c Which element has a mass number of 32? (★★) ....

d Which element is a noble gas? ....

e Which element is a non-metal in group 3? (★★★) ....

f Which element is a non-metal in period 4? (★★★) ....

g Which element forms a 2⁺ ion? (★★★) ....

h Which element forms a 3⁻ ion? (★★★★) ....

(3) **Barium is a reactive element found in group 2 of the periodic table.**

a **Is barium a metal or a non-metal?** (1 mark, ★)

....

b **How many electrons does barium have in its outer shell?** (1 mark, ★)

....

c **Which two properties would you expect barium to have? Circle the correct answer.** (2 marks, ★★)

| low melting point   good electrical conductor   brittle   shiny |

Group 1 – the alkali metals

(1) **Explain, using electron configuration, why all the group 1 metals have similar chemical properties.** (1 mark, ★★)

....

....

(2) **Circle which group 1 metal is represented by the symbol K.** (1 mark, ★)

| Lithium | Sodium | Potassium | Krypton |

(3) **Circle which is the most reactive group 1 metal.** (1 mark, ★)

| Sodium | Caesium | Lithium | Francium |

(4) **The diagram shows the electronic structure of a group 1 metal.** (1 mark, ★★★)

What is the symbol for this metal?

| N | K | Na | Li |

Symbol: ....

(5) **A student observes the reaction of lithium with water.**

State **three** observations the student would see during the reaction. (3 marks, ★★★)

....

....

....

(6) **Potassium reacts with water in a similar way to lithium.**

State **two** observations that would be different. (2 marks, ★★★)

....

....

....

Group 7 – the halogens

1. **Circle the chemical symbol for fluorine.** (1 mark, ★)

| Fl | Fr | F | Fe |

2. **Circle the most reactive halogen.** (1 mark, ★)

| Bromine | Iodine | Chlorine | Fluorine |

3. **Circle the correct formula for a molecule of bromine.** (1 mark, ★★★)

| Be | Br | B_2 | Br_2 |

4. **Circle which halogen has the electronic configuration 2,8,7.** (1 mark, ★★★)

| Chlorine | Bromine | Fluorine | Iodine |

NAILIT!

The halogens can react with other non-metals to form **covalent** substances. They can also react with metals to form **ionic** substances called halide (1-) ions.

DOIT!

When the halogens react, they change the ending of their name from **ine** to **ide**. Practise writing simple word equations to get used to this. For example:

sodium + chlorine → sodium chloride

5. **A student watches the reaction between lithium and chlorine, and lithium and iodine.**

   a **Which would be the most vigorous reaction? Explain why.** (1 mark, ★★)

   ....

   b **Write a word equation for the reaction between lithium and chlorine.** (1 mark, ★★)

   ....

   c **Write a balanced chemical equation for the reaction between lithium and iodine.**
   (2 marks, ★★★★)

   ....

6. **The reactivity of chlorine, bromine and iodine can be shown by carrying out reactions between these halogens and aqueous solutions of their salts, some of these reactions are shown below.**

	Chlorine	Bromine	Iodine
Potassium chloride	X	No reaction	
Potassium bromide	Orange solution formed	X	No reaction
Potassium iodide			X

   a **Complete the table, stating any colour change that would take place.** (3 marks, ★★)

   b **Write a word equation for the reaction between chlorine and potassium bromide.** (1 mark, ★★)

   ....

   c **On a separate piece of paper, suggest an experiment that you could carry out to prove that iodine is more reactive than astatine. State what you would observe and write down a chemical equation and an ionic equation for this reaction.** (4 marks, ★★★★★)

The transition metals

① **Which of the following metals are transition metals? Circle three elements.** (3 marks, ★★)

| silver | tin | mercury | magnesium | tungsten |

DO IT!

You need to be able to compare the properties of the transition metals with those of group 1. Construct a table like this to show the similarities and differences.

Property	Group 1 metal	Transition metals
Melting and boiling points		
Electrical conductivity		
Reactivity		
Density		

② **Palladium (Pd) is a transition metal which is used in jewellery and also in catalytic converters in cars.**

  a **Suggest a property of palladium that makes it suitable for use in jewellery.** (1 mark, ★)

  b **Predict three properties of palladium that would be different from sodium.** (3 marks, ★★)

③ **A student watches the reaction between sodium and chlorine. The reaction is vigorous and the sodium burns brightly with a yellow flame, producing a solid product.**

  a **Name the solid formed.** (1 mark, ★)

NAILIT!

Make sure you know the differences between the properties of the metals and their compounds. For example, copper metal is orange/bronze-coloured, but copper compounds are usually blue or green.

  b **State the colour of the solid formed.** (1 mark, ★★)

  c **Write a balanced chemical equation for this reaction.** (2 marks, ★★★★)

④ **Iron also reacts with chlorine. In this reaction there are two possible products, iron(II) chloride and iron(III) chloride.**

Would the reaction of iron with chlorine be more or less vigorous than the reaction of sodium with chlorine? Explain your answer. (1 mark, ★★)

Bonding, structure and the properties of matter

Bonding and structure

① **Complete the diagram below by choosing the correct words which represent these changes of state.** (4 marks, ★)

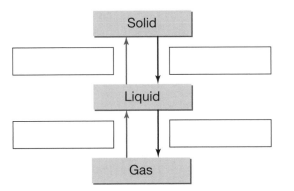

Condensing

Dissolving

Distillation

Freezing

Subliming

Boiling

Melting

NAILIT!

The **boiling point** is the temperature at which a liquid boils and turns into a gas, **or** condenses from a gas to a liquid.

The **melting point** is the temperature at which a solid melts, **or** when a liquid freezes and turns into a solid.

② **Water freezes at 0°C and turns into ice. It boils at 100°C and turns into water vapour.** (2 marks, ★★)

a What is the melting point of water? ....

b At what temperature will water vapour condense back into a liquid? ....

③ **Mercury (Hg) melts at −39°C and boils at 357°C. Use this information to predict the state of mercury at the following temperatures.** (3 marks, ★★★)

a **500°C** ....   b **−40°C** ....

c **Room temperature, 25°C** ....

④ **Air consists of a mixture of several different gases, some of which are shown in the table below.**

Gas	Boiling point/°C
Nitrogen	−196
Oxygen	−183
Argon	−186

The gases can be separated by fractional distillation; this involves cooling the air down and removing each gas as it condenses. (4 marks, ★★★)

a Which gas has the highest boiling point? ....

b Which gas has the lowest boiling point? ....

c Which gas would condense first when air is cooled? ....

d Which gas has the strongest forces between its particles? ....

Ions and ionic bonding

① **Complete the following passage using the words below. Some words may be used more than once.**

Magnesium is a metal which is found in group .... of the periodic table. This means it has .... electrons in its outer shell. When it reacts, it loses .... electrons and forms an ion with a .... charge. Fluorine is a non-metal which is found in group .... of the periodic table. When it reacts, it .... 1 electron to form an ion with a .... charge. When magnesium reacts with fluorine, it forms magnesium fluoride which has the formula .... (8 marks, ★★)

MgF	1	2	3	gains	Mg_2F	6
7	loses	MgF_2		1⁻	2⁻	1⁺	2⁺

② **Match the compound to its correct formula.** (4 marks, ★★)

DOIT!

Practise writing out formulae by using the group numbers of the elements to find out the charge on the ions formed. Remember, **metals** form **positive ions (cations)** and **non-metals** form **negative ions (anions)**. Then, work out the number of each ion needed to make the charges add up to zero.

For example, potassium is in group 1 so forms an ion with a 1⁺ charge, K^+.

Oxygen is in group 6 so forms an ion with a 2⁻ charge, O^{2-}.

K^+ O^{2-}

There are 2 negative charges, but only 1 positive charge. Therefore, 2 positive charges are needed to cancel out the 2 negative charges which means we need to multiply the K^+ by 2.

$2 \times K^+$ O^{2-}

Overall, the formula is K_2O.

Potassium chloride K_2Cl

MgO_2

Magnesium oxide $MgCl_2$

Al_3F

Magnesium chloride   KCl

AlF_3

Aluminium fluoride   MgO

KCl_2

③ **Draw dot-and-cross diagrams (outer electrons only) to show the formation of the ionic compounds below. For each diagram, work out the formula of the compound formed.**

   a Lithium chloride (3 marks, ★★)   **b Barium bromide** (3 marks, ★★★)

The structure and properties of ionic compounds

1 Tick **three** boxes that describe the correct properties of ionic compounds. (3 marks, ★★)

High melting points	☐
Made of molecules	☐
Conduct electricity when solid	☐
Conduct electricity when molten or in solution	☐
Made of non-metals bonded together	☐
Made of ions	☐

2 From the diagrams below, give **one** substance A, B or C that:

a **represents sodium chloride, NaCl.** (1 mark, ★) ....

b **represents magnesium chloride, MgCl$_2$.** (1 mark, ★★) ....

c **represents sodium oxide.** (1 mark, ★★★) ....

> **NAILIT!**
>
> Remember, ionic compounds only conduct electricity when molten or dissolved in water, because the ions are free to move, not the electrons. Make sure you use the correct charge carrier.

A   B   C

3 Complete the following passage about the structure of ionic compounds, choosing the correct words from the box below. (3 marks, ★★)

Ionic bonds are formed when .... react with .... Atoms either lose or gain .... to become positive or negative particles called ions. The ions are held together in a giant ionic .... by strong .... forces of attraction acting in all ....

magnetic	protons	metals	areas	electrostatic	molecules
directions	neutrons	lattice	non-metals	electrons	

4 Potassium iodide is a substance that is often added to table salt in countries where people have little iodine in their diets. A deficiency of iodine can cause many long-term health problems but is also easily preventable. Use your ideas about structure and bonding to make predictions about the properties of potassium iodide. (6 marks, ★★★★)

....

....

....

....

....

....

Covalent bonds and simple molecules

① **Which of the following substances are covalent? Tick the correct answers.** (2 marks, ★★)

NaCl	
CaO	
NH$_3$	
Potassium nitrate	
Water	

NAILIT!

Remember, covalent substances are only made from non-metals. Make sure you know where the non-metals are found in the periodic table!

② **The compounds drawn below all have covalent bonds.**

  a **Complete the dot-and-cross diagrams below to show the covalent bonding in each molecule.** (6 marks, ★★)

  Hydrogen

  Methane

  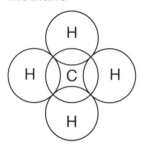

  b **Write out the formula of each substance.** (2 marks, ★★)

  Hydrogren ....

  Methane ....

③ a **Draw a dot-and-cross diagram to show the bonding in a molecule of nitrogen, N$_2$.** (2 marks, ★★★★)

  b **What type of covalent bond does it have?** (1 mark, ★★★★) ....

④ a **Ethene is a hydrocarbon with the formula C$_2$H$_4$. Draw a dot-and-cross diagram to show its bonding.** (2 marks, ★★★★★)

  b **What type of covalent bonds does it have?** (2 marks, ★★★★) ....

Diamond, graphite and graphene

1 The diagram below shows three giant covalent substances. Choose the correct letter to answer each question. (2 marks, ★★)

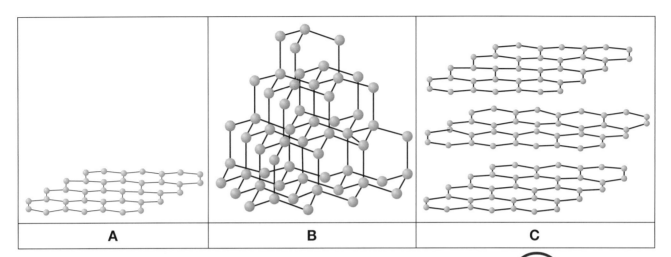

| A | B | C |

a Which substance is graphene? ....

b Which substance has weak intermolecular forces? ....

NAILIT!

The properties of diamond and graphite are often assessed in exams.

2 This question is about the properties of diamond and graphite.

a Use your knowledge about their structure and bonding to explain why diamond and graphite both have high melting points. (2 marks, ★★★)

....

....

b **Explain why diamond is hard.** (2 marks, ★★★)

....

....

c Although graphite is a non-metal, like metals it conducts electricity. Explain what feature both graphite and metals have that enable them to conduct electricity. (1 mark, ★★★)

....

3 Silicon dioxide (SiO_2) is the main component of sand. It has a giant covalent structure, shown below.

a SiO_2 does *not* conduct electricity. Suggest why. (1 mark, ★★★)

....

b **Predict two further properties of SiO_2.** (2 marks, ★★★)

....

....

Fullerenes and polymers

1. The diagram below shows four different substances made from carbon. Choose the correct letter to answer each question. (4 marks, ★★)

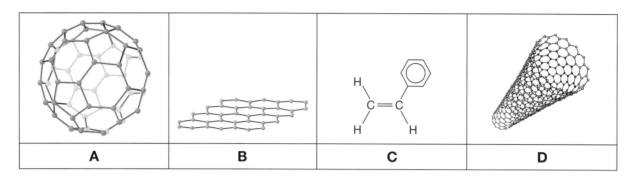

| A | B | C | D |

a Which substance has a very high length to diameter ratio? ....

b Which substance could be used to make a polymer? ....

c Which substance is buckminsterfullerene? ....

d Which substance is made from a single layer of graphite? ....

2. The structures of fullerenes and nanotubes are unique, which gives them many uses. Explain how their structure makes them suitable for the following:

a Fullerenes can be used to deliver drugs to targeted areas inside the body. (1 mark, ★★★)

....

b Nanotubes make excellent catalysts. (1 mark, ★★★)

....

3. Polyethene is a polymer made from many ethene molecules joined together in a long chain.

a Which type of bonds are found in polymers? (1 mark, ★)

....

The table below shows some of the properties of ethene and polyethene.

	Ethene	Polyethene
Melting point/°C	−169	Approximately 120
Size of molecules	Small	Large
State at room temperature	Gas	Solid

b Use this information to explain why ethene is a gas at room temperature yet polyethene is a solid. (3 marks, ★★★)

....

....

....

Giant metallic structures and alloys

DO IT!

The properties of metals depend on their structure and bonding. Practise drawing *labelled* diagrams to represent metallic bonding. This will help you to gain marks in exam questions.

NAILIT!

The difference in the properties between pure metals and alloys is all down to the *sizes* of the atoms or metal ions, and the *distortion* of the regular layers of atoms.

(1) **Use the words in the box below to complete the following passage about metals. You will not need to use all of the words.** (4 marks, ★★)

Metals are .... structures.

The particles are arranged in ....

The outer shell electrons become detached from the rest of the atom and are said to be .... This means they are free to move throughout the whole metal.

Metallic bonding is strong because of the .... attraction between the positive metal ions and the electrons.

layers	magnetic	giant	electrostatic	small	delocalised

(2) **Explain, with the aid of a labelled diagram, why metals are good electrical conductors.** (4 marks, ★★★★)

....

....

....

....

(3) **Iron is the fourth most abundant element found in the Earth's crust, and has many different uses.**

a **The melting point of pure iron is 1538°C. Explain this in terms of metallic bonding.** (2 marks, ★★)

....

....

Pure iron is relatively soft, so is often mixed with other elements to form alloys. Steel is made when small amounts of carbon are added to iron.

b **Explain why steel is harder than pure iron.** (2 marks, ★★★)

....

....

Nanoparticles

(1) **Which is the correct size range of a nanoparticle?**
Tick one box. (1 mark, ★)

1–1000 nm	
1–100 mm	
1–100 nm	
1–1000 mm	

NAILIT!

Surface area of a cube = side^2 × volume of a cube = side^3

Surface area to volume ratio = surface area/volume

WORKIT!

Convert 15 nanometres to metres and express your answer in standard form. (1 mark, ★★★)

- First, convert 15 nanometres to metres. 1 nanometre is equivalent to 0.000000001, or 1 × 10^{-9} metres. Therefore, 15 nanometres is 0.000000015 metres.
- Look for the first number which is not 0 after the decimal point. In this case it's number 1.
- Count how many places it is after the decimal point – it's 8 places after. This means that your answer must have 10^{-8} in it.

0	.	0	0	0	0	0	0	0	1	5
			1	2	3	4	5	6	7	8	9

- Finally, look at the numbers which aren't 0. Put a decimal point after the first number which gives us 1.5.

Put everything together to get the final answer of 1.5 × 10^{-8} m.

(2) **Convert the following measurements to metres, expressing your answer in standard form.**
(4 marks, ★★★)

a 86 nm ....

b 14.6 nm ....

c 158.6 nm ....

d 8.2 nm ....

e **Which of the above measurements does not correspond to a nanoparticle? Explain your answer.** (2 marks, ★★)

....

....

(3) **A cube with sides of 50 nm has a surface area to volume ratio of 0.12.**

a **Calculate the surface area to volume ratio of a cube with sides of 5 nm.** (3 marks, ★★★)

....

....

....

b **What is the relationship between the length of the side of the cube and the surface area to volume ratio?** (2 marks, ★★★★)

....

....

Quantitative chemistry

Conservation of mass and balancing equations

1. **Magnesium burns in oxygen to produce magnesium oxide.**

   a **Write a word equation for this reaction.** (2 marks, ★)

   .... → ....

   b **Identify the reactants and products in this reaction.** (2 marks, ★)

Reactants	Products

   The reaction can also be written in a balanced equation as:

   $2Mg + O_2 \rightarrow 2MgO$

   c **If 12g of magnesium reacts with 8g of oxygen, what is the mass of MgO product?** (2 marks, ★)

   ....

NAILIT!

Don't forget that in all chemical reactions, the mass before and after the reaction is the same.

Think of it as like making a cake – the amount of flour, sugar, butter and eggs doesn't change after you bake them – they just react and turn into something new!

WORKIT!

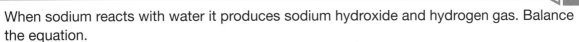

When sodium reacts with water it produces sodium hydroxide and hydrogen gas. Balance the equation.

Step 1 Write a word equation for the reaction and identify the reactants and products.

Reactants		Products	
sodium + water	→	sodium hydroxide + hydrogen	

Step 2 Write a symbol equation for the reaction.

Na + H_2O → $NaOH$ + H_2

Step 3 Count the number of atoms before and after the reaction.

$Na = 1$ → $Na = 1$

$O = 1$ → $O = 1$

$H = 2$ → $H = 3$

We can see here that we end up with more hydrogen atoms than we started with – that's impossible!

Continued

WORKIT!

Step 4 Balance the equation by writing the number in front of the reactants or products, keeping count of the atoms as you go.

$$2Na \quad + \quad 2H_2O \quad \rightarrow \quad 2NaOH \quad + \quad H_2$$

$$Na = 2 \qquad\qquad\qquad \rightarrow \quad Na = \underline{2}$$

$$O = 2 \qquad\qquad\qquad\qquad O = \underline{2}$$

$$H = 4 \qquad\qquad\qquad\qquad H = \underline{4}$$

Step 5 Write the balanced equation.

$$2Na \quad + \quad 2H_2O \quad \rightarrow \quad 2NaOH \quad + \quad H_2$$

Balancing and interpreting equations are really important skills that will be useful elsewhere in the exam, so spend some extra time making sure you're happy with them before moving on.

② **The production of ammonia by reacting nitrogen and hydrogen is shown in the unbalanced equation below:** (4 marks, ★★★)

$N_2(g) + H_2(g) \rightarrow NH_3(g)$

a **Write a word equation for the reaction.**

....

b **Identify the number of atoms before and after the reaction in the unbalanced equation.**

	Reactants	Products
N		
H		

c **Write a balanced equation for this reaction.**

....

③ **Write a balanced equation for the reaction of iron oxide (Fe_2O_3) with carbon monoxide to produce iron and carbon dioxide.** (2 marks, ★★★★)

....

NAILIT!

Double check that you've balanced the equation correctly – count the number of atoms again! Remember, the number of atoms in the reactants and the products should be the same – if they aren't, it isn't balanced.

Relative formula masses

(1) **Match the following terms to their definition.** (2 marks, ★★)

The relative atomic mass (symbol = A_r)	of a compound is calculated by adding up all the relative atomic masses of all the atoms present in the formula of the compound.
The relative formula mass (symbol = M_r)	of an element is the weighted average mass of its naturally occurring isotopes.
In equations, the relative formula masses of diatomic molecules, such as oxygen, bromine and nitrogen,	means that in a chemical reaction the sum of the relative formula masses of the reactants is equal to the sum of the relative formula masses of the products.
The law of mass conservation	are twice their relative atomic masses.

(2) **Find the A_r for the following elements.** (3 marks, ★★)

Carbon	Oxygen	Chlorine	Iron
12			

(3) **A neutralisation reaction of sodium hydroxide and sulfuric acid is shown in the balanced equation:**

$$2NaOH + H_2SO_4 \rightarrow Na_2SO_4 + 2H_2O$$

a Find the M_r for each of the reactants and products. (4 marks, ★★)

NaOH	H_2SO_4	Na_2SO_4	H_2O

b Calculate how much water is formed when 10 g of sulfuric acid reacts with excess sodium hydroxide. (2 marks, ★★★★)

....

....

c Calculate how much sodium hydroxide is needed to make 5 g of sodium sulfate. (2 marks, ★★★★)

....

....

d Suggest one reason why it is important for a company that produces sodium sulfate to know the mass of reactants. (1 mark, ★★★★)

....

NAILIT!

- Remember that some elements are diatomic. HONCIBrIF is one way to help you remember them.

- You will be given a periodic table in the exam – make sure you know which numbers refer to the relative atomic mass.

The mole and reacting masses

(1) **Calculate the number of moles for the following.** (4 marks, ★★)

a 2.3 g of sodium ....

c 0.2 g of SO_2 ....

b 1.6 g of CH_4 ....

d 2.2 g of CO_2 ....

(2) **Calculate the mass of the following.** (4 marks, ★★)

a 1.0 mol HCl ....

c 0.3 mol Na_2CO_3 ....

b 1.5 mol NaOH ....

d 0.5 mol $Al_2(SO_4)_3$ ....

(3) The labels on the containers of chemical substances in a laboratory have worn away and some of the information is missing. The information still visible has been recorded in the table below.

Substance	A_r or M_r	Mass/g	Moles	Comments
Sodium	23.0	2.30	0.1	soft metal
		0.32	0.01	gas
CH_4		1.60		gas

a **Use the information available to complete the table.** (4 marks, ★★★)

Another bottle contains hydrochloric acid (HCl) diluted in water. The label reads '50 g HCl'.

b **Calculate the number of moles of HCl in the solution.** (2 marks, ★★★)

....

(4) Iron is an essential part of the human diet. Breakfast cereals often contain anhydrous iron(II) sulfate to supplement the iron from other sources in a person's diet. The formula for iron(II) sulfate is $FeSO_4$. Assume 1 mole of iron(II) sulfate produces 1 mole of iron.

a **Calculate the M_r of $FeSO_4$.** (1 mark, ★★)

....

b **Calculate the mass of 0.25 moles of $FeSO_4$.** (1 mark, ★★★)

....

c **Calculate the mass of $FeSO_4$ needed to provide 7 g of iron.** (2 marks, ★★★★)

....

d **Calculate the number of atoms of iron in 7 g.** (2 marks, ★★★★)

....

(5) Calcium carbonate undergoes thermal decomposition to produce calcium oxide and carbon dioxide as shown in the equation below:

$$CaCO_3(s) \rightarrow CaO(s) + CO_2(g)$$

a Calculate the mass of calcium oxide produced if 25 g of calcium carbonate decomposes. (2 marks, ★★★)

....

....

Carbon capture, storing carbon dioxide from the atmosphere in other forms, has been suggested as a way to reduce climate change caused by increased carbon dioxide in the atmosphere. Experiments have been conducted to find out whether calcium carbonate can be used in this way by reversing the thermal decomposition equation given above.

b Calculate the mass of calcium carbonate that would be produced by storing 500 kg of carbon dioxide. (2 marks, ★★★)

....

....

(6) A pharmaceutical company produces tablets of the medicine paracetamol ($C_8H_9NO_2$), which contain 0.5 g of paracetamol.

a Calculate the number of moles of paracetamol in each tablet. (2 marks, ★★★)

....

....

b The same company produces the medicine aspirin by the following reaction:

$$C_7H_5O_3 + C_4H_6O_3 \rightarrow C_9H_8O_4 + CH_3COOH$$

salicylic acid + ethanoic anhydride → aspirin + ethanoic acid

$(M_r = 138)$ $(M_r = 180)$

Calculate the number of moles of aspirin produced if 4 g of salicylic acid is used. (2 marks, ★★★★)

....

....

c Calculate the number of molecules of salicylic acid that produce 0.5 g of aspirin. (2 marks, ★★★★)

....

....

....

MATHS SKILLS

Use the formulae for your calculations:

$n = m/M_r$, $m = n \times M_r$; no. of particles $= n \times N_A$

N_A = Avogadro's number

Don't forget to put the units in your answer and use standard form (e.g. 6.5×10^{-5} instead of 0.000065) when appropriate.

Limiting reactants

NAILIT!

A reaction stops when all the particles of one of the reactants are used up. In a reaction involving two reactants:

- the limiting reactant is the one that is all used up at the end of the reaction
- the reactant in excess is still there at the end of the reaction (although in a smaller amount than at the start).

① **After a reaction of magnesium and hydrochloric acid, there is magnesium left behind.**

  a **Which is the limiting reactant?** (1 mark, ★) ....

  b **Which reactant was in excess?** (1 mark, ★) ....

WORKIT!

In an experiment, 3.2 g of NH_3 reacts with 3.5 g of O_2. Find the limiting reactant.

$$NH_3 \quad + \quad O_2 \quad \rightarrow \quad NO \quad + \quad H_2O$$

Step 1 Balance the equation.

$$4NH_3 \quad + \quad 5O_2 \quad \rightarrow \quad 4NO \quad + \quad 6H_2O$$

Step 2 Calculate the number of moles for each of the reactants.

NH_3: $3.25g / 17 gmol^{-1} = 0.19$ moles O_2: $3.5g / 32 gmol^{-1} = 0.11$ moles

Step 3 Compare the ratios of what we have versus what the balanced equation tells us we need.

From the equation we can see that 4 moles of NH_3 react with 5 moles of O_2. This tells us that if we have 0.19 moles of NH_3 we need 0.23 moles of O_2.

What we actually have is 0.19 moles of NH_3 reacting with 0.11 moles of O_2.

This tells us that NH_3 was added to excess and O_2 is the limiting factor for the reaction.

② **Hydrogen reacts with oxygen to produce water: $2H_2(g) + O_2(g) \rightarrow 2H_2O(l)$**

  If 1 mole of hydrogen is reacted with 1 mole of oxygen, determine the limiting reactant and the reactant in excess by matching the questions on the left to the correct answer on the right. (3 marks, ★★★)

How many moles of water can be produced by 1 mole of H_2?	1
How many moles of water can be produced by 1 mole of O_2?	2
Which is the limiting reactant?	1
How much H_2O is produced in the reaction?	O_2
Which reactant is in excess?	H_2
How many moles of O_2 is used in the reaction?	1

MATHS SKILLS

- To identify the limiting reactant from a chemical equation, work out the number of moles of each reactant and compare this ratio with what is needed by looking at the ratio in the chemical equation for the reaction.

- To convert the ratio in the equation to match the numbers you're told, find the factor by dividing one by the other, depending on the direction you're going. For the worked example above, the ratio is 4:5, which means that for every 4 units of NH_3 you needed 5 units of O_2. You knew the '4' units of NH_3 was 0.19, so to work out how much O_2 needed, simply divide 5 by 4 = 1.25 (i.e. 5 is 1.25 times bigger than 4!) and multiply that by 0.19 = 0.23.

③ **Copper reacts with oxygen in the air to produce copper(I) oxide. The reaction is shown in the equation below:**

...... $Cu(s) +$ ...... $O_2(g) \rightarrow$ ...... $Cu_2O(s)$

In an experiment to investigate this reaction, 80 g of copper was reacted with 50 g of oxygen.

a **Balance the equation.** (2 marks, ★★)

b **Calculate the number of moles of the two reactants.** (2 marks, ★★)

....

....

c **Identify the limiting reagent and explain your choice.** (2 marks, ★★★)

....

....

④ **Propane is a fuel that is commonly used in portable stoves and increasingly in vehicles, where it is known as liquid petroleum gas (LPG). It completely combusts in the presence of excess oxygen. The chemical equation is shown below:**

...... $C_3H_8(l) +$ ...... $O_2(g) \rightarrow$ ...... $CO_2(g) +$ ...... $H_2O(g)$

To develop an efficient car engine, a manufacturer is testing mixes with different amounts of oxygen and propane. In this test, 14.8 g of C_3H_8 reacts with 3.44 g of O_2.

a **Balance the equation.** (2 marks, ★★)

b **Calculate the mass of carbon dioxide produced in the reaction.** (2 marks, ★★★)

....

....

c **Identify the limiting reagent and suggest how the manufacturer could change the quantities of propane and oxygen to maximise the efficiency of an engine.** (5 marks, ★★★★)

....

....

....

....

Concentrations in solutions

(1) **Two solutions are shown below in diagrams (1) and (2).**

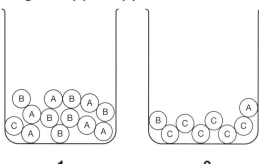

1   **2**

a **Which of the two solutions has the highest concentration of solute A?**

(1 mark, ★) ....

b **Which of the two solutions has the highest concentration of solute C?**

(1 mark, ★) ....

MATHS SKILLS

Concentration (in g/dm³ or mol/dm³) = amount in mol or mass in g/volume (in dm³).

To convert from mol/dm³ to g/dm³, multiply the amount of the solute in 1 dm³ by its M_r.

> For a 0.2 mol/dm³ solution of hydrochloric acid HCl (M_r = 36.5):
>
> 0.2 moles × 36.5 = 7.3 g
> so the concentration is 7.3 g/dm³

We can also convert from g/dm³ to mol/dm³ by dividing by the M_r.

> For a 5 g/dm³ solution of HCl:
>
> 5 g / 36.5 = 0.14 moles
> so the concentration is 0.14 mol/dm³

Remember that there are a thousand cubic centimetres in a cubic decimetre. So if you are given a volume in cubic centimetres, you need to divide by a thousand.

(2) **A student dissolved sodium chloride (NaCl) into three beakers of water as shown in the table below.**

Test	Mass of solute/g	Volume/dm³
1	5	0.020
2	10	0.025
3	20	0.035

M_r NaCl = 58.5

a **Calculate the concentration of the solute in each of the three tests.** (3 marks, ★★)

Test 1 .... g/dm³

Test 2 .... g/dm³

Test 3 .... g/dm³

b **Calculate the number of moles of solute in each solution.** (3 marks, ★★)

Test 1 .... moles

Test 2 .... moles

Test 3 .... moles

(3) **The organisers of a swimming competition need to calculate how much cleaning agent to add to the pool to keep it free of harmful microorganisms. The pool contains 2.5×10^6 dm³ water and the instructions on the box of the cleaning agent state that the pool must contain 0.01 mol/dm³ of calcium oxychloride (Ca(ClO)₂) before swimming.**

a **Calculate the M_r of Ca(ClO)₂.** (1 mark, ★★) ....

b **Calculate the concentration of Ca(ClO)₂ required, in g/mol³.** (1 mark, ★★★) ....

c **Calculate the amount of cleaning agent, in g, that must be added for the pool to contain the correct concentration. Give your answer in standard form.** (3 marks, ★★★★)

....

....

Moles in solution

NAILIT!

- Be careful with your units and orders of magnitude – it is easy to get confused!
- If you're given a volume or concentration with the units cm^3 or mol/cm^3, divide by 1000.
- Don't forget to write and balance the chemical equation – check the ratio of moles in the equation and change your initial answer accordingly.

(1) **A student has 50 cm^3 of 5.0 mol/dm^3 hydrochloric acid (HCl) which is titrated with sodium hydroxide (NaOH).**

  a **How many moles of NaOH are needed to neutralise the HCl? Circle the correct answer.**
  (1 mark, ★★)

0.25 moles	4 moles	250 moles	0.1 moles

  b **What is the concentration of NaOH if 25 cm^3 was used? Circle the correct answer.** (1 mark, ★★)

10 mol/dm^3	0.1 mol/dm^3	5 mol/dm^3	0.5 mol/dm^3

(2) **An orange juice company wanted to find out the concentration of acid in its juice. The acid in 25.0 cm^3 of the orange juice reacted completely with 12.5 cm^3 of 0.1 mol/dm^3 sodium hydroxide. Calculate the concentration of acid in the orange juice. A previous investigation had shown that 1 mole of the acid reacted with 1 mole of sodium hydroxide to produce 1 mole of salt and water.** (3 marks, ★★★)

....

....

(3) **In a titration, a student finds that 12.6 dm^3 of 2.5 mol/dm^3 sulfuric acid (H_2SO_4) neutralises 0.025 dm^3 of sodium hydroxide (NaOH). Calculate the concentration of the sodium hydroxide.** (3 marks, ★★★★)

....

....

MATHS SKILLS

- The key equation you will use in titration-related questions is $n = c \times V$.
- You need to be able to rearrange that equation – try using equation triangles.
- A common stumbling block for students answering exam questions on this topic is jumbling up the information that is given. One way to avoid this is to create a table that will tell you exactly what is known and what is unknown, like this:

Value	Solution 1/acid	Solution 2/alkali
Concentration/c(mol/dm^3)		
Moles/n(moles)		
Volume/V(dm^3)		

Moles and gas volumes

(1) Fill in the gaps to complete the definition of Avogadro's Gas Law.

At the same temperature and pressure equal .... of different gases contain the same number of molecules.

This means that under the same conditions, equal volumes of gases have the same number of .... present.

At .... (20°C) and ...., together known as ...., 1 mole of any gas occupies a volume of 24 dm³.

atmospheric pressure	room temperature	room temperature and pressure (RTP)
	volumes gases moles	

(2) A car reacts petrol with oxygen, in its engine, at a rate of 6 g of carbon per km. Calculate the volume of carbon dioxide produced in a 12 km journey. (2 marks, ★★★)

....

....

(3) A plant scientist wants to investigate the air conditions in a plant laboratory to understand the optimal conditions for maximum plant growth. The volume of air in the laboratory is 2000 dm³. A meter on the wall measures the percentage composition of the air once a day, as shown in the table below:

Gas	Per cent in the air (%)
Nitrogen	78.1
Oxygen	20.9
Argon	0.9
Carbon dioxide	0.1

a **Calculate the number of moles of gas in the laboratory.** (1 mark, ★★★)

....

....

b **Calculate the number of moles of carbon dioxide (CO_2) in the laboratory.** (1 mark, ★★★)

....

....

c **Calculate the mass of carbon dioxide (CO_2) in the laboratory.** (1 mark, ★★)

....

....

Percentage yield and atom economy

1 TitaniMine, a titanium mining and processing company, are trying to decide which of two methods to use to produce titanium from its ore, TiO_2. The two methods to extract titanium from titanium ore (TiO_2) include:

1 Displacement by magnesium – $TiO_2 + 2Mg \rightarrow Ti + 2MgO$

2 Electrolysis – $TiO_2 \rightarrow Ti + O_2$

One way that the company could compare the two methods is by calculating the atom economy of each reaction.

a Give the formula for working out the atom economy. (1 mark, ★)

....

b Explain why it is useful for chemists to understand the atom economy for a reaction. (2 marks, ★★)

....

c Calculate the atom economy for the **two** methods of producing titanium from its ore. (4 marks, ★★★)

1 ....

....

2 ....

....

d Oxygen is a useful product that can be sold. Explain how this might affect the company's decision in terms of the atom economy. (2 marks, ★★★)

....

....

2 A student heats 12.5g of calcium carbonate ($CaCO_3$) producing 6.5g of calcium oxide, as shown in the equation below: $CaCO_3(s) \rightarrow CaO(s) + CO_2(g)$

a Determine the M_r of $CaCO_3$ and CaO. (1 mark, ★)

$CaCO_3$ .... CaO ....

b What is the correct atom economy of the reaction? Tick **one** box. (2 marks, ★★★)

56%	
44%	
87%	
50%	

c Calculate the maximum theoretical mass of CaO that could be made. (2 marks, ★★)

....

d Calculate the percentage yield of the reaction. (3 marks, ★★★)

....

....

Metal oxides and the reactivity series

1 **Magnesium reacts with oxygen to form a white solid.**

   a **Write a word equation for this reaction.** (1 mark, ★★)

....

   b **Write a balanced chemical equation for this reaction.** (2 marks, ★★★)

....

....

   c **In this reaction, magnesium is oxidised. Explain what is meant by oxidation.** (1 mark, ★)

....

....

NAILIT!

More reactive metals will **displace** less reactive metals from metal salts.
This means that the metals swap places in the reaction. For example:

sodium + lead oxide → lead + sodium oxide

---

2 **Use the reactivity series to predict the outcome of the following reactions.** (4 marks, ★★)

   a **Aluminium + lead chloride →** ....

   b **Silver + copper oxide →** ....

   c **Calcium + zinc nitrate →** ....

   d **Iron chloride + copper →** ....

3 **A student has an unknown metal, X, and carries out some experiments in order to determine its reactivity. The student's results are in the table below.**

1	X + copper sulfate solution	A red/orange solid is formed
2	X + sodium sulfate solution	No reaction
3	X + magnesium sulfate	A silvery grey solid is produced
4	X + hydrochloric acid	X dissolves vigorously and a gas is produced

Metal	Reactivity
Copper	
Sodium	1
Magnesium	
X	

   a **Use the student's results to place the metals in order of reactivity, with 1 being the most reactive and 4 being the least reactive. The most reactive is done for you.** (2 marks, ★★)

   b **What is the name of the red/orange solid formed in experiment 1?** (1 mark, ★★★)

....

Extraction of metals and reduction

(1) Magnesium cannot be extracted from its ore by heating with carbon. Explain why. (1 mark, ★★)

....

....

(2) Why does gold not need to be extracted from an ore? (1 mark, ★★)

....

....

(3) Tin is extracted from its ore by heating it with carbon. The main tin ore is called cassiterite and it contains tin(IV) oxide, SnO_2.

a **Write a word equation for this reaction.** (2 marks, ★★★)

....

....

b **Which substance is oxidised in this reaction?** (1 mark, ★★)

....

(4) Copper can also be extracted from its ore with carbon. Many copper containing ores contain copper(II) oxide, CuO.

a **Write a balanced chemical equation for this reaction. Include state symbols.** (2 marks, ★★★)

....

....

b **Using the reactivity series, predict another element which could be used to extract copper from its ore. Suggest why this element is not used in practice.** (2 marks, ★★★)

....

....

....

....

DO IT!

Make sure that you always refer to the reactivity series when answering questions about metal extraction. Remember, any metal above carbon is extracted from its ore using electrolysis.

The blast furnace

1 Iron is extracted from its ore in the blast furnace. The iron ore, which contains mostly iron(III) oxide, is mixed with coke (a form of carbon), limestone and air and heated to around 1500°C.

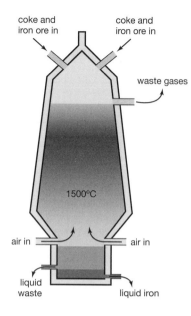

coke and iron ore in   coke and iron ore in

waste gases

1500°C

air in   air in

liquid waste   liquid iron

There are several reactions that take place in the blast furnace. Although carbon can be used to extract iron from its ore, during this reaction, carbon monoxide (CO) is formed and this then reacts with the iron(III) oxide to form iron.

The first reaction is between carbon and oxygen to form carbon dioxide.

a Write a word equation for this reaction. (1 mark, ★)

....

The carbon dioxide then reacts with further carbon to form carbon monoxide.

b Write a balanced chemical equation for this reaction. Include state symbols.
(2 marks, ★★★★)

....

The following reaction then takes place.

Iron(III) oxide + carbon monoxide → iron + carbon dioxide

c What type of reaction is this? (1 mark, ★★)

....

d Balance the symbol equation for this reaction below. (2 marks, ★★★★)

___Fe_2O_3 (s) + ___CO(g) → ___Fe (l) + ___CO_2 (g)

e How can you tell from this equation that the reaction is carried out at a high temperature?
(1 mark, ★★★)

....

The final stage of this reaction produces the waste product, calcium silicate (slag). This is formed when impurities such as sand (silicon dioxide) react with the limestone.

f What is the chemical formula for slag? (1 mark, ★★)

....

g On the diagram, label where the slag is formed. (1 mark, ★★)

NAILIT!

Learn the equations for each of the four stages in this metal extraction, and make sure you know which involve oxidation/reduction and which equation is an acid/base reaction.

The reactions of acids

1. State **one similarity** and **one difference** between bases and alkalis. (2 marks, ★★★)

....

....

....

2. Choose **two** chemicals from the table below that could be used to make the following salts.
(3 marks, ★★)

a **Sodium chloride** ....

b **Potassium nitrate** ....

c **Copper sulfate** ....

Copper chloride	Sodium hydroxide	Sulfuric acid
Nitric acid	Chlorine	Potassium carbonate
Sodium sulfate	Hydrochloric acid	Copper oxide

3. Magnesium oxide and magnesium carbonate are both white solids that will react with dilute acids, including hydrochloric acid, HCl.

A student adds HCl to separate portions of magnesium oxide and magnesium carbonate and makes observations.

a **State one observation that the two reactions would have in common.** (1 mark, ★★)

....

b **State one observation that would be different.** (1 mark, ★★)

....

c **Write the word equation for the reaction between magnesium oxide and hydrochloric acid.** (1 mark, ★★)

....

d **What is the formula for magnesium carbonate?** (1 mark, ★★★) ....

4. Write chemical equations for these reactions, including state symbols. (6 marks, ★★★★)

a **Magnesium + hydrochloric acid** ....

b **Lithium oxide + sulfuric acid** ....

c **Copper(II) oxide + hydrochloric acid** ....

5. The reaction between calcium and hydrochloric acid is a redox reaction. This means that both oxidation and reduction take place at the same time.

a **Write an ionic equation for this reaction. Include state symbols.** (3 marks, ★★★★★)

....

b **State which species is oxidised and which species is reduced.** (2 marks, ★★★★)

....

The preparation of soluble salts

① A sample of copper sulfate can be formed by reacting together solid copper carbonate and dilute sulfuric acid.

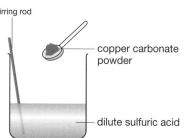

stirring rod

copper carbonate powder

dilute sulfuric acid

> **NAILIT!**
>
> The preparation of soluble salts can be summarised as follows:
>
> • heat acid (to increase the rate of reaction)
> • add insoluble base until no more reacts
> • filter excess base
> • allow solution to crystallise.
>
> This is the standard method regardless of which type of base is used.

a **Complete the word equation for this reaction.** (1 mark, ★★)

Copper carbonate + sulfuric acid → copper sulfate + ... + ...

b **State two observations that would be seen during this reaction.** (2 marks, ★★)

....

c **The copper carbonate needs to be added until it is in excess. Explain why this is necessary.** (1 mark, ★★)

....

d **How is the excess copper carbonate removed?** (1 mark, ★)

....

e **State another chemical that reacts with sulfuric acid to form copper sulfate.** (1 mark, ★★)

....

f **When soluble salts are prepared in this way, the percentage yield is generally less than 100%. Suggest one reason why.** (1 mark, ★★)

....

② A soluble salt is formed in the reaction between calcium and nitric acid.

Calcium + nitric acid → calcium nitrate + hydrogen

a **Write a balanced chemical equation for this reaction, including state symbols.** (3 marks, ★★★★)

....

b **A student carried out the experiment above and made 2.6 g of calcium nitrate. If the theoretical yield is 3.0 g, what is the percentage yield? Quote your answer to one decimal place.** (2 marks, ★★★)

....

....

③ On a separate piece of paper, describe how to make a pure, dry sample of zinc chloride. Include an equation and a full equipment list. (6 marks, ★★★★)

Oxidation and reduction in terms of electrons

① **Magnesium reacts with a solution of copper(II) chloride to form a solution of magnesium chloride and solid copper.**

a **Write an ionic equation, including state symbols, for this reaction.** (3 marks, ★★★★)

....

b **Which species is oxidised and which is reduced?** (1 mark, ★★★)

....

WORKIT!

Step 1 Write a balanced chemical equation, including state symbols.

$Mg(s) + CuCl_2(aq) \rightarrow MgCl_2(aq) + Cu(s)$

Step 2 Any aqueous solution will split up into its ions. Rewrite the equation to show this.

$Mg(s) + Cu^{2+}(aq) + 2Cl^-(aq) \rightarrow Mg^{2+}(aq) + 2Cl^-(aq) + Cu(s)$

Step 3 Cancel out any species that appear on both sides of the equation. These are **spectator ions** and don't take part in the reaction.

$Mg(s) + Cu^{2+}(aq) + \cancel{2Cl^-(aq)} \rightarrow Mg^{2+}(aq) + \cancel{2Cl^-(aq)} + Cu(s)$

Step 4 Rewrite the equation with the remaining ions.

$Mg(s) + Cu^{2+}(aq) \rightarrow Mg^{2+}(aq) + Cu(s)$

Step 5 Finish with a conclusion. The Mg has lost electrons and formed a positive ion, so according to OILRIG, it has been oxidised. The Cu^{2+} has gained electrons and has therefore been reduced.

② **Write ionic equations for the following reactions. In each case, state which species has been oxidised and which has been reduced.**

a **Zinc(II) nitrate reacts with magnesium to form magnesium nitrate and solid zinc.**
(4 marks, ★★★★★)

....

b **Sodium reacts with a solution of zinc(II) chloride to form a solution of sodium chloride and solid zinc.**
(4 marks, ★★★★★)

....

c **Silver(I) sulfate reacts with copper to form copper(II) sulfate and silver metal.** (4 marks, ★★★★)

....

d **Calcium reacts with a solution of iron(III) chloride to form solid iron and a solution of calcium chloride.** (4 marks, ★★★★★)

....

NAILIT!

Writing ionic equations is tricky and you need to make sure you can write formulae correctly. You cannot always use the periodic table to work out the charges on metal ions, as the transition metals often form more than one ion. Here are some common ones.

Zinc – Zn^{2+} Iron(II) – Fe^{2+}

Copper – Cu^{2+} Iron(III) – Fe^{3+}

Silver – Ag^+

pH scale and neutralisation

① Match each solution with its correct pH value and colour that universal indicator would change to. The first one is done for you. (4 marks, ★★)

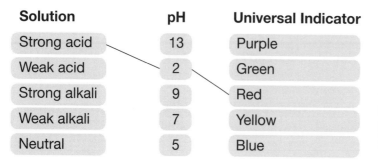

Solution	pH	Universal Indicator
Strong acid	13	Purple
Weak acid	2	Green
Strong alkali	9	Red
Weak alkali	7	Yellow
Neutral	5	Blue

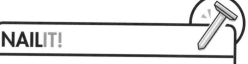

NAILIT!

All neutralisation reactions between an acid and an alkali can be simply represented by this ionic equation:

$H^+(aq) + OH^-(aq) \rightarrow H_2O(l)$

Always include this if you are asked about neutralisation; equations are an excellent way of gaining marks.

② State the **name** of the ion that causes solutions to be alkaline. (1 mark, ★) ....

③ State the **formula** of the ion that causes solutions to be acidic. (1 mark, ★) ....

④ Which of these solutions has the greatest concentration of H^+ ions? Tick **one** box. (1 mark, ★★)

pH 3 ☐

pH 1 ☐

⑤ Which of these solutions has the lowest concentration of OH^- ions? Tick **one** box. (1 mark, ★★)

pH 14 ☐

pH 12 ☐

⑥ Potassium sulfate (K_2SO_4) can be produced in the reaction between sulfuric acid and an alkali.

a State the name of the alkali that could be used. (1 mark, ★)

....

b Write a balanced chemical equation for this reaction. (2 marks, ★★★★)

....

c Write the ionic equation for this reaction. (1 mark, ★★★)

....

⑦ Ammonia gas (NH_3) forms an alkaline solution when dissolved in water. Suggest the formulae of the two ions formed. (2 marks, ★★★★★)

....

Strong and weak acids

WORKIT!

Hydrochloric acid, HCl, is a strong acid and ethanoic acid, CH_3COOH, is a weak acid. Write equations to show how they ionise in aqueous solution. (2 marks, ★★★)

Strong acids completely ionise (split up into ions) when they are in solution.

$$HCl(aq) \rightarrow H^+(aq) + Cl^-(aq)$$

Weak acids only partially ionise when they are in solution. This is represented by using the reversible arrow ($\rightleftharpoons$) in the equation. ←

$$CH_3COOH(aq) \rightleftharpoons CH_3COO^-(aq) + H^+(aq)$$

> Reversible reactions are discussed more on page 243.

---

(1) **Write equations to show how the following acids ionise in solution.** (3 marks, ★★★)

a **Nitric acid, HNO_3 (strong acid)**

....

b **Methanoic acid, HCOOH (weak acid)**

....

c **Sulfuric acid, H_2SO_4 (strong acid)**

....

(2) **Explain the difference between a weak acid and a dilute acid.** (2 marks, ★★★)

....

....

....

(3) **An acid with pH 3 has a hydrogen ion concentration of 0.001 mol/dm³.**

a **Express this value in standard form.** (1 mark, ★★★)

....

b **What is the hydrogen ion concentration of an acid with a pH of 1? Express your answer in standard form.** (3 marks, ★★★★★)

....

....

....

NAILIT!

Strong and concentrated do not mean the same thing!

Concentration refers to how much of a solute is dissolved in a solution. More solute means a **higher** concentration.

If an acid is strong, this means that it completely splits or **dissociates** into its ions in solution.

Electrolysis

① **Label the diagram choosing the correct words from the box below.** (3 marks, ★★)

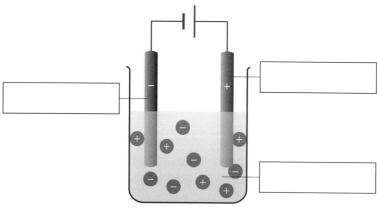

cathode	electrolyte	electroplating	anode

② **Why can ionic compounds conduct electricity when melted or in solution, but not when they are solids?** (2 marks, ★★)

....

③ **Predict the products formed when these compounds undergo electrolysis.** (3 marks, ★★)

a **Molten zinc(II) chloride** ....

b **Molten silver iodide** ....

c **Molten copper(II) oxide** ....

④ **Molten lead bromide undergoes electrolysis to form lead and bromine.**

a **Complete the half equations for this reaction.** (2 marks, ★★★) ◄——— Remember that half equations only show one species being oxidised or reduced.

  • $Pb^{2+} +$ .... $\rightarrow Pb$

  • $2Br^- \rightarrow Br_2 +$ ....

b **Which species is oxidised and which is reduced?** (1 mark, ★★★)

....

DO IT!

Practise writing half equations for simple ionic compounds.

Step 1 Use the charges on ions to write a formula, e.g. K^+ and Cl^- forms KCl.

Step 2 Write out the half equations:

$K^+ \rightarrow K$

$Cl^- \rightarrow Cl_2$

Step 3 Balance any atoms:

$K^+ \rightarrow K$ *already balanced*

$2Cl^- \rightarrow Cl_2$ *2Cl- needed*

Step 4 Add electrons to balance the charges.

$K^+ + e^- \rightarrow K$

$2Cl^- \rightarrow Cl_2 + 2e^-$

NAILIT!

Electrons are always **added** in half equations. If you can't remember which side to put the electrons on, remember that the **charges need to be balanced**.

For example, during electrolysis of NaCl, Na^+ ions form Na metal.

$Na^+ \rightarrow Na$

There is a **positive** charge on the **left-hand side**, which means that **one electron** needs to be added to the **right-hand side** to balance the charge.

$Na^+ \rightarrow Na + \textbf{e}^-$

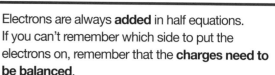

Electrolysis of copper(II) sulfate and electroplating

① The diagram shows an experiment to show the apparatus used to electrolyse a solution of copper(II) sulfate. The electrodes are made of graphite and are inert.

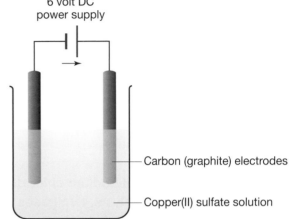

6 volt DC
power supply

Carbon (graphite) electrodes

Copper(II) sulfate solution

a What is meant by the word 'inert'? (1 mark, ★★)

....

b What is the name of the electrolyte? (1 mark, ★★)

....

c Oxygen is produced at the anode (positive electrode). Describe how you would test for this gas. (1 mark, ★)

....

d What would you see formed at the cathode (negative electrode)? Write an equation for this reaction. (2 marks, ★★★★)

....

e Copper(II) sulfate solution is blue. Explain what happens to the colour of the solution during this experiment. (2 marks, ★★★)

....

f A different reaction takes place if **copper electrodes** are used instead of **graphite electrodes. State two differences that you would see.** (2 marks, ★★★★)

....

② Electroplating is an application of electrolysis that allows a thin layer of metal to be coated onto another, this could be to make them look nicer or increase protection. Bathroom taps are often plated in **chromium** which gives them a very shiny coating.

a In this reaction:

i What would the anode be made of? (1 mark, ★★★)

....

ii What would the cathode be made of? (1 mark, ★★★)

....

b Suggest a substance that could be used as the electrolyte. (1 mark, ★★★)

....

c Write a half equation to show what would happen at the cathode. Assume that the chromium ion formed is Cr^{3+}. (2 marks, ★★★★★)

....

NAILIT!

Remember these rules for electroplating.
- The electrolyte must contain the metal ion that is being used to coat the object.
- The cathode must be the metal that is being used to coat the object.
- The anode must be the object that is being plated.

The electrolysis of aqueous solutions

1 State the products formed when the following **aqueous** solutions undergo electrolysis.
(4 marks, ★★★)

a Copper(II) chloride ....

b Potassium bromide ....

c Zinc(II) sulfate ....

d Sodium carbonate ....

NAILIT!

Learn these rules to predict the products of the electrolysis of aqueous solutions.

Positive ion	Cathode
Copper and below in reactivity series	Metal
Anything above hydrogen in reactivity series	Hydrogen

Negative ion	Anode
Chloride, bromide, iodide	Halogen
Sulfate, nitrate, carbonate	Oxygen

2 When a solution of sodium chloride undergoes electrolysis, two gases are formed at the electrodes.

a The gas formed at the cathode is hydrogen. Complete the half equation for this reaction. (2 marks, ★★★)

.... H^+ + ... $\rightarrow$ .... H_2

b What is the name of the gas formed at the anode? Write a half equation to show how it is formed. (3 marks, ★★★★)

....

....

3 A solution of lithium iodide (LiI) undergoes electrolysis.

a This solution contains a mixture of ions, including iodide, I^-, ions. State the other **three** ions present. (2 marks, ★★★)

....

b Explain what happens to the iodide ions during electrolysis. (3 marks, ★★★★)

....

....

c What is the name of the remaining solution? (1 mark, ★★★★) ....

4 When a solution of copper(II) sulfate undergoes electrolysis, one of the products formed is oxygen.

a At which electrode is the oxygen formed? (1 mark, ★) ....

b Write a half equation to show the formation of oxygen. (3 marks, ★★★★★)

....

....

The extraction of metals using electrolysis

(1) **Aluminium is extracted from its ore by electrolysis. The most common aluminium ore is called bauxite and this is purified to produce aluminium oxide, Al_2O_3. The aluminium oxide is heated to around 950 °C and dissolved in another aluminium compound called cryolite. The mixture then undergoes electrolysis and forms aluminium and oxygen.**

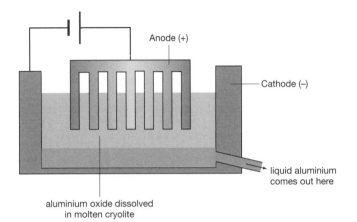

Anode (+)

Cathode (−)

liquid aluminium comes out here

aluminium oxide dissolved in molten cryolite

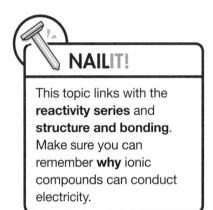

NAILIT!

This topic links with the **reactivity series** and **structure and bonding**. Make sure you can remember **why** ionic compounds can conduct electricity.

a **Aluminium oxide has a high melting point. Use your ideas about structure and bonding to explain why.** (2 marks, ★★★)

....

....

b **Why does the aluminium oxide need to be heated?** (1 mark, ★★)

....

c **Why is cryolite added to the aluminium oxide?** (2 marks, ★★★)

....

d **The reaction that takes place at the anode is replaced with: $2O^{2-} \rightarrow O_2 + 4e^-$**

This equation shows oxidation. Explain why. (1 mark, ★★)

....

e **Aluminium is produced at the cathode. Write a half equation to show this reaction.**
(2 marks, ★★★)

....

f **With the help of an equation, explain why graphite anodes require frequent replacing.**
(2 marks, ★★★)

....

....

g **Aluminium was not discovered until around 200 years ago, yet there is evidence to suggest that iron was used by humans over 7000 years ago. Suggest why it took a long time for aluminium to be discovered.** (1 mark, ★★)

....

....

Practical investigation into the electrolysis of aqueous solutions

Hypothesis: The product produced at the cathode when an aqueous solution undergoes hydrolysis depends on the reactivity of the metal in the salt solution.

A student carries out the following experiment with four different metal salt solutions, all of which have a concentration of $1\,mol/dm^3$. The salt solutions are:

- **Iron(III) chloride, $FeCl_3(aq)$**
- **Sodium chloride, $NaCl(aq)$**
- **Copper(II) chloride, $CuCl_2(aq)$**
- **Magnesium chloride, $MgCl_2(aq)$**

Method

- **Measure out $100\,cm^3$ of iron(III) chloride solution in a measuring cylinder and pour into a beaker.**
- **Place two inert electrodes into the beaker and attach to a power pack.**
- **Set voltage to 4 V, switch on the power pack and observe the product formed at the cathode.**
- **If a gas is produced, test to see if it is hydrogen.**
- **Repeat for the remaining salt solutions.**

(1) a **In the table below, state the variables in this experiment.** (4 marks, ★★★)

Independent variable	Dependent variable	Control variables

b **Describe how this experiment is valid.** (1 mark, ★)

....

(2) **Describe the test for hydrogen gas.** (2 marks, ★★) ....

....

(3) a **In the table below, predict the products that will be formed at the cathode.** (2 marks, ★★★)

Salt solution	Product produced at the cathode
$FeCl_3$	
$NaCl$	
$CuCl_2$	
$MgCl_2$	

b **Justify your predictions.** (2 marks, ★★★)

....

....

(4) **All four solutions will produce the same product at the anode. Name this gas, and describe a test to identify it.** (2 marks, ★★★)

....

....

Titrations

1 **The results from a titration are shown below.**

	Rough	1	2	3
Final volume/cm^3	15.60	30.50	45.85	14.80
Initial volume/cm^3	0.00	15.60	30.50	0.00
Titre/cm^3	15.60			

a **Calculate the titre values for experiments 1, 2 and 3.** (2 marks, ★★)

b **Calculate the mean titre.** (2 marks, ★★★) ....

c **How many times should a titration be carried out?** (1 mark, ★★★) ....

2 **Work out the unknown concentrations and volumes in the table below.** (3 marks, ★★★)

The equation for the reaction is: NaOH + HCl → NaCl + H$_2$O

Volume NaOH (cm^3)	Concentration NaOH (mol/dm^3)	Volume HCl (cm^3)	Concentration HCl (mol/dm^3)
25.00	0.1	25.00	0.1
25.00	0.1	50.00	
12.50	0.2		0.1
20.00	0.5	10.00	

3 **A student has a solution of sodium hydroxide (NaOH) and a solution of nitric acid (HNO$_3$).**

On a separate piece of paper, describe how they could carry out an experiment to find out the exact volumes of these solutions that would react together. Include an equipment list.
(6 marks, ★★★)

4 **In a titration, 25 cm^3 of 0.1 mol/dm^3 of sodium hydroxide (NaOH) reacts with 21.60 cm^3 of nitric acid, HNO$_3$. NaOH + HNO$_3$ → NaNO$_3$ + H$_2$O**

Calculate the concentration of nitric acid in:

a **mol/cm^3** (3 marks, ★★★★★) ....

b **g/dm^3, [H = 1, N = 14, O = 16]** (2 marks, ★★★) ....

5 **In another titration, 25 cm^3 of 0.2 mol/dm^3 of calcium hydroxide (Ca(OH)$_2$) reacts with 36.50 cm^3 of hydrochloric acid (HCl).**

The unbalanced chemical equation for the reaction is:

Ca(OH)$_2$ + HCl → CaCl$_2$ + H$_2$O

a **Balance the equation for this reaction.** (1 mark, ★★)

....

b i **Calculate the concentration of the hydrochloric acid in mol/dm^3.** (3 marks, ★★★★★)

....

ii **Calculate the concentration of the hydrochloric acid in g/dm^3, [H = 1, Cl = 35.5]**
(2 marks, ★★★)

....

Exothermic and endothermic reactions

1. **Explain what happens to the temperature of the surroundings during 'endothermic' and 'exothermic' reactions.** (2 marks, ★)

   a **Endothermic** ....
   ....

   b **Exothermic** ....
   ....

2. **A student set up an experiment as shown in the image below. The initial temperature of solution was 23.7°C. At the end of the reaction the temperature was 15.4°C.**

   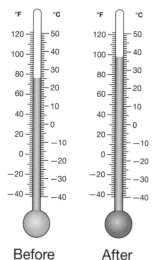

   a **Calculate the temperature change of the reaction and state whether the reaction is exothermic or endothermic.** (3 marks, ★★)
   ....
   ....
   ....

   b **Another student repeated the experiment with different reactants. They recorded the temperature at the start and at the end of the reaction as shown below.**

   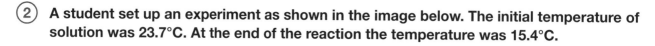

   Before   After

   i **Calculate the temperature change of the reaction.** (2 marks, ★★)
   ....
   ....

   ii **State whether the reaction is endothermic or exothermic.** (1 mark, ★★)
   ....

NAILIT!

Exothermic reactions include combustion (burning) reactions, most oxidation reactions and neutralisation reactions.

Endothermic reactions include *thermal decomposition* (breaking up of a compound using heat) and the reaction of citric acid with sodium hydrogen carbonate.

Practical investigation into the variables that affect temperature changes in chemical reactions

1. A student is comparing the temperature change in the reaction of iron with oxygen. She set up the experiment as shown in the diagram below.

   a Label the diagram to identify the equipment the student used. (4 marks, ★)

   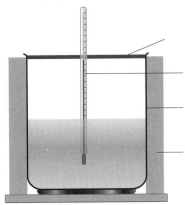

   b **Suggest why the student wrapped the calorimeter in wool.** (2 marks, ★★)

   ....

   ....

   The results of the experiment are shown below.

	Iron filings	Iron ball bearings	A large piece of iron
Initial temperature / °C	24.2	23.9	24.1
Final temperature / °C	60.1	37.3	24.3

   c **What conclusions could be made from these results?** (2 marks, ★★)

   ....

   ....

   d **Explain why it is important that the student kept the volume of air the same in all three tests.** (2 marks, ★★★)

   ....

   ....

2. **On a separate piece of paper, describe how you would set up an experiment to investigate how the concentration of hydrochloric acid affects the temperature change during its reaction with calcium carbonate.** (6 marks, ★★★★)

   Your answer should include:

   - **an explanation for your choice of equipment**

   - **the hypothesis you will be testing**

   - **a prediction of what you think will happen and why**

   - **how you would ensure valid results**

   - **how you would record your results.**

NAILIT!

If asked why a student has kept a variable the same, it is usually not enough to simply say 'to ensure valid results' – you will typically be expected to explain what could happen if that variable was changed. For example, if a student is investigating the effect of particle size, it is important to keep the concentration the same, because increasing concentration can increase the rate of reaction and so would also affect the temperature change.

Reaction profiles

1. **Fill the gaps to complete the sentence about reaction profiles for endothermic and exothermic reactions.** (4 marks, ★)

   A .... shows how the energy changes from reactants to products.

   In a reaction profile for an .... reaction the products are lower in energy than the reactants because .... is released to the surroundings during the reaction.

   In a reaction profile for an .... reaction the .... are higher in energy than the .... because energy is taken in from the .... during the reaction.

   Chemical reactions occur when reacting particles collide with enough energy to react. This energy is called the .... (E_a).

surroundings	energy	products	reaction profile
reactants	activation energy	endothermic	exothermic

2. **A student reacts barium hydroxide ($Ba(OH)_2.8H_2O(s)$) with ammonium chloride ($NH_4Cl(s)$) as shown in the balanced equation below:**

   $$Ba(OH)_2.8H_2O(s) + 2NH_4Cl(s) \rightarrow 2NH_3(g) + 10H_2O(l) + BaCl_2(s)$$

   The student predicts that the reaction will be exothermic.

   a **Use the reaction profile diagram below to suggest whether the student's prediction is correct. Explain your answer.** (3 marks, ★★★)

   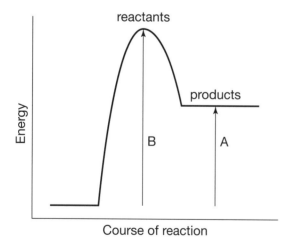

   ....

   ....

   ....

   ....

   b **Identify what is shown on the diagram by labels A and B.** (2 marks, ★★)

      i **A** ....

      ii **B** ....

   c **On a separate piece of paper, draw a diagram to show how a catalyst might change the reaction profile.** (2 marks, ★★★)

The energy changes of reactions

(1) **1 mole of hydrogen and 1 mole of chlorine react to form 2 moles of hydrogen chloride gas, as shown below.**

Bond	Bond energy (kJ per mol)
H–H	436
Cl–Cl	243
H–Cl	432

NAILIT!

You will be given information about the bond energy of different bonds in the exam (usually the ones you need and a couple just there to distract you!) – don't try to remember them all!

H–H + Cl–Cl → 2 × (H–Cl)

a **Calculate the amount of energy required to break both the H–H and Cl–Cl bonds.**
(2 marks, ★★)

H–H ....

Cl–Cl ....   **Sum (bond breaking)** ....

b **Calculate the amount of energy released as the H–Cl bonds are formed.** (2 marks, ★★)

....

c **Suggest whether the reaction is exothermic or endothermic.** (1 mark, ★★★)

....

d **Calculate the energy change of the reaction.** (1 mark, ★★★)

....

(2) **Two moles of hydrogen bromide produce one mole of hydrogen and bromine gas.**

$2HBr(g) \rightarrow H_2(g) + Br_2(g)$

Bond	Bond energy (kJ per mol)
H–Br	366
Br–Br	193
H–Cl	432

NAILIT!

It is important to remember that the units for bond energy are given in kJ per mole – so you need to multiply the value you are given by the number of moles you have.

a **Draw the bonds present in the molecules.** (3 marks, ★★)

b **Calculate the energy change of the reaction and identify whether the reaction is endothermic or exothermic.** (★★★★, 3 marks)

....

....

....

Chemical cells and fuel cells

① **A student put strips of copper and zinc into a lemon and created a circuit using two wires and an LED bulb, as shown in the picture below.**

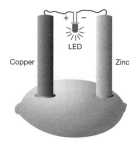

a **Identify the most reactive metal in the circuit.** (1 mark, ★)

....

b **Identify the electrolyte in the circuit.** (1 mark, ★) c **Draw an arrow on the picture to show the flow of electrons.** (1 mark, ★★)

....

② **A battery company produces 9 volt batteries by connecting 1.5V cells in series. Calculate the number of cells in the battery.** (2 marks, ★★)

....

....

③ **A significant amount of research in battery technology has involved hydrogen fuel cells which may in future replace traditional chemical cells and the combustion of fossil fuels to provide the energy we need for our electronic devices and cars.**

a **Identify the reaction that occurs that produces water from hydrogen.** (1 mark, ★★)

....

b **Compare the advantages and disadvantages of hydrogen fuel cells as a replacement for chemical cells.** (6 marks, ★★★)

....

....

....

....

....

c **Write the half equations for the electrode reactions in the hydrogen fuel cell.** (2 marks, ★★)

....

....

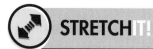 **STRETCH**IT!

The two half equations for a zinc-copper cell are shown below.

$$Zn(s) \rightarrow Zn^{2+}(aq) + 2e^-$$

$$Cu^{2+}(aq) + 2e^- \rightarrow Cu$$

Try writing the half equations for a cell that uses the reaction:

$$Ni(s) + 2Fe^{3+} \rightarrow Ni^{2+} + 2Fe^{2+}$$

Rates of reaction and equilibrium

Ways to follow a chemical reaction

(1) A student wants to investigate how the size of marble chips affects the rate of reaction with hydrochloric acid. The chemical equation for the reaction is:

$$CaCO_3(s) + 2HCl(aq) \rightarrow CO_2(g) + H_2O(l) + CaCl_2(s)$$

a Identify the independent variable in this experiment. (1 mark, ★)

....

b What else does the student need to record to be able to calculate the **rate** of the reaction? (1 mark, ★)

....

c Suggest what the student could use as the dependent variable in the experiment. Explain your answer. (2 marks, ★★)

....

d Suggest what variables the student would need to control to ensure the investigation results were valid. (2 marks, ★★)

....

(2) In an experiment to investigate the effect of concentration on the rate of reaction, a student is given sodium thiosulfate ($Na_2S_2O_3$) and $2\,mol/dm^3$ hydrochloric acid (HCl). The chemical equation for the reaction is:

$$2HCl(aq) + Na_2S_2O_3(aq) \rightarrow 2NaCl(aq) + SO_2(g) + S(s) + H_2O(l)$$

The student marks a sheet of paper with an X and places it under the flask in which the reaction will take place.

a Suggest what the student is using to identify the progress of the reaction. (1 mark, ★)

....

b Identify the independent variable in the experiment. (1 mark, ★)

....

c What variables should be controlled to ensure the experiment is valid? (2 marks, ★★)

....

d Explain how this experiment could be improved to reduce errors. (2 marks, ★★★)

....

....

(3) On a separate piece of paper, describe how you would use the equipment listed below to investigate how the concentration of hydrochloric acid affects the rate of its reaction with magnesium. Explain how you will ensure the experiment is valid. (6 marks, ★★★)

- magnesium ribbon
- hydrochloric acid
- safety goggles
- conical flask
- bung and delivery tube to fit conical flask
- trough or plastic washing-up bowl
- measuring cylinder
- clamp stand, boss and clamp
- stop clock

Calculating the rate of reaction

(1) **Describe how you could calculate the rate of a reaction from the amount of product formed.** (1 mark, ★)

....

(2) **For each of the graphs below, describe what is shown in terms of the rate of reaction.** (4 marks, ★★)

a 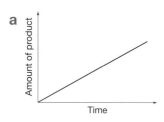   b    c    d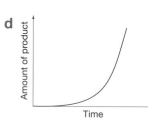

....

(3) **In a reaction between magnesium and hydrochloric acid, hydrogen gas is given off. The volume of hydrogen was recorded every 10 seconds, as shown in the table.**

Time/s	0	10	20	30	40	50	60	70	80	90	100	110	120
Volume of H_2/cm³	0	21	39	55	67	76	84	91	95	97	98	99	99

a **Write a balanced chemical equation for the reaction.** (1 mark, ★)

....

b **Calculate the mean rate of the reaction in cm³/s.** (2 marks, ★★)

....

c **On a piece of graph paper draw a graph of the results.** (3 marks, ★★)

d **Draw a tangent to the curves on your graph at 30s, 60s and 90s.** (3 marks, ★★★)

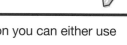

NAILIT!

To calculate the rate of reaction you can either use the amount of reactant used:

$$\text{Mean rate of reaction} = \frac{\text{Amount of reactant used up}}{\text{Time taken}}$$

Or the product formed:

$$\text{Mean rate of reaction} = \frac{\text{Amount of product formed}}{\text{Time taken}}$$

e **Calculate the rate of reaction at 30s, 60s and 90s from the tangents of your graph.** (3 marks, ★★★★)

....

....

f **Calculate the rate of the reaction in moles/second of hydrogen gas produced at 30s and 60s.** (4 marks, ★★★★)

....

....

The effect of concentration on reaction rate and the effect of pressure on the rate of gaseous reactions

(1) **Fill the gaps to complete the sentence.** (3 marks, ★)

For a reaction to happen, particles must .... with sufficient .... The minimum amount of .... that particles must have for a specific reaction is known as the .... The rate of a reaction can be increased by increasing the .... of collisions and increasing the .... of collisions.

frequency	activation energy	energy	collide	(some words are used more than once)

(2) **A student planned to investigate the effect of concentration on the rate of reaction. The student predicted that the rate of reaction would increase as the concentration increased.**

Give two reasons why the student's prediction is correct. Tick two boxes. (2 marks, ★★)

There are more particles	
The particles have more energy	
The particles have a larger surface area	
The frequency of successful collisions increases	
The particles have greater mass	

(3) **A student investigated how pressure affects the rate of reaction between two gases.**

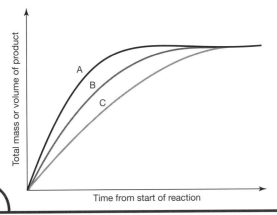

a **Identify which curve represents the lowest pressure.** (1 mark, ★★) ....

b **Identify which curve represents the highest pressure.** (1 mark, ★★) ....

NAILIT!

Remember that concentration is the number of moles of a substance per unit of volume.

- If you increase the moles but keep the volume the same, you've increased the concentration. Increasing the concentration means it is more likely that the particles will collide successfully.

- Similarly, if you keep the same number of moles but decrease the volume, you've also increased the concentration.

- Concentration = number of moles/volume

For gases, increasing pressure has the same effect – and you can increase the pressure by reducing the size of the container or increasing the number of particles.

(4) Another student investigated the reaction between marble chips and hydrochloric acid. The student collected the carbon dioxide (CO_2) given off and recorded the amount at intervals of 10 s. The results are shown below.

Time (s)	0	10	20	30	40	50	60	70
Volume of CO_2 (cm^3)	0.0	1.4	2.4	2.9	3.5	3.9	4.1	4.1

a **Plot this data on a graph, including a line of best fit.** (3 marks, ★★)

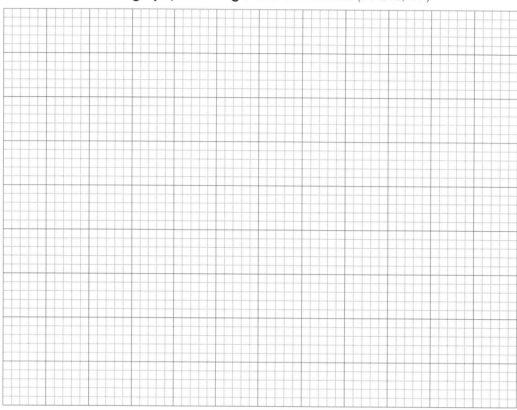

b **Use your graph to describe how the rate of the reaction changes with time.** (2 marks, ★★)

....

....

c **The reaction eventually stops. Pick the correct explanation for this. Tick one box.** (1 mark, ★★★)

The catalyst has been used up	
The particles do not have enough energy	
The pressure reduces	
One (or more) of the reactants has been used up	
The temperature reduces	

d **Sketch on your graph what you would expect to see if the concentration of hydrochloric acid was halved.** (2 marks, ★★★★)

e **Explain, in terms of particles, the reason for this difference.** (3 marks, ★★★★)

....

....

....

Rates of reaction – the effect of surface area

(1) A student is investigating how surface area affects the rate of the reaction of calcium carbonate ($CaCO_3$) and hydrochloric acid (HCl).

A

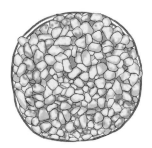

B

a Identify which sample of calcium carbonate has the larger surface area. (1 mark, ★) ....

b Predict which you think will give the fastest rate of reaction. (1 mark, ★★) ....

c Explain, in terms of particles, your answer to (b). (2 marks, ★★)

....

....

d Marshmallows are made primarily of sugar. They are produced by mixing finely powdered sugar, water, gelling agent and flavourings. When exposed to a flame, marshmallows burn slowly.

Explain why factories producing marshmallows often have strict rules in place to prevent explosive fires. (2 marks, ★★★)

....

....

....

(2) A pharmaceutical company produces medicine in the form of effervescent tablets that dissolve in water. As the tablet dissolves, carbon dioxide bubbles are produced. Following feedback from patients, the company want to investigate how they can reduce the time it takes for the medicine to dissolve.

a Suggest how the company could vary the surface area of the tablets. (2 marks, ★★)

....

....

b The company recorded the loss of mass as a tablet dissolved in a beaker of water, as shown in the graph. Sketch onto the graph what you would expect to find if the tablet were crushed into powder. (1 mark, ★★★)

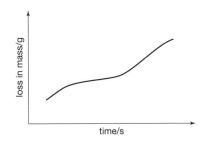

c Suggest another method the company could use in their experiment to follow the rate of the reaction. (2 marks, ★★)

....

....

239

The effects of changing the temperature and adding a catalyst

① A student wanted to investigate the effect of temperature on the rate of a reaction. The student put 10 cm³ of sodium thiosulfate ($Na_2S_2O_3$) in a beaker with 10 cm³ of hydrochloric acid and recorded the time it took for a cross to become obscured. The student predicted that the rate of reaction would increase with increasing temperature.

a Give **two** reasons why the student's prediction is correct. (2 marks, ★)

....

b At 20°C the student found that it took 40 s for the cross to disappear. Predict how long it would take for the cross to disappear at 40°C. (2 marks, ★★)

....

② The Haber process produces ammonia (NH_3) by passing nitrogen and hydrogen over iron.

a State the role of iron in this reaction. (1 mark, ★★)

....

b Explain how iron increases the rate of the reaction. (2 marks, ★★★)

....

c Complete the diagram below by labelling the line representing the reaction with and without iron. (2 marks, ★★★)

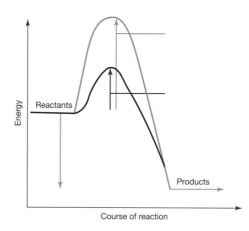

③ Hydrogen peroxide (H_2O_2) decomposes at room temperature to produce water and oxygen, as shown in the balanced equation below:

$$2H_2O_2\,(aq) \rightarrow 2H_2O(l) + O_2\,(g)$$

a How could you measure the rate of the reaction? (1 mark, ★★★)

....

b Manganese oxide (MnO_2) can be used as a catalyst to increase the rate of decomposition of hydrogen peroxide. Catalase is an enzyme found in the liver where it also increases the decomposition of hydrogen peroxide. On a separate piece of paper, explain how you would set up an experiment to investigate which is more effective at increasing the rate of decomposition. State how you would ensure valid results in your answer. (4 marks, ★★★★)

An investigation into how changing the concentration affects the rate of reaction

(1) You are given sodium thiosulfate ($Na_2S_2O_3$) and hydrochloric acid (HCl) and asked to investigate how changing the concentration of sodium thiosulfate or hydrochloric acid affects the rate of reaction. The chemical equation for the reaction is:

..........$HCl(aq)$ + ...$Na_2S_2O_3(aq)$ → ....$NaCl(aq)$ + ...$SO_2(g)$ + ...$S(s)$ + ...$H_2O(l)$

a Balance the chemical equation above. (1 mark, ★)

b Suggest a suitable hypothesis for the investigation. (1 mark, ★★)

....

c Make a prediction for your investigation. Explain your prediction. (3 marks, ★★★)

....

....

....

d Describe the method you would use to test your hypothesis. Suggest how you would ensure the experiment was valid. (4 marks, ★★★)

....

....

....

....

e Explain how a change in temperature could affect your results.
(2 marks, ★★★)

....

....

....

....

f Evaluate **two** different methods you could use to measure the progress of the reaction. (4 marks, ★★★)

....

....

MATHS SKILLS

- You should be comfortable developing hypotheses and making predictions.
- The hypotheses in these reactions will always be that increasing concentration of a reactant increases the reaction rate.
- Your prediction should include whether or not you think the hypothesis is true, and an explanation, i.e. I think the hypothesis is true because…
- When answering questions about valid results it's always a good idea to explain why it is important to keep a particular variable the same, in terms of what might happen if it changed. For example, in an investigation about the effect of concentration on the rate of reaction, it's important to keep the temperature the same, because increasing temperature also increases the rate of reaction.

....

....

....

(2) A student carried out a reaction between limestone ($CaCO_3$) and hydrochloric acid (HCl). To find out the effect of changing the concentration of acid on the rate of reaction, the student used four different concentrations of hydrochloric acid and measured the carbon dioxide gas given off, and recorded the following results.

Time/s	Volume of carbon dioxide / cm³ for each concentration of HCl			
	0.5 mol/dm³	1 mol/dm³	1.5 mol/dm³	2 mol/dm³
30	0	0	0	0
60	5	10	15	20
90	10	20	30	40
120	15	30	45	60
150	20	40	60	80
180	25	50	70	85
210	30	60	80	90
240	35	65	85	95
270	40	70	90	97
300	45	80	92	98
330	47.5	85	95	99
360	50	88	97	99.5
390	51	90	95	100
420	52	92	99	100
450	53	94	100	100
480	54	95	100	100

a **Plot a graph of the results.** (5 marks, ★★★)

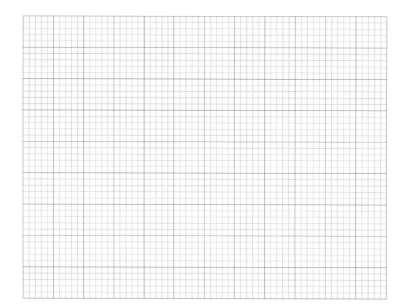

b **Use your graph to calculate the overall rate of reaction for each concentration of concentration of acid.** (4 marks, ★★★)

....

MATHS SKILLS

Remember that the independent variable (the one you change) goes on the x-axis on your graph. The dependent variable (the one you measure) goes on the y-axis.

Reversible reactions

(1) The decomposition of ammonium chloride is a reversible reaction:

ammonium chloride $\rightleftharpoons$ ammonia + hydrogen chloride

$$NH_4Cl(s) \rightleftharpoons NH_3(g) + HCl(g)$$

a What symbol tells you that the reaction is reversible? (1 mark, ★)

> **NAILIT!**
>
> Relatively few reactions are reversible – for example, most combustion reactions are generally irreversible!

b Which of the following statements about reversible reactions is correct?
Tick **one** box. (1 mark, ★)

Reversible reactions can go both forwards and backwards in certain conditions.	
All reactions are reversible to some extent.	
Reversible reactions stop when they reach equilibrium.	
If the forward reaction is endothermic, the backward reaction must also be endothermic.	

> **NAILIT!**
>
> When a reversible reaction reaches a dynamic equilibrium the reaction does not stop. The forwards reaction is simply happening at the same rate as the backwards reaction. The concentration of reactants and products stays the same.

c Explain what is meant by the term **dynamic equilibrium.** (2 marks, ★★)

(2) A student heats limestone ($CaCO_3$) to produce lime (CaO) and carbon dioxide, as shown below:

$$CaCO_3 \rightleftharpoons CaO + CO_2$$

The reaction is reversible. The student collects the carbon dioxide in an upturned measuring cylinder in a trough of water.

> **NAILIT!**
>
> Remember that for reversible reactions if the forward reaction (left to right) is exothermic, the backward reaction (right to left) must be endothermic.

a Explain what is meant by the term **reversible reaction.** (2 marks, ★★)

b Determine whether the backwards reaction is endothermic or exothermic. Explain your answer. (3 marks, ★★★)

c Explain why, after some time, the volume of carbon dioxide stops increasing and remains the same. (3 marks, ★★★★)

The effect of changing conditions on equilibrium

(1) **Complete the sentence about dynamic equilibrium below.** (1 mark, ★)

At dynamic equilibrium, the rate of the forward reaction is ....

....

(2) **Give three factors that can be changed that may change the position of equilibrium.** (3 marks, ★)

a ....

b ....

c ....

> **NAILIT!**
>
> If the temperature is increased the equilibrium will shift in favour of the reaction which is accompanied by a decrease in temperature. This means that if the backward reaction is endothermic, like in the Haber process, then more reactants are formed.

(3) **Define Le Chatelier's Principle.** (3 marks, ★★)

....

....

....

(4) **In the Haber process, nitrogen and hydrogen produce ammonia, a valuable product which has many uses. The process is shown in the reaction shown below:**

~400°C
~200atm pressure
Iron catalyst
$N_2(g) + 3H_2(g) \rightleftharpoons 2NH_3(g)$ (+ heat)

> **NAILIT!**
>
> If you increase the concentration of one of the products then the system will try to lower its concentration by forming more reactants.

a **Describe what would happen if the temperature was increased.** (3 marks, ★★★)

....

....

b **Suggest a possible reason the reaction isn't carried out at room temperature.** (1 mark, ★★★)

....

....

c **Explain the effect that the iron catalyst has on the reaction.** (3 marks, ★★★)

> **NAILIT!**
>
> A catalyst has no effect on the position of equilibrium. It speeds up how quickly equilibrium is reached.

....

....

d **Explain why the Haber process is carried out at high pressure.** (2 marks, ★★★★)

....

....

Organic chemistry

(1) **Explain each of the following facts about alkanes.**

    a **Alkanes are hydrocarbons.** (1 mark, ★)

    ....

    b **Alkanes are described as saturated.** (1 mark, ★★)

    ....

    c **Alkanes form a homologous series.** (2 marks, ★★★)

    ....

> **NAILIT!**
>
> The trends in the physical properties of alkanes are linked to the number of carbon atoms they have.
>
> As the number of carbon atoms increases, boiling points and viscosity increase, the colour darkens and flammability decreases.
>
> Viscosity is a measure of how easily fluids flow.

(2) **State the formulae for the following alkanes.** (4 marks, ★★)

    a **Alkane with 20 carbon atoms.** ....

    b **Alkane with 18 hydrogen atoms.** ....

(3) **Complete the dot-and-cross diagram to show the bonding in ethane.** (2 marks, ★★)

> **DOIT!**
>
> Remember the general formula for alkanes, C_nH_{2n+2}. You can then use this to predict the formula of any alkane if you are given the number of carbon or hydrogen atoms.

(4) **Heptane is an alkane which contains seven carbon atoms.**

    a **Draw out its displayed formula.** (1 mark, ★★)

    b **State its molecular formula.** (1 mark, ★★) ....

(5) **Which of these alkanes is the most flammable? Tick one box.** (1 mark, ★★)

CH_4	
C_3H_8	

(6) **Which of these alkanes has the highest boiling point? Tick one box.** (1 mark, ★★)

Propane	
Pentane	

(7) **Which of these alkanes is the most viscous? Tick one box.** (1 mark, ★★)

C_2H_6	
C_4H_{10}	

Fractional distillation

(1) **Crude oil is separated into fractions by fractional distillation. Fractions are mixture of hydrocarbons which contain similar numbers of carbon atoms, and therefore have similar physical properties.**

Describe how fractional distillation separates crude oil into fractions. (4 marks, ★★★★)

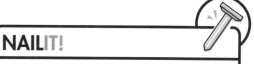

NAILIT!

Note: use the key words **heat**, **evaporate**, **condense** and **boiling points** when describing fractional distillation.

....

....

(2) **Two of the fractions produced during fractional distillation are in the table below.**

Name of fraction	Use	Example of alkane in this fraction	Molecular formula of alkane	Boiling point of alkane/°C
Petroleum gases	Household fuels	Methane	CH_4	−162
Kerosene		Dodecane		214

Kerosene contains an alkane called dodecane, which has 12 carbon atoms.

a **State a use for kerosene.** (1 mark, ★★) ....

b **What is the molecular formula for dodecane?** (1 mark, ★★) ....

c **Explain why dodecane has a higher boiling point than methane.** (1 mark, ★★)

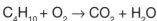

....

WORKIT!

Balance the chemical equation to show the **complete combustion** of butane, C_4H_{10}.

$C_4H_{10} + O_2 \rightarrow CO_2 + H_2O$

Step 1 Balance the carbon atoms. There are 4 in butane, so this means 4 × CO_2

$C_4H_{10} + O_2 \rightarrow 4CO_2 + H_2O$

Step 2 Balance the hydrogen atoms. There are 10 in butane, which means 5 × H_2O

$C_4H_{10} + O_2 \rightarrow 4CO_2 + 5H_2O$

Step 3 Finally, balance the oxygen atoms. There are now 9 in total. Remember, you have O_2, so you need to halve 9. It's ok to use a fraction - half of 9 is 9/2 or 4½

$C_4H_{10} + 4½O_2 \rightarrow 4CO_2 + 5H_2O$

(3) **Write balanced symbol equations to show the complete combustion of:**

a **Ethane** (2 marks, ★★★) ....

b **Propane** (2 marks, ★★★) ....

c **Pentane** (2 marks, ★★★) ....

Cracking and alkenes

1. Explain why alkenes are described as **unsaturated hydrocarbons.** (2 marks, ★★★)

....

....

NAILIT!

- Learn the products for the addition reactions for alkenes.
- Alkene + hydrogen → **alkane**
- Alkene + steam → **alcohol**
- Alkene + halogen → **dihaloalkane (an alkane with two halogens attached to it)**

2. Alkenes undergo addition reactions with hydrogen, steam and halogens.

   a Write out the structural formula for these reactions, ensuring that the organic reactants and products are fully displayed.

      i **Pentene + hydrogen** (2 marks, ★★★) ....

      ii **Butene + steam** (2 marks, ★★★) ....

      iii **Propene + chlorine** (2 marks, ★★★) ....

   b **Explain why the addition reactions of alkenes show 100% atom economy.** (1 mark, ★★)

   ....

3. Complete these equations to show the missing substances. (5 marks, ★★★)

   a $C_8H_{18} \rightarrow C_5H_{12} +$ ....

   b $C_{18}H_{38} \rightarrow C_3H_6 +$ ....

   c .... $\rightarrow C_4H_8 + C_9H_{20}$

   d $C_{14}H_{30} \rightarrow C_4H_{10} + C_6H_{12} +$ ....

   e $C_{14}H_{30} \rightarrow C_8H_{18} + 2$ ....

4. Decane is an alkane with ten carbon atoms. Two possible products when it undergoes cracking are hexane (C_6H_{14}) and an unknown compound Z, which decolourises bromine water.

   a **What is the formula for decane?** (1 mark, ★) ....

   b **Suggest a use for hexane.** (1 mark, ★★) ....

   c **Why does compound Z decolourise bromine water?** (1 mark, ★★) ....

   d **Suggest a use for compound Z.** (1 mark, ★★) ....

   e **Work out the formula for compound Z and use this to construct the overall chemical equation for the cracking of decane.** (1 mark, ★★★)

   ....

Alcohols

(1) Some alcohols are shown in the table below.

CH₃CH₂CH₂OH	H H H H | | | | H—C—C—C—C—O—H | | | | H H H H
A	**B**
H H | | H—C—C—O—H | | H H	CH₃OH
C	**D**

Which letter represents:

a **Butanol?** (1 mark, ★★) ....

b **Methanol?** (1 mark, ★★) ....

c **The alcohol with the molecular formula C_3H_8O?** (1 mark, ★★)

....

d **The alcohol formed when sugars are fermented?** (1 mark, ★★)

....

e **The alcohol with the highest boiling point?** (1 mark, ★★★) ....

(2) Alcohols make excellent fuels and when they burn in plenty of air, complete combustion takes place.

Complete the word and balanced chemical equations to show the complete combustion of the following alcohols. (4 marks, ★★★)

a **Methanol + oxygen →** .... + ...

.... CH_3OH + ... O_2 → .... + ...

b **Propanol + oxygen →** .... + ...

.... $CH_3CH_2CH_2OH$ + ... O_2 → .... + ...

> **NAILIT!**
>
> Don't forget the extra 'O' in the alcohol when you are balancing combustion equations.

(3) Describe what would be seen in the following experiments.

a **A small piece of sodium is added to butanol.** (2 marks, ★★★)

....

b **Ethanol is added to water.** (1 mark, ★★)

....

c **Propanol is mixed with acidified potassium manganate(VII).** (1 mark, ★★)

....

Carboxylic acids

1. Some organic substances with four carbon atoms are shown in the table below.

C_4H_8		$CH_3CH_2CH_2CH_2OH$
A	**B**	**C**
	C_4H_{10}	
D	**E**	

Which letter represents:

a **Butane?** (1 mark, ★★) ....

b **A substance that will decolourise bromine water?** (1 mark, ★★) ....

c **Butanol?** (1 mark, ★★) ....

d **A substance that will produce carbon dioxide when added to sodium carbonate?**
(1 mark, ★★★) ....

e **A substance that is formed when a carboxylic acid and alcohol are heated with an acid catalyst?** (1 mark, ★★★) ....

f **The substance that can be oxidised to form butanoic acid?** (1 mark, ★★★★) ....

DO IT!

Carboxylic acids are **weak** acids. Review the topic about strong and weak acids to remind you about full and partial ionisation of acids in solution.

2. The general formula for carboxylic acids is $C_nH_{2n}O_2$.

a **State the formula of the carboxylic acid with eight carbon atoms.** (1 mark, ★★)

....

b **State the formula and the name of the carboxylic acid with six hydrogen atoms.** (2 marks, ★★)

....

3. The pH of 0.1 mol/dm³ hydrochloric acid is 1.00, whilst the pH of ethanoic acid of the same concentration is 2.88.

Explain the difference in these pH values. You should use an equation in your answer.
(5 marks, ★★★★)

....

....

....

....

Addition polymerisation

① The alkenes below undergo addition polymerisation to form polymers.

For each monomer, draw out the repeating unit, and name the **polymer** formed. (8 marks, ★★★★)

Monomer	Repeating unit	Name of polymer
Propene		
Chloroethene		
Ethenol		
Butene		

② Draw out the displayed formulae for the monomers that would be used to make the polymers below. (2 marks, ★★★)

Repeating unit	Monomer

③ Pentene can undergo addition polymerisation to form a polymer.

a The formula for pentene is C_5H_{10}. Write an equation using displayed formulae, to show the formation of the polymer. (2 marks, ★★★★)

....

b **Name the polymer formed.** (1 mark, ★) ....

Condensation polymerisation

(1) **Five compounds are represented by the letters A, B, C, D and E.**

HO–CH$_2$–CH$_2$–OH	CH$_3$—CH$_2$–OH	H$_2$O	HOOC—CH$_2$–CH$_2$–CH$_2$–CH$_2$–COOH	CH$_3$–CH$_2$–COOH
A	**B**	**C**	**D**	**E**

a **Which two substances could be used to form a condensation polymer?** (2 marks, ★★★)

....

b **What other product would be formed when these two substances react together?**
(1 mark, ★★) ....

c **Name the functional group found in both A and B.** (1 mark, ★★) ....

d **Name the functional group found in both D and E.** (1 mark, ★★) ....

(2) **The general equation to form a condensation polymer can be represented as follows:**

a **Write an equation like this for the reaction between ethanedioic acid and ethanediol. Their structures are shown below.** (3 marks, ★★★★★)

HOOC—CH$_2$–CH$_2$–COOH	HO—CH$_2$–CH$_2$–OH
Ethanedioic acid	**Ethanediol**

> **NAILIT!**
>
> For condensation polymerisation to occur there must be:
>
> • **two** different monomers
> • each monomer must have **two** functional groups.

....

b **Explain why the atom economy for condensation polymerisation will always be less than 100%.** (1 mark, ★★★)

....

c **Name the functional group formed during this type of polymerisation.** (1 mark, ★★)

....

(3) **Deduce the monomers used to form the condensation polymer below.** (2 marks, ★★★★★)

> **DO IT!**
>
> Learn the differences between addition and condensation polymerisation. Compare the atom economy, number of monomers, functional groups and number of products.

....

....

Amino acids and DNA

(1) **Choose the words from the box to complete the sentences below.** (4 marks, ★★)

Two amino acids can join together by .... polymerisation to form polypeptides
and ....

Each amino acid contains two functional groups, a .... acid group which has the
formula –COOH and an amine group, which has the formula –NH$_2$. The –COOH on one
amino acid reacts with the –NH$_2$ group on another amino acid forming a polymer, with the
elimination of ....

carboxylic hydrogen addition strong water condensation weak proteins starch

(2) **The simplest amino acid is called *glycine*, and has the formula H$_2$NCH$_2$COOH. When it
undergoes polymerisation it forms the polypeptide shown in the equation below.**

n H$_2$NCH$_2$COOH → (–HNCH$_2$COO–)$_n$ + nH$_2$O

Another amino acid *alanine*, has the formula H$_2$NCH(CH$_3$)COOH

**Different amino acids can be combined to form proteins. The amino acids are linked by
the peptide bond:**

–NHCO–

a **Write out a chemical equation to show the polymerisation of alanine.** (2 marks, ★★★★)

....

....

b **Write out a chemical equation to show how glycine and alanine can combine together
to form a polymer.** (3 marks, ★★★★★)

....

....

(3) **DNA is a naturally occurring polymer which is essential for life. State the name of the
monomers used to form DNA.** (1 mark, ★★)

....

(4) **Starch and glucose are both polysaccharides. What type of monomers are used to form
polysaccharides?** (1 mark, ★★)

....

DO IT!

Create a table of naturally occurring polymers
and the names of the types of polymers
which they are made from.

Chemical analysis

Testing for gases

① **Match the gas to its test and result if it is present. Chlorine has been done for you.** (3 marks, ★)

Hydrogen	a glowing splint put into a test tube of the gas	is extinguished with a 'pop'
Oxygen	bubble the gas through a solution of limewater	produces solid calcium carbonate, turning the limewater cloudy
Carbon dioxide	expose to litmus or UI paper	colour change and bleaches the paper
Chlorine	a lighted splint put into a test tube of the gas	relights

② **For each of the following, identify the gas being tested.** (4 marks, ★★)

a **The gas turns limewater turns cloudy.** ....

b **The gas bleaches litmus paper.** ....

c **The gas extinguishes a lighted splint with a pop.** ....

d **The gas relights a glowing splint.** ....

③ **For the following reactions, describe the test that could be used to confirm the gases produced.** (4 marks, ★★)

a $CH_4 + 2O_2 \rightarrow CO_2 + 2H_2O$ ....

b $Mg + H_2SO_4 \rightarrow MgSO_4 + H_2$ ....

c $CO_2 + H_2O \rightarrow C_6H_{12}O_6 + O_2$ ....

d $HCl + MnO_2 \rightarrow MnCl_2 + 2H_2O + Cl_2$ ....

④ **A student sets up an experiment using limewater to test the gases produced by a lit candle.**

Explain what the student will observe, and how they could find out whether the candle produces other gases. (6 marks, ★★★).

NAILIT!

Chlorine gas is toxic – reactions involving the production of it should be done in small quantities and in a fume cupboard.

NAILIT!

Hydrogen is actually a very flammable gas and can cause explosions. The pop you hear is actually a tiny explosion!

NAILIT!

You are expected to remember each of the tests for gases.

- Carbon dioxide – limewater
- Oxygen – relight
- Hydrogen – pop
- Chlorine – bleach

....

....

....

....

....

....

....

Identifying metal ions using flame tests, flame emission spectroscopy and sodium hydroxide

(1) **Match the metal salt to the colour of the flame when heated on a Bunsen burner.** (5 marks, ★)

Lithium carbonate	Lilac
Sodium chloride	Crimson
Potassium sulfate	Orange-red
Calcium nitrate	Green
Copper phosphate	Yellow

(2) **A flame emission spectroscope was used to identify a mixture of metal salts. Four known ions were analysed, followed by the unknown sample, Y.**

Lithium
Potassium
Sodium
Copper
Y

a **Identify the two ions in Y.** (2 marks, ★★)

....

....

....

b **To calibrate the spectroscope, a student ran solutions of pure lithium of increasing concentration and recorded the line intensity in the table below.**

Concentration in mg/cm³	0.00	0.10	0.20	0.40	0.80	1.00
Line intensity/arbitrary units	0.000	0.013	0.026	0.055	0.110	0.124

 i **Plot a graph of the data.** (2 marks, ★★)

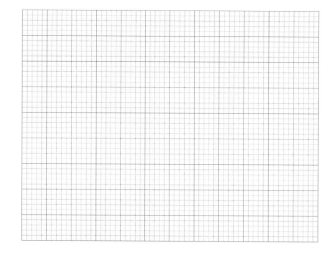

 ii **Use your graph to determine the concentration of a sample which gives a line intensity of 0.041.** (1 mark, ★★★)

....

 iii **Use your graph to predict the line intensity of a sample which contains 0.6 mg/cm³ of lithium.** (1 mark, ★★★)

....

Testing for negative ions (anions) in salts

1. **Match the negative ion with the procedure to test for it and what would happen in a positive test.** (5 marks, ★)

Chloride (Cl⁻)	Hydrochloric acid then pass gas formed through limewater	White precipitate (of silver chloride)
Bromide (Br⁻)	Hydrochloric acid followed by barium chloride solution	Cream precipitate (of silver bromide)
Iodide (I⁻)	Nitric acid followed by silver nitrate solution	Yellow precipitate (of silver iodide)
Sulfate (SO_4^{2-})	Nitric acid followed by silver nitrate solution	White precipitate (of barium sulfate)
Carbonate (CO_3^{2-})	Nitric acid followed by silver nitrate solution	Effervescence and gas turns limewater cloudy/milky

2. **A student wanted to find out what other substances are added to table salt (NaCl).**

   The student conducted an investigation and recorded the results as shown below.

Test	Description	Observations
1	Dilute nitric acid was added to the table salt and the gas passed through limewater	The mixture effervesced and the gas turned limewater cloudy
2	Nitric acid was added to the salt, and then silver nitrate solution was added	A white precipitate formed

a **What does this tell you about the negative ions in the table salt?** (2 marks, ★★)

....

....

b **Explain why the student used nitric acid in test 1 rather than hydrochloric acid.** (2 marks, ★★★)

....

....

c **Identify the white precipitate that formed in test 2.** (1 mark, ★★★) ....

d **Write a balanced chemical equation for the reaction that takes place in test 1.**
   (1 mark, ★★★)

....

NAILIT!

If you are asked to write the symbol equations for the reactions of halides and sulfate you must remember that the negative ion combines with the metal in the test reagent to form a solid. So for potassium bromide:

ionic equation   balanced chemical equation

$Ag^+(aq) + Br^-(aq) \rightarrow AgBr(s)$ $AgNO_3(aq) + KBr(aq) \rightarrow KNO_3(aq) + AgBr(s)$

Identifying ions in an ionic compound

(1) A compound contains either calcium or lithium ions, and either chloride or bromide ions.

   a Suggest how you would identify which of the **positive** ions the compound contains. You must include what colours you could expect to find in your answer. (1 mark, ★)

   ....

   b Suggest how you would identify which of the **negative** ions the compound contains. You must include what colours you could expect to find in your answer. (1 mark, ★)

   ....

(2) Explain how you would identify the ions in sodium sulfate. (4 marks, ★★)

   ....

   ....

(3) A student carries out a series of experiments to identify **four** unknown compounds, as shown in the table below.

Substance	Flame test	Sodium hydroxide	Barium chloride solution	Silver nitrate solution	Hydrochloric acid
A	Lilac	No reaction	No reaction	No reaction	Effervescence and gas turned limewater milky
B	Red	White precipitate	White precipitate	No reaction	No reaction
C	No colour	White precipitate, dissolves in excess	No reaction	Cream precipitate	No reaction
D	Orange-brown	Brown precipitate	No reaction	Yellow precipitate	No reaction

Identify substances A to D. (4 marks, ★★★)

A ....   B ....

C ....   D ....

(4) A student reacts hydrochloric acid with calcium carbonate, producing water, carbon dioxide and a salt.
Explain how you would identify the ions in the salt and what you would expect to find.
(4 marks, ★★★)

....

....

NAILIT!

In the exam, you may be asked about colour changes you don't recognise. Where that happens, focus on the colour changes you do recognise as they may provide a clue.

NAILIT!

Check back through your notes for this topic to answer these questions.

The composition and evolution of the Earth's atmosphere

1 **a** Tick **two** processes that reduced the amount of carbon dioxide in the atmosphere. (2 marks, ★)

Carbonate rock formation	
Respiration by animals	
Fossil fuel combustion	
Fossil fuel formation	

b What reduced the amount of water vapour in the atmosphere? (1 mark, ★★)

....

....

....

c Explain how this affected the amount of carbon dioxide in the atmosphere? (2 marks, ★★)

....

d Photosynthesis by algae, bacteria and later, plants, is thought to have significantly reduced the amount of carbon dioxide in the atmosphere. Write the balanced chemical equation for the reaction. (2 marks, ★★)

....

2 Some students set up an experiment to investigate what percentage of air is oxygen, as shown in the diagram below.

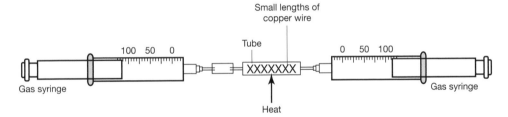

100 cm³ of air is drawn into the syringe. When heated, the oxygen in the air reacts with the copper in the tube. At the end of the experiment, the volume of gas in the syringe had reduced to 78.5 cm³. The equation for the reaction is:

..........$Cu + O_2 \rightarrow$ ....CuO

a Balance the equation. (1 mark, ★)

b Calculate the percentage of oxygen in the 100 cm³ sample of dry air. (1 mark, ★★)

....

....

c Explain why it is important to allow the apparatus to cool before recording the result. (2 marks, ★★)

....

....

....

Climate change

(1) It is known that some gases are greenhouse gases that have the potential to increase global temperatures. It is also known that human activity has increased the amount of some of these greenhouse gases in the atmosphere. To understand the possible consequences, scientists have created climate models that they use to try to predict future changes to the Earth's climate.

a Give **one** reason why it is difficult to create models to predict future climate change.
(1 mark, ★)

....

b Describe what is meant by the term **peer review.** (1 mark, ★★)

....

c Identify **two** greenhouse gases. (2 marks, ★)

....

d Describe how human activity has increased the amount of these two gases in the atmosphere. (4 marks, ★★)

....

....

....

....

(2) The graph below shows how temperatures and the proportion of CO_2 have changed over the last 400 000 years.

a Suggest **two** conclusions you could make from the data in the graph. (2 marks, ★★★)

....

....

b One theory about climate change is that temperatures on Earth have always changed with natural increases and decreases in the amount of CO_2 in the atmosphere and that the current situation is no different. Use the data in the graph and your knowledge to **evaluate** this theory. (4 marks, ★★★★)

....

....

....

....

The carbon footprint and its reduction

(1) **Match the method of reducing the carbon footprint to the description of how it works.**
(3 marks, ★★)

Alternative energy

Energy conservation

Carbon Capture and Storage (CCS)

Carbon taxes

Carbon offsetting

Using plants as biofuels

Removing the carbon dioxide given out by power stations by reacting it with other chemicals. The product of this reaction can then be stored deep under the sea in porous sedimentary rocks.

Plants take in carbon dioxide as they grow, when they are burned they only release the same amount of carbon dioxide. This makes them carbon neutral.

Renewable energy sources such as solar cells, wind power and wave power do not rely on the burning of fossil fuels.

Reducing the amount of energy used by using energy-saving measures such as house insulation, using devices that use less energy, reduces the demand for energy.

Penalising companies and individuals who use too much energy by increasing their taxes reduces the demand for energy.

Removing carbon dioxide from the air using natural biological processes such as photosynthesis. This is achieved by planting trees and increasing marine algae by adding chemicals to the oceans.

(2) **The table shows the annual carbon footprint (in tonnes per person) of some countries in 1990 and 2011.**

Country	Carbon footprint (tonnes/person) 1990	Carbon footprint (tonnes/person) 2011
Qatar	25.2	44.0
USA	19.1	17
UK	10	7.1
Greece	7.2	7.6
New Zealand	7.1	7.1
China	2.2	7.2
India	0.7	1.2

a **Suggest two reasons that countries such as the USA and Qatar have carbon footprints much higher than China or India.** (2 marks, ★★)

b **Describe how the carbon footprint in the UK has changed since 1990.**
(1 mark, ★)

c **Explain why some countries have seen an increase in their carbon footprints since 1990.** (3 marks, ★★★)

Atmospheric pollutants

(1) **Match the pollutant with its effects and ways to reduce its release in the atmosphere.**
(4 marks, ★★)

Soot	Dissolves in clouds to cause acid rain and causes respiratory problems	Ensure complete combustion of fossil fuels
Carbon monoxide	A toxic gas which binds to haemoglobin in the blood, preventing the transport of oxygen around the body	Desulfurisation of petrochemicals before combustion
Sulfur dioxide	Global dimming and lung damage	Ensure complete combustion of fossil fuels
Oxides of nitrogen	Dissolves in clouds to cause acid rain and causes respiratory problems	Catalytic converters used after combustion

(2) **The table below shows information about the pollutants emitted by cars which use diesel and petrol fuels.**

Fuel	Relative proportion of CO_2	Relative proportion of SO_2	Relative amount of particulate matter	Relative amount of oxides of nitrogen
Diesel	80	40	100	30
Petrol	100	10	0	20

a **Compare the pollutants from cars using petrol as their fuel to those using diesel.** (3 marks, ★★)

....

....

....

b **Electric cars emit no pollutants directly and are powered by batteries that are recharged by plugging them into an electrical plug socket. Suggest how powering these vehicles may still release pollutants into the atmosphere.** (2 marks, ★★)

....

....

(3) **The use of coal to produce electricity has in recent decades reduced in many countries. However, with reducing oil supplies, some countries are considering building new coal power stations. The chemical reaction for the complete combustion of coal is:**

$$4C_{240}H_{90}O_4NS + 1053O_2 \rightarrow 960CO_2 + 174H_2O + 4HNO_3 + 4H_2SO_4$$

a **Calculate the number of moles of carbon dioxide released when 8 moles of coal is burned in an excess of oxygen.** (2 marks, ★★)

....

b **In the 1950s, thousands of people in London died during the 'London Smog'. Many of these deaths were due to high levels of sulfur dioxide in the atmosphere released by the burning of fossil fuels such as coal. Using the balanced equation above, explain how burning coal can also cause damage to limestone buildings, trees and plant crops.** (2 marks, ★★★)

....

....

Using resources

Finite and renewable resources, sustainable development

(1) Fill the gaps to complete the sentence about finite and renewable resources. (5 marks, ★)

The .... used by chemists to make new materials can be divided into
two categories – .... and .... resources will run out.
Examples are fossil fuels and various metals. .... resources are ones that can be
replaced at the same rate as they are used up. They are derived from plant materials.

.... meets the needs of present development without depleting
natural resources for future generations.

natural resources	finite	renewable	sustainable development

(some words are used twice)

(2) State four characteristics of a sustainable process. (4 marks, ★)

....

....

....

....

> **NAILIT!**
>
> Look over your notes on atom economy and percentage yield as you may be asked to compare the sustainability of reactions in terms of quantitatively using them.

(3) Explain how the use of catalysts helps make chemical reactions more sustainable. (2 marks, ★★)

....

....

(4) Two companies produce a plastic used to manufacture goods. Company A uses a method where they expect to produce 25 kg. Company B uses a method where they expect to produce 19 kg. Company A actually produces 22 kg and Company B actually produces 18 kg.

a Calculate the percentage yield for both companies. (2 marks, ★★)

....

....

....

b Suggest which company uses the more sustainable method. (1 mark, ★★)

....

....

....

....

> **NAILIT!**
>
> Sustainable processes:
>
> - have reactions with high atom economy with as few waste products as possible;
> - use renewable resources from plant sources;
> - have as few steps as possible to eliminate waste and increase the yield;
> - use catalysts to save energy.

Life cycle assessments (LCAs)

(1) **Explain what is meant by the term life cycle assessment.** (2 marks, ★)

....

....

(2) **List the stages of a life cycle assessment.** (2 marks, ★)

....

....

(3) **a** **Complete the table of the life cycle assessments of paper and plastic shopping bags.**
(4 marks, ★★)

Stage of LCA	Plastic bag	Paper bag
Source of raw materials		Come from trees
Production	Simple process involving no chemical change	
Use	Reusable	
End of life	Decompose slowly but produce less	Decompose quickly but generate more ....

b **Use the information in the table to compare the life cycle assessments of the paper and plastic shopping bags.** (2 marks, ★★★)

....

....

....

(4) **A supermarket that supplies its customers with plastic carrier bags ran the following advert:**

'Our carrier bags are environmentally friendly as their manufacture produces no harmful pollutants. They're also reusable.'

Explain why the advert is misleading. (2 marks, ★★★)

....

....

....

Alternative methods of copper extraction

(1) **a** **Complete the flow chart below to show how copper ores that are rich in copper can be extracted.** (1 mark, ★★)

copper rich ores → [........................] .... → [........................] → copper

b **Suggest a reason why the copper produced by smelting may need to undergo electrolysis.** (1 mark, ★★)

....

(2) **Tick two potential problems when using these processes.** (2 marks, ★)

Smelting and electrolysis use a lot of energy	☐
Copper-rich ores are scarce	☐
Copper is less reactive than iron	☐
Copper is used in many products	☐
Electrolysis is not necessary	☐

NAILIT!

Copper is a widely used metal – it is in coins, electrical wiring and motors, because it conducts heat and electricity well.

NAILIT!

Copper-rich ores are scarce because copper is so widely used. Using traditional methods for ores that are low in copper is uneconomical – it costs more than the value of the copper produced. Developing alternative processes is an active area of research.

(3) **a** **Tick three alternative methods that can be used to extract copper from low-grade ores.** (3 marks, ★)

Distillation using heat	☐
Bioleaching using bacteria	☐
Phytomining using plants	☐
Displacement using silver	☐
Displacement using iron	☐

NAILIT!

This is another topic where it's useful to know the order of reactivity of metals!

b **Identify one advantage and one disadvantage for each of these methods.** (3 marks, ★★)

i Method ....

Advantage: .... Disadvantage: ....

ii Method ....

Advantage: .... Disadvantage: ....

iii Method ....

Advantage: .... Disadvantage: ....

Making potable water and waste water treatment

(1) **State what is meant by the term potable water.** (1 mark, ★)

....

(2) **Explain why potable water can't be described as 'pure water'.** (2 marks, ★)

....

(3) **The flow chart below shows the different stages in the production of potable water.**

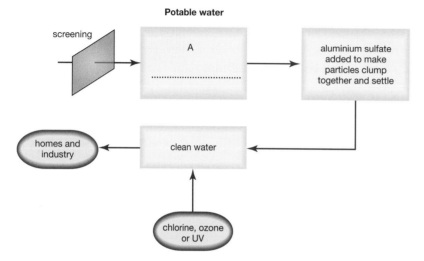

a **Fill in the gap in the box marked 'A' to identify what happens at that stage of potable water production.**
(1 mark, ★)

b **Suggest why chlorine, ozone or UV is used in this process.** (1 mark, ★★)

....

....

(4) **One way to obtain potable water from salt water is by distillation.**

a **Identify one other way to obtain potable water from salt water.** (1 mark, ★)

....

b **Explain why distillation requires energy to heat the salt water.** (2 marks, ★★)

....

....

(5) **The flow chart below shows how waste water is treated.**

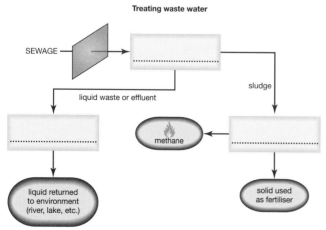

a **Complete the diagram to identify the stages of waste water treatment.**
(4 marks, ★★)

b **Suggest what additional treatment may be needed for industrial waste before it can be released into the environment.** (1 mark, ★★★)

....

....

Ways of reducing the use of resources

1 **There are many benefits to reusing and recycling materials like glass, plastic and metal.**

   a **Tick two statements which are not benefits of reusing glass bottles.** (2 marks, ★)

Reduces use of limited raw materials to make glass bottles	
Reduces use of glass bottles	
Reduces demand for energy from limited resources	
Melting glass bottles to form new products requires energy	
Reduces use of limited raw materials to make other glass products	

NAILIT!

Remember that steel is an alloy of iron with specific amounts of carbon and other metals.

   b **Tick three statements which are processes involved in recycling metals.** (3 marks, ★)

Separation	
Distillation	
Reforming	
Demineralisation	
Melting	
Cracking	

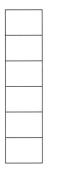

NAILIT!

Extracting metals from their ores is energy intensive. Look back at the metals topic to see how metals are extracted and how the reactivity of a metal impacts the amount of energy required to extract it.

2 **The table below shows data about the extraction and recycling of iron and aluminium.**

	Iron		Aluminium	
	Extraction	Recycling	Extraction	Recycling
Relative energy use	70	30	95	5
Relative CO$_2$ emissions	70	30	95	5
Relative impact on ore deposits	100	0	100	0
Comments	Magnetic		Reactive	

   a **Suggest why iron is easy to separate from other metals.** (1 mark, ★)

   ....

   b **Describe how recycled iron can reduce the amount of raw materials required to produce steel.** (2 marks, ★★)

   ....

   ....

   c **Explain why increasing the amount of aluminium that is recycled is important.** (3 marks, ★★★)

   ....

   ....

Rusting

(1) **Define the term corrosion.** (1 mark, ★)

....

(2) **A student ran an experiment to investigate the effectiveness of different methods to prevent rust. The student recorded the mass of five nails and put them in different test tubes as shown below. The student left them for 14 days and then recorded the mass again.**

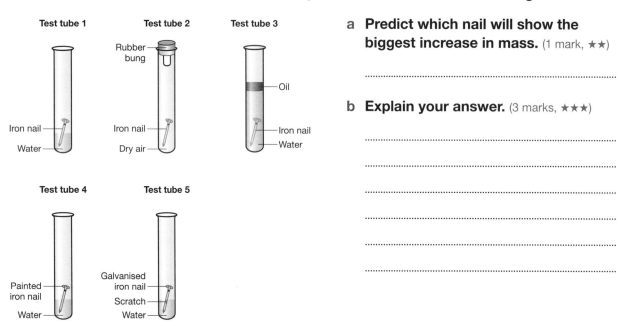

a **Predict which nail will show the biggest increase in mass.** (1 mark, ★★)

....

b **Explain your answer.** (3 marks, ★★★)

....

....

....

....

....

....

c **Rust is hydrated iron(III) oxide. Write the word equation for the reaction.**

.... + ... + ... → ....

The results of the experiment are shown in the table below.

Test tube	Mass before (g)	Mass after 14 days (g)
1	7.02	7.74
2	7.04	7.04
3	6.99	6.99
4	7.86	7.86
5	8.17	8.17

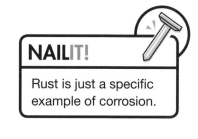

NAILIT!

Rust is just a specific example of corrosion.

d **Explain why the mass of the nails in test tubes 2 to 5 did not increase.** (4 marks, ★★★)

Test tube 2: ....

Test tube 3: ....

Test tube 4: ....

Test tube 5: ....

e **Suggest a metal that could have been used to galvanise the nail in test tube 5. Explain your answer.** (3 marks, ★★★)

....

....

Alloys as useful materials

(1) Circle the correct words to complete the sentence below. (1 mark, ★)

mixture		non-metals.
An alloy is a compound	of	compounds.
solution		metals.

SNAP IT!

Some alloys and their uses

car bodywork

low carbon steel

kitchen knives — stainless steel — Steels — medium carbon steel — girders

high carbon steel

drills

tin → bronze statues

copper alloys +

zinc → brass instruments

(2) Most pure metals are soft. They can be made harder by creating alloys.

a **Suggest why the gold medals given at sporting events are usually made with an alloy containing gold, rather than pure gold.** (2 marks, ★★)

....

....

b **Tick two statements that explain why pure gold is soft.** (2 marks, ★★★)

Gold ions are joined by strong ionic bonds	
Gold ions are arranged in layers	
Gold ions can slide over each other	
Gold ions are joined by strong covalent bonds	

c **Explain how adding copper to gold makes it harder.** (2 marks, ★★★)

....

(3) A company that manufactures steel is testing samples of the steel they have produced so that it can be sent to the companies that use it. The results of the tests are shown in the table below.

	Steel sample A	Steel sample B	Steel sample C
Mass of iron (g)	25.40	24.80	25.10
Mass of carbon (g)	0.45	0.21	0.03

a **Explain why a car bodywork manufacturer uses mild steel.** (2 marks, ★★★)

....

....

b **Suggest which sample of steel would be most suitable for a bodywork manufacturer. Explain your answer.** (2 marks, ★★★)

....

....

c **Calculate the number of moles and percentage composition of iron and carbon in steel sample B.** (2 marks, ★★★★)

....

....

Ceramics, polymers and composites

1. **a Match the materials to their properties and components.** (1 mark, ★)

Borosilicate glass	Strong and light	Metal ions and covalent structures
Fibre glass	High melting point	Strands of glass fibre and plastic resin
Ceramics	Hard, brittle, electrical insulators, waterproof	Silicon dioxide and boron trioxide

b Identify what type of material house bricks are made of. Tick one box. (1 mark, ★)

Fibre glass	
High-density polyethene	
Composite	
Ceramic	

c What is the function of the glass fibres and plastic resin in fibre glass? (2 marks, ★★)

....

d What is fibre glass an example of? (1 mark, ★) ....

e Explain why fibre glass is used to make cycling equipment. (2 marks, ★★)

....

2. **The diagrams below show four different polymers.**

a Identify each type of polymer.

i .... ii ....

iii .... iv ....

b Explain the differences and similarities between HDPE and LDPE. (4 marks, ★★)

....

....

....

c Explain why milk bottles are easily recycled but plastic electrical components are more difficult to recycle. (4 marks, ★★★)

....

....

....

The Haber process

① What is the product of the Haber process? Tick **one** box. (1 mark, ★)

Ammonia	
Nitrogen	
Nitrates	
Nitrites	

② Write a balanced chemical equation for the reaction. (2 marks, ★)

....

....

③ Which of these describes the Haber process best? Tick **one** box. (1 mark, ★★)

The reaction is reversible and the forward reaction is exothermic. This means that the backward reaction is endothermic.	
The reaction is reversible and the forward reaction is endothermic. This means that the backward reaction is exothermic.	
The reaction is not reversible and the reaction is endothermic.	
The reaction is not reversible and the reaction is exothermic.	

④ Describe the conditions of the Haber process. (3 marks, ★★)

....

....

⑤ Explain the compromised conditions used in the Haber process. (6 marks, ★★★)

....

....

....

....

⑥ The graph below shows the percentage yield of ammonia changes with pressure at different temperatures.

a Explain why the percentage yield of ammonia is higher at higher pressure. (2 marks, ★★)

....

....

b Explain why 350°C is described as a 'compromise'. (2 marks, ★★)

....

....

c Determine the percentage yield of ammonia at:

i 300 atmospheres and 400°C ....

ii 200 atmospheres and 350°C. ....

Production and uses of NPK fertilisers

(1) **Using the words in the box below, fill the gaps to complete the sentence about fertilisers.** (3 marks, ★)

Plants need compounds of ...., ... and .... for growth and carrying

out photosynthesis. .... containing these three elements are called ....

| nitrogen (N)   phosphorous (P)   potassium (K)   fertilisers   NPK fertilisers |

(2) **Match the component compound of fertilizer to its source.** (3 marks, ★★)

Ammonium nitrate, NH_4NO_3	Obtained by mining.
Ammonium hydrogen phosphate, $(NH_4)_2HPO_4$	Ammonia from the Haber process is oxidised to form nitric acid, which is then reacted with ammonia.
	Mined phosphate rock is reacted with nitric acid to form phosphoric acid (H_3PO_4), which is reacted with ammonia.
Potassium chloride, KCl	

(3) **Fertilisers used by farmers usually has a label similar to the one below.**

| NPK 12:9:11 |

Explain why this information is useful to farmers. (2 marks, ★★)

....

....

(4) **Complete the table below.**

Fertiliser	Acid	Alkali
Ammonium nitrate		ammonia
Ammonium phosphate		ammonia
Ammonium sulfate		ammonia
Potassium nitrate		potassium hydroxide

(5) **Calculate the percentage of phosphorous in ammonium hydrogen phosphate, $(NH_4)_2HPO_4$.** (2 marks, ★★★)

....

....

(6) **Calculate the number of moles of nitrogen in 500 g of ammonium nitrate, NH_4NO_3.** (3 marks, ★★★)

....

....

1.1 The three states of matter can be represented by the simple particle model.

a **Match each diagram to the correct state of matter.** (3 marks)

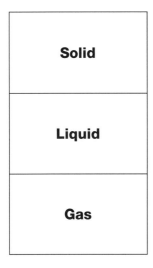 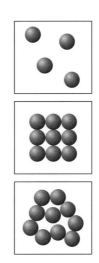

The temperature at which a substance changes from a liquid to a solid is known as the **freezing point**. This can be investigated by heating a solid until it melts and then recording the temperature at regular intervals as it cools.

Some results of an experiment are shown below.

Time/minutes	Temperature/°C
0	80
1	76
2	73
3	72
4	72
5	72
6	72
7	71
8	68
9	64
10	60

b **Choosing a suitable scale, plot these points on graph paper.** (3 marks)

c **Join up the points with a line and state the freezing point of this solid.** (2 marks)

d **State one limitation of the simple particle model when it is used to explain changes of state.** (1 mark)

....

1.2 Lithium reacts with chlorine to form lithium chloride.

    a What is the correct formula for lithium chloride? Tick **one** box. (1 mark)

Li_2Cl	
$LiCl_2$	
$LiCl$	
Li_2Cl_2	

    b Lithium also reacts with water to form an alkaline solution.

       Identify the ion responsible for making the solution alkaline. Tick **one** box.
(1 mark)

OH^+	
H^+	
H^-	
OH^-	

    c The formula for lithium oxide is Li_2O.

       What is its relative formula mass? Tick **one** box. (1 mark)

14	
30	
22	
39	

1.3 Lithium exists as two stable isotopes, ^6_3Li and ^7_3Li.

Complete the table below to show the number of sub-atomic particles
in each isotope. (3 marks)

Isotope	Number of protons	Number of electrons	Number of neutrons
^6_3Li			
^7_3Li			

1.4 The most abundant isotope of lithium is ^7_3Li, which accounts for 92.5% of naturally
occurring lithium.

    a Calculate the percentage abundance of the ^6_3Li isotope. (1 mark)

....

    b Use the information to work out the relative atomic mass of lithium to one
decimal place. (3 marks)

....

....

2.1 **The table below shows some of the properties of calcium, chlorine and calcium chloride.**

Substance	Formula	Type of bonding	Melting point	Electrical conductivity
Calcium	Ca		842	Good
Chlorine	Cl_2		−102	Does not conduct
Calcium chloride	$CaCl_2$		772	Conducts only when molten or in solution

a **Complete the table to show the type of bonding in these substances.** (3 marks)

....

....

b **Explain why calcium can conduct electricity.** (2 marks)

....

....

c **Complete the dot-and-cross diagram to show the bonding in a molecule of chlorine.**
(2 marks)

d **Use your ideas about structure and bonding to explain the melting points of calcium, chlorine and calcium chloride.** (6 marks)

....

....

....

....

....

2.2 **Sodium is also in group 1.**

   a **Complete the diagram of the sodium atom.** (1 mark)

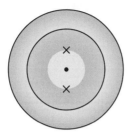

   b **Explain why an atom of sodium is termed as neutral.** (1 mark)

....

2.3 **In a reaction, 5 g of sodium reacts with an excess of oxygen to form sodium oxide.**

   The balanced chemical equation for this reaction is as follows:

$$4Na(s) + O_2(g) \rightarrow 2Na_2O(s)$$

   a **Explain what happens, in terms of electrons, when sodium reacts with oxygen. You can include diagrams in your answer.** (4 marks)

....

....

....

   b **Sodium oxide does not conduct electricity when solid, but will when molten or in solution. Explain why.** (3 marks)

....

....

....

   c **Calculate the maximum mass of sodium oxide that could be formed in this reaction.** (4 marks)

   [Na = 23, O = 16]

....

....

....

....

3.1 Soluble salts can be formed by reacting dilute acids with bases. These are neutralisation reactions.

a **Which of the following does not act as a base? Tick one box.**

(1 mark)

Calcium carbonate	
Lithium sulfate	
Potassium oxide	
Ammonia	

b **What is the pH of a neutral solution? Tick one box.**

(1 mark)

7	
14	
1	
3	

c **Which of the following is a weak acid? Tick one box.** (1 mark)

Sulfuric acid	
Ethanoic acid	
Nitric acid	
Hydrochloric acid	

3.2 A student carries out an experiment to make magnesium chloride by reacting magnesium carbonate with hydrochloric acid. Carbon dioxide and water are also produced in the reaction.

The equation for this reaction is: $MgCO_3(s) + 2HCl(aq) \rightarrow MgCl_2(aq) + CO_2(g) + H_2O(l)$

a **What is meant by the symbol (aq)?** (1 mark) ....

During this experiment, an excess of magnesium carbonate is added to $20\,cm^3$ of $2\,mol/dm^3$ hydrochloric acid. The excess magnesium carbonate is removed by filtration, and the resulting solution is heated over a water bath to evaporate the water, leaving solid magnesium chloride.

b **State one observation the student would see in this reaction.** (1 mark)

....

c **How would the student know that he had added excess magnesium carbonate?** (1 mark)

....

....

d How many moles of HCl are there in 20 cm³ of 2 mol/dm³ hydrochloric acid? (2 marks)

.... moles

e Use the equation and your answer to (d) to calculate the volume of carbon dioxide (CO_2) produced in this reaction. If you could not answer part (d), use 0.1 moles as the amount of hydrochloric acid used. This is **not** the answer to part (d). Give your answer in dm³. (2 marks)

....

....

3.3 This experiment produced 1.18 g of magnesium chloride.

The theoretical yield of magnesium chloride in this reaction is 1.90 g.

a Calculate the percentage yield. Quote your answer to one decimal place. (3 marks)

....

....

b State **one** reason why the percentage yield is less than 100%. (1 mark)

....

Magnesium chloride is also formed when hydrochloric acid reacts with solid magnesium oxide.

c Write a balanced chemical equation for this reaction. Include state symbols. (3 marks)

....

3.4 Titrations can be carried out to find out the unknown concentration of solutions.

A student carried out a titration to find out the concentration of a solution of potassium hydroxide.

She placed 25 cm³ of the potassium hydroxide to a conical flask and added a few drops of phenolphthalein indicator.

She then added a standard solution 0.15 mol/dm³ nitric acid to the conical flask until the solution went from pink to colourless.

The equation for the reaction is as follows:

$$KOH(aq) + HNO_3(aq) \rightarrow KNO_3(aq) + H_2O(l)$$

The table below shows her results.

	Rough	2	3	4
Volume of 0.15 mol/dm³ nitric acid added/cm³	20.10	19.70	23.20	19.80

a **How many times should a titration be carried out?** (1 mark)

....

b **Calculate the mean volume of nitric acid used in the titration.** (2 marks)

....

....

c **Calculate the concentration of the potassium hydroxide, in mol/dm³.** (3 marks)

....

....

d **Calculate the concentration of the potassium hydroxide, in g/dm³.** (2 marks)
   K = 39, O = 16, H = 1

....

....

One of the products formed in this reaction is water.

e **Name the other product.** (1 mark) ....

The reaction that takes place is a neutralisation reaction.

f **Write the ionic equation for this reaction, including state symbols.** (2 marks)

....

4.1 **Electrolysis can be used to break down ionic compounds into their elements, and is often used to extract metals from their ores.**

a **Explain why potassium cannot be extracted from its ore using carbon.** (1 mark)

....

....

Molten potassium chloride (KCl) consists of potassium ions and chloride ions. It undergoes electrolysis to form potassium and chlorine.

b **What is the name of the electrolyte?** (1 mark) ....

c **State the formula of the potassium ion.** (1 mark) ....

The chloride ions are attracted to the positive electrode.

d **Complete and balance the half equation for the reaction that takes place at the positive electrode.** (1 mark)

...........Cl^- $\rightarrow$ ....Cl_2^+ ....

e **What type of reaction is this?** (1 mark) ....

4.2 **A student carried out the electrolysis of aqueous solutions of potassium chloride.**

She was surprised to find that during the electrolysis of aqueous potassium chloride that bubbles of gas were produced at each electrode.

a **Name the gas produced at the negative electrode and explain why this is formed rather than potassium.** (2 marks)

....

....

b **Write a half equation for this reaction.** (2 marks)

....

c **What is the name of the remaining solution?** (1 mark)

....

5.1 **A student investigated the reactivity of four different metals by measuring the temperature change when they were reacted with hydrochloric acid. The equipment they used is shown below.**

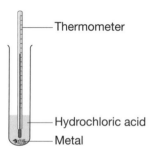

Thermometer

Hydrochloric acid
Metal

The student used the same amount of metal in each experiment.

a **State two further variables that would need to be controlled.** (2 marks)

....

....

b **What is the independent variable in this reaction?** (1 mark)

....

The table below shows the results of the experiment. The student concluded that the higher the temperature rise, the more reactive the metal.

Metal	Temperature change/°C
Zinc	5.5
Iron	0.5
Calcium	15.0
Magnesium	12.0

c Place the metals in order of reactivity, from most reactive to least reactive. (2 marks)

Most reactive	
Least reactive	

All of these reactions are **exothermic**.

d Complete the word equation for the reaction between calcium and hydrochloric acid. (2 marks)

Calcium + hydrochloric acid → .... + ...

e Draw a reaction profile diagram for this reaction on a separate piece of paper. (3 marks)

5.2 Ethanol is a very useful fuel as it can be produced from renewable sources. It has the formula C_2H_5OH.

The equation below shows the complete combustion of ethanol.

$$
\begin{array}{c}
H \quad H \\
| \quad | \\
H-C-C-O-H \\
| \quad | \\
H \quad H
\end{array}
+
\begin{array}{c}
O=O \\
O=O \\
O=O
\end{array}
\longrightarrow
\begin{array}{c}
O=C=O \\
O=C=O
\end{array}
+
\begin{array}{c}
H \quad O \quad H \\
H \quad O \quad H \\
H \quad O \quad H
\end{array}
$$

The table below shows the bond energies of some common bonds.

Bond	Bond energy (kJ per mol)
C–C	350
C–H	415
O=O	500
C=O	800
O–H	465
C–O	360

a Use this information to work out the energy change in this reaction. (3 marks)

....

....

....

b State, with a reason, if this reaction is exothermic or endothermic. (2 marks)

....

....

For an additional practice paper, visit: www.scholastic.co.uk/gcse

Answers

Atomic structure and the periodic table

Atoms, elements and compounds

1 a Atom – The smallest part of an element that can exist; Element – A substance made of only one type of atom; Compound – A substance that contains two or more elements chemically combined; Mixture – A substance that contains two or more elements not chemically combined.

  b Br_2; Ar c B d 9 e 3

2 a Any two from fluorine, chlorine, bromine, iodine or astatine (must be the name, not the symbol).

  b Any two from Li, Na, K, Rb, Cs or Fr (not H as not in group 1 of the periodic table).

Mixtures and compounds

1 Element: hydrogen, oxygen; Compound: sodium hydroxide, water; Mixture: air, salty water.

2 Heat the solution; Allow water to evaporate/leave to form crystals.

3 a Condenser

  b Water boils and turns into a gas/vapour; The vapour is then cooled in the condenser and turns back into water; The salt remains in the flask as it has a higher melting/boiling point than water.

4 Any four from: Crush rock salt; Add rock salt to water; Heat/stir until NaCl dissolves; Filter to remove sand; Heat remaining solution; Leave to crystallise/allow water to evaporate.

Pure substances and formulations

1 Pure substances are either single elements or single compounds.

2 a Although milk doesn't contain additives; it is a mixture of compounds.

  b You could heat the mixture and using a thermometer; observe a range of boiling points; pure substances have a specific boiling/melting point. (No mark for 'separate the mixture'.)

3 It is not pure – it contains other elements or compounds.

4 a
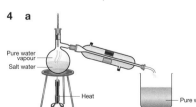

Pure water vapour
Salt water
Heat
Pure water

  b The salt water is heated; water boils at 100°C; the water vapour rises up the round-bottomed flask and enters a condenser where it cools and turns into a liquid; the salt is left behind as it boils at a higher temperature.

5 a A formulation is a mixture that is designed to be an improvement on the activate substance on its own – the lubricant stops the paracetamol sticking/makes it easier to swallow.

  b 0.5g + 0.25g + 1.25g = 2g
     0.5g/2g = 0.25 × 100 = 25%

  c i Paracetamol = 151 → 0.5/151
       = 0.003 moles or 3 × 10⁻³ moles

    ii Starch = 162 → 1.25/162
       = 0.008 moles or 8 × 10⁻³ moles

   iii Magnesium stearate = 591 → 0.25/591 = 0.0004 moles or 4 × 10⁻⁴ moles

  d 0.003 + 0.008 + 0.004 = 0.0114. 0.003/0.0114 × 100 = 26.3%

Chromatography

1 Chromatography is a technique that can be used to separate mixtures into their components; Chromatography works because different compounds have different levels of attraction for the paper and the solvent.

2 a Water line is above the base line; which will cause the inks to disperse in the water rather than up the paper; The base line is drawn in ink; which may contain colours that could contaminate the chromatogram/which could interfere with the experiment.

  b R_f = distance travelled/solvent front = 22/25 = 0.88. C is yellow.

Scientific models of the atom

1 Before the discovery of the electron, atoms were thought to be tiny spheres that could not be divided.

2 Ball/sphere of positive charge; electrons embedded in the sphere.

3 a Positive

  b Most of the atom is empty space.

  c Only part of the atom has a positive charge.

  d Mass of the atom is concentrated in the middle/nucleus; this positive charge is found in the middle of the atom/nucleus.

  e Neutrons

Atomic structure, isotopes and relative atomic mass

1
Sub-atomic particle	Relative charge	Relative mass
Proton	+1	1
Electron	−1	Very small
Neutron	0	1

2 There are equal numbers of protons and electrons/6 protons and electrons; The positive and negative charges cancel each other out.

3 a 74 protons and 74 electrons; 110 neutrons.

  b Gold (not Au)

4 Atomic; mass; protons; neutrons; 6; 6; 7

5 Both isotopes have 35 protons; and 35 electrons; Br-79 has 44 neutrons and Br-81 has 46 neutrons or Br-81 has 2 more neutrons than Br-79.

6 The other isotope makes up 25%; (35 × 75) + (Cl × 25)/100 = 35.5; Cl = 37.

The development of the periodic table and the noble gases

1 a 4 b 4

  c Same number of electrons/5 electrons in outer shell

  d Same number of electron shells

2 a Periods

  b For missing/undiscovered elements

  c By increasing atomic/proton number

  d They are unreactive.

3 a Increase down the group.

  b Any number between −185 and −109

Electronic structure

1 a Nucleus

  b Protons; and neutrons

  c Aluminium or Al d 14

2 a C b A c B, E
  d B, F e D f A

Metals and non-metals

1 Malleable – Can be hammered into shape; Ductile – Can be drawn into wires; Sonorous – Makes a ringing sound when hit.

2 a Na d Ar g Ca
  b Au e B h N
  c Si f Br

3 a Non-metal b 2

  c Good electrical conductor; shiny.

Group 1 – the alkali metals

1 They all have 1 electron in their outer shell.

2 Potassium

3 Francium

4 Na

5 Any three from: Fizzing/bubbling/effervescence, not gas given off; Lithium floats; Lithium moves on the surface; Lithium dissolves/gets smaller/disappears.

6 Any two from: Potassium melts/forms a ball; Potassium catches fire; Lilac/purple; Reaction is faster/more vigorous.

Group 7 – the halogens

1 F 　　　　　　**2** Fluorine

3 Br_2 　　　　　**4** Chlorine

5 **a** Lithium and chlorine, as chlorine is more reactive.

　　b Lithium + chlorine → lithium chloride

　　c $2Li + I_2 \rightarrow 2LiI$ (correct; balanced)

6 **a**

	Chlorine	Bromine	Iodine
Potassium chloride	x	No reaction	**No reaction**
Potassium bromide	Orange solution formed	x	No reaction
Potassium iodide	**Brown solution formed**	**Brown solution formed**	x

　　b Chlorine + potassium bromide → bromine + potassium chloride

　　c Add iodine to potassium astatide (or any astatide salt); Brown colour of iodine disappears/solution turns darker.

　　　$I_2 + 2At^- \rightarrow 2I^- + At_2$

The transition metals

1 Silver; mercury; tungsten.

2 **a** Any from: shiny; unreactive; hard; strong.

　　b Any three from: High melting points; High density; Unreactive [if not given in (a)]; Hard [if not given in (a)]; Strong [if not given in (a)].

3 **a** Sodium chloride 　**b** White

　　c $2Na + Cl_2 \rightarrow 2NaCl$ (correct; balanced)

4 Less, as iron is less reactive.

Bonding, structure and the properties of matter

Bonding and structure

1

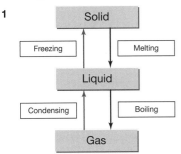

2 **a** 0°C 　　　**b** 100°C

3 **a** Gas 　　　**b** Solid

　　c Liquid

4 **a** Oxygen 　**b** Nitrogen

　　c Oxygen 　**d** Oxygen

Ions and ionic bonding

1 Magnesium is a metal which is found in group **2** of the periodic table. This means it has **2** electrons in its outer shell. When it reacts, it loses **2** electrons and forms an ion with a **2**$^+$ charge. Fluorine is a non-metal which is found in group **7** of the periodic table. When it reacts, it **gains** 1 electron to form an ion with a **1**$^-$ charge. When magnesium reacts with fluorine, it forms magnesium fluoride which has the formula **MgF_2**.

2 Potassium chloride, KCl; Magnesium oxide, MgO_2; Magnesium chloride, $MgCl_2$; Aluminium fluoride, AlF_3.

3 **a** Formula = $LiCl$

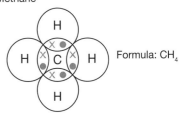

　　　(correct ion; correct formula)

　　b Formula = $BaBr_2$

　　　$Ba^x_x + 2\cdot\ddot{Br}\colon_2 \longrightarrow \left[Ba \right]^{2+} \left[\colon\ddot{Br}\colon \right]^-$

　　　(correct ion; correct formula)

The structure and properties of ionic compounds

1 High melting points; Conduct electricity when molten or in solution; Made of ions.

2 **a** B 　**b** A 　　**c** C

3 Ionic bonds are formed when **metals** react with **non-metals**. Atoms either lose or gain **electrons** to become positive or negative particles called ions. The ions are held together in a giant ionic **lattice** by strong **electrostatic** forces of attraction acting in all **directions**.

4 Level 1 (marks 1–2)

KI is ionic/made of ions/consists of a giant ionic lattice.

KI will have a high melting point *or* will conduct electricity when molten or in solution.

Level 2 (marks 3–4)

KI will have a high melting point because the ions are strongly attracted together/lots of energy is needed to break the strong ionic bonds *or*

KI will conduct electricity when molten or in solution/dissolved because the ions are free to move.

Level 3 (marks 5–6)

KI will have a high melting point because the ions are strongly attracted together/lots of energy is needed to break the strong ionic bonds *and*

KI will conduct electricity when molten or in solution/dissolved because the ions are free to move *and*

KI will not conduct electricity when solid as the ions do not move/are in fixed positions.

Covalent bonds and simple molecules

1 NH_3; Water.

2 **a** and **b**

Hydrogen

Formula: H_2

Methane

Formula: CH_4

3 **a**

　　b Covalent bond – triple bond

4 **a**

　　　(each single bond; correct double bond)

　　b Covalent bonds – 4 × single and 1 × double

Diamond, graphite and graphene

1 **a** A 　　**b** C

2 **a** Strong covalent bonds; large amounts of energy needed to overcome/break covalent bonds.

　　b Each carbon is bonded to 4 other carbon atoms; covalent bonds are very strong.

　　c Both have delocalised electrons; both conduct electricity.

3 **a** Does not have delocalised electrons. (do not allow free/mobile ions).

　　b High melting/boiling points hard. (due to no delocalised electrons).

Fullerenes and polymers

1 **a** D 　　**b** C

　　c A 　　**d** B

2 **a** Hollow/spherical

　　b Large surface area

3 **a** Covalent

　　b Polyethene is a bigger molecule so has larger intermolecular forces;

More energy needed to overcome these intermolecular forces; Increases the melting point; Allow reverse argument.

Giant metallic structures and alloys

1   Metals are **giant** structures. The atoms are arranged in **layers**.

The outer shell electrons become detached from the rest of the atom and are said to be **delocalised**. This means they are free to move throughout the whole metal.

Metallic bonding is strong because of the **electrostatic** attraction between the positive metal ions and the electrons.

2   **free electrons** from outer shells of metal atoms

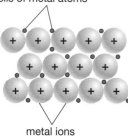

metal ions

Giant structure; Positive metal ions drawn and labelled; Delocalised electrons drawn and labelled; Electrons can carry charge throughout the metal.

3   a   Strong electrostatic attraction between positive metal ions and delocalised electrons; Lots of energy needed to overcome the strong attraction.

b   Carbon/different sized atoms distort the regular lattice; Layers cannot slide over each other.

Nanoparticles

1   1–100 nm

2   a 8.6×10^{-8} m

b 1.46×10^{-8} m

c 1.58×10^{-7} m

d 8.2×10^{-9} m

e   c– because the value is > 100 nm (both points needed)

3   a   • Surface area = $5^2 \times 6$ = 150 nm²; [units not needed]

• Volume = 5^3 = 125 nm³;

• SA:volume ratio = 150/125 = 1.2.

b   As length of the side increases, ratio increases; by a factor of 10.

Quantitative chemistry

Conservation of mass and balancing equations

1   a   Magnesium + oxygen → magnesium oxide

b   Reactants: Magnesium, oxygen; Products: Magnesium oxide.

c   12 + 8 = 20 g

2   a   Nitrogen + hydrogen → ammonia

b

	Reactants	Products
N	2	1
H	2	3

c $N_2(g) + 3H_2(g) \rightarrow 2NH_3(g)$

3   $Fe_2O_3 + 2CO \rightarrow 2Fe + 2CO_2$

Relative formula masses

1   The relative atomic mass (symbol = A_r) of an element is the weighted average mass of its naturally occurring isotopes;

You calculate the relative formula mass (symbol = M_r) of a compound by adding up all the relative atomic masses of all the atoms present in the formula of the compound;

The elements hydrogen, oxygen, nitrogen, chlorine, bromine, iodine and fluorine exist as diatomic molecules- in equations their relative formula masses are twice their relative atomic masses;

The law of mass conservation means that in a chemical reaction the sum of the relative formula masses of the reactants is equal to the sum of the relative formula mass of the products.

2   Carbon — 12; Oxygen — 16; Chlorine 35.5; Iron — 55.8

3   a   NaOH — 40; H_2SO_4 — 98; Na_2SO_4 — 142; H_2O — 18

b   10 g/98 = 0.010 → 0.010 × 18 = 1.84 g

c   5 g/142 = 0.35 → 0.035 × 40 × 2 = 2.82 g

d   So they know how much product will be made OR to avoid waste.

The mole and reactive masses

1   a   0.1 moles   b   0.1 moles

c   0.003 (or 3.125×10^{-3}) moles

d   0.5 moles

2   a   36.5 g   b   60 g

c   31.8 g   d   171 g

3   a

Substance	A_r or M_r	Mass/g	Moles
sodium	23.0	2.30	0.1
sulfur	32	0.32	0.01
CH_4	16	1.60	0.1

b   1.37 moles

4   a   152   b   38 g

c   19 g   d 7.5×10^{22}

5   a   14 g

b   1 136 364 (or 1.13664×10^6) g

6   a   0.003 moles   b   0.02 moles

c 2.29×10^{23}

Limiting reactants

1   a   Hydrochloric acid

b   Magnesium

2   How many moles of water can be produced by 1 mole of H_2? 1

How many moles of water can be produced by 1 mole of O_2? 2

Which is the limiting reactant? H_2

How much H_2O is produced in the reaction? 1

Which reactant is in excess? O_2

How many moles of O_2 is used in the reaction? 1

3   a $4Cu + O_2 \rightarrow 2Cu_2O$

b   Cu → 1.26 moles; O_2 → 1.56 moles

c   Copper; because in the equation, the ratio of moles is Cu:O_2 4:1, however in the experiment there was only 1.26:1.56 moles.

4   a $C_3H_8 + 5O_2 \rightarrow 3CO_2 + 4H_2O$

b   5.68 g

c   The limiting reactant is oxygen; because in the balanced equation the ratio is 1:5 (0.3:1.5), but the engine only has 0.3:0.1; they could make the engine more efficient by increasing the amount of oxygen.

Concentrations in solutions

1   a   1   b   2

2   a   Test 1 — 250 g/dm³

Test 2 — 400 g/dm³

Test 3 — 571 g/dm³

b   Test 1 — 0.09 moles

Test 2 — 0.17 moles

Test 3 — 0.34 moles

3   a   143

b   0.01 moles/143 g/mol = 1.43 g = 1.43 g/dm³

c   3 575 000 g; 3.575×10^6 g

Moles in solution

1   a   0.25 moles   b   10 mol/dm³

2   0.05 mol/dm⁻³

3   1 260 mol/dm⁻³

Moles and gas volumes

1   At the same temperature and pressure equal **volumes** of different gases contain the same number of molecules.

This means that under the same conditions, equal volumes of gases have the same number of **moles** present.

At room temperature (20°C) and **atmospheric pressure,** together known as **room temperature and pressure (RTP),** 1 mole of any gas occupies a volume of 24 dm³.

2   144 dm³

3 a 83.3 moles **b** 0.083 moles

 c 3.66 g

Percentage yield and atom economy

1 a

$$\frac{\text{Relative formula mass of desired product}}{\text{Sum of relative formula masses of reactants}} \times 100$$

 b They would understand how much of the desired product is made from the reactants and how much is wasted; it can inform decisions about the sustainability of different methods/percentage yield gives no information about the quantity of wasted atoms.

 c 1 $\frac{48}{128} \times 100 = 38\%$

  2 $\frac{48}{80} \times 100 = 60\%$

 d It would increase the atom economy of method to 100%; making method even more favourable.

2 a $CaCO_3 = 100$; $CaO = 56$

 b 56%

 c 7g

 d $\frac{6.5}{7} \times 100 = 92.9\%$

Chemical changes

Metal oxides and the reactivity series

1 a Magnesium + oxygen → magnesium oxide

 b $2Mg(s) + O_2(g) \rightarrow 2MgO(s)$ (correct; balanced)

 c Oxygen is gained/electrons are lost.

2 a Aluminium + lead chloride → aluminium chloride + lead

 b Silver + copper oxide → no reaction

 c Calcium + zinc nitrate → calcium nitrate + zinc

 d Iron chloride + copper → no reaction

3 a 1-Sodium, 2-X, 3-Magnesium, 4-Copper.

 b Copper

Extraction of metals and reduction

1 Carbon is less reactive than magnesium ore.

2 It's unreactive/doesn't easily form compounds.

3 a Tin(IV) oxide + carbon → carbon oxide/dioxide + tin

 b Carbon

4 a $2CuO(s) + C(s) \rightarrow CO_2(g) + 2Cu(s)$ or (l)

 b Any metal above iron in the reactivity series; Too expensive/metals above carbon extracted by electrolysis so require more energy.

 c Iron is a liquid.

 d Carbon is more reactive than iron.

 e Any metal above iron in the reactivity series; Too expensive/metals above carbon extracted by electrolysis so require more energy.

The blast furnace

1 a Carbon + oxygen → carbon dioxide (1)

 b $C(s) + CO_2(g) \rightarrow 2CO(g)$ − 1 mark for correct formulae and balancing, 1 mark for state symbols

 c Reduction/redox (1)

 d $2Fe_2O_3(s) + 3C(s) \rightarrow 4Fe(l) + 3CO_2(g)$

 e Iron is a liquid

 f $CaSiO_3$

 g

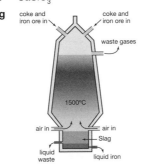

The reactions of acids

1 Both neutralise acid; Bases are insoluble/alkalis are soluble bases/alkalis form hydroxide/OH^- ions ins solution.

2 a Sodium chloride – sodium hydroxide and hydrochloric acid.

 b Potassium nitrate – potassium carbonate and nitric acid.

 c Copper sulfate – copper oxide and sulfuric acid.

3 a Solid dissolves/colourless solution forms.

 b Fizzing occurs with magnesium carbonate.

 c Magnesium oxide + hydrochloric acid → magnesium chloride + water

 d $MgCO_3$

4 a $Mg(s) + 2HCl(aq) \rightarrow MgCl_2(aq) + H_2(g)$

 b $Li_2O(s) + H_2SO_4(aq) \rightarrow Li_2SO_4(aq) + H_2O(l)$

 c $CuO(s) + 2HCl(aq) \rightarrow CuCl_2(aq) + H_2O(l)$

5 a $Ca(s) + 2H^+(aq) \rightarrow Ca^{2+}(aq) + H_2(g)$ (reactants; products; state symbols)

 b Ca oxidised; H^+/hydrogen reduced.

The preparation of soluble salts

1 a Copper carbonate + sulfuric acid → copper sulfate + water + carbon dioxide

 b Any two from: Copper carbonate dissolves; Fizzing/bubbles/effervescence; Blue/green solution forms.

 c To ensure all the acid reacts

 d Filtration

 e Copper oxide/copper hydroxide

 f Any one from: Salt lost from spitting during evaporation; Solution left in container; Not all the solution crystallises.

2 a $Ca(s) + 2HNO_3(aq) \rightarrow Ca(NO_3)_2(aq) + H_2(g)$ (reactants; products; state symbols)

 b % yield = 2.6/3.0 x 100; 87.7%

3 Possible steps to include: Reactants (zinc/zinc hydroxide/zinc oxide/zinc carbonate) and hydrochloric acid; Correct equation for chosen reactants; Heat acid; Add base until no more reacts/dissolves so the base is in excess; Filter unreacted base; Heat solution on a steam bath until half the water has evaporated; Leave remaining solution to cool so crystals form.

Equipment list: Bunsen burner; Heatproof mat; Tripod; Gauze; Beaker; Evaporating dish; Funnel; Filter paper; Conical flask; Spatula; Measuring cylinder; Safety glasses.

Oxidation and reduction in terms of electrons

1 a $Mg(s) + Cu^{2+}(aq) \rightarrow Mg^{2+}(aq) + Cu(s)$

 b Mg is oxidised and Cu is reduced.

2 a $Mg(s) + Zn^{2+}(aq) \rightarrow Mg^{2+}(aq) + Zn(s)$; Mg oxidised, Zn reduced.

 b $2Na(s) + Zn^{2+}(aq) \rightarrow 2Na^+(aq) + Zn(s)$; Na oxidised, Zn reduced.

 c $Cu(s) + 2Ag^+(aq) \rightarrow Cu^{2+}(aq) + 2Ag(s)$; Cu oxidised, Zn reduced.

 d $3Ca(s) + 2Fe^{3+}(aq) \rightarrow 3Ca^{2+}(aq) + 2Fe(s)$; Ca oxidised, Fe reduced.

pH scale and neutralisation

1 Strong acid — pH 2 — Red, Weak acid — pH 5 — Yellow, Strong alkali — pH 13 — Purple, Weak alkali - pH 9 — Blue, Neutral — pH 7 — Green.

2 Hydroxide ion

3 H^+

4 pH1

5 pH12

6 a Potassium hydroxide

 b $2KOH + H_2SO_4 \rightarrow K_2SO_4 + 2H_2O$

 c $H^+ + OH^- \rightarrow H_2O$ *or* $2H^+ + 2OH^- \rightarrow 2H_2O$

7 OH^- and NH_4^+

Strong and weak acids

1 a $HNO_3(aq) \rightarrow H^+(aq) + NO_3^-(aq)$

 b $HCOOH(aq) \rightarrow H^+(aq) + COO^-(aq)$

 c $H_2SO_4(aq) \rightarrow 2H^+(aq) + SO_4^{2-}(aq)$ *or* $H_2SO_4(aq) \rightarrow H^+(aq) + HSO_4^-(aq)$

2 Weak acid only partially ionises in solution; Dilute acid has fewer moles of solute dissolved.

3 a 1×10^{-3}

 b Answer is 100 times greater as if pH decreases by 1, H^+ concentration increases by 10; 0.1 (overrides previous mark); 1×10^{-1}

Answers

Electrolysis

1

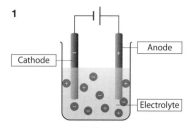

Cathode | Anode | Electrolyte

2 Ions are free to move when molten/ aqueous; Ions in fixed positions/ions can't move in solid lattice.

3
a Zinc and chlorine

b Silver and iodine

c Copper and oxygen.

4
a $Pb^{2+} + 2e^- \rightarrow Pb$; $2Br^- \rightarrow Br_2 + 2e^-$

b Lead/lead ions reduced and bromine/bromide ions oxidised.

Electrolysis of copper(II) sulfate and electroplating

1
a Unreactive

b Copper(II) sulfate

c Relights a glowing splint

d Copper

$Cu^{2+} + 2e^- \rightarrow Cu$

e Fades,

Copper ions form copper

f Any 2 from: Solution does not fade; No oxygen given off; Anode gets smaller; Cathode gets bigger.

2
a In this reaction:

i Pure chromium

ii Should be the tap

b Any chromium compound

c $Cr^{3+} + 3e^- \rightarrow Cr$

The electrolysis of aqueous solutions

1
a Copper chloride – copper and chlorine

b Potassium bromide – hydrogen and bromine

c Zinc sulfate – zinc and oxygen

d Sodium carbonate – hydrogen and oxygen

2
a $2H^+ + 2e^- \rightarrow H_2$

b Chlorine; $2Cl^- \rightarrow Cl_2 + 2e^-$

3
a H^+/hydrogen; Li^+/lithium; OH^-/ hydroxide.

b I^-/iodide ions attracted to anode/ positive electrode; Lose electron/ an electron; Form iodine; $2I^- \rightarrow I_2 + 2e^-$.

c Lithium hydroxide/LiOH

4
a Anode

b $4OH^- \rightarrow O_2 + 2H_2O + 4e^-$; OH^- and H_2O (correct; balanced)

The extraction of metals using electrolysis

1
a Strong ionic bonds/strong electrostatic attraction between oppositely charged ions; Requires lots of energy to overcome.

b So the ions are free to move.

c Reduce the operating temperature; Saves energy/reduces energy costs.

d Electrons are lost.

e $Al^{3+} + 3e^- \rightarrow Al$ (correct; balanced electrons)

f They react with the oxygen produced; Carbon + oxygen → carbon dioxide/$C + O_2 \rightarrow CO_2$

g Electricity wasn't discovered/ electricity not needed to extract iron.

Practical investigation into the electrolysis of aqueous solutions

1
a Independent – Metal/metal ion in salt; Dependent variable – Product formed at cathode; Control variables – Volume of solution, Concentration of solution, Negative ion in salt, Voltages.

b Only 1 variable is changed.

2 Place a lighted splint into the gas; Positive test – burns with a squeaky pop.

3
a $CuCl_2$ – Copper; all others – Hydrogen.

b Solutions containing metals above hydrogen in the reactivity series produce hydrogen on electrolysis; Solutions containing metals below hydrogen in the reactivity series produce the metal on electrolysis.

4 Chlorine; Bleaches blue litmus paper **or** bleaches UI in solution.

Titrations

1
a Titre 1: $14.90\,cm^3$; Titre 2: $15.35\,cm^3$; Titre 3: $14.80\,cm^3$ (Must be to 2 decimal places.)

b 14.85 (2 marks as outlier ignored); 15.02 (1 mark if outlier included)

c Until consistent/concordant results/ two titres within $0.10\,cm^3$

2

Volume NaOH (cm^3)	Concentration NaOH (mol/dm^3)	Volume HCl (cm^3)	Concentration HCl (mol/dm^3)
25.00	0.1	25.00	0.1
25.00	0.1	50.00	**0.05**
12.50	0.2	**25.00**	0.1
20.00	0.5	10.00	**1.0**

3 Possible steps to include: Use of pipette to measure out alkali; Place this solution into a conical flask; Add an indicator; Place conical flask onto a white tile; Fill burette with acid; Carry out rough titration; Add acid to alkali until there is a colour change; Record readings to nearest $0.05\,cm^3$; Repeat, slowing down addition of acid when close to rough titration reading; Continue until consistent results obtained/two results within $0.10\,cm^3$ of each other.

Equipment: Conical flask; Pipette (and filler); Burette; White tile; Indicator.

4
a Moles NaOH = conc × vol = 0.1 × 0.025 = 0.0025; moles HNO_3 = 0.0025; Conc HNO_3 = moles/vol = 0.0025/0.0216 = 0.116 mol/dm^3

b Formula mass HNO_3 = 63; Conc HNO_3 = 63 x 0.116 = 7.29 g/dm^3

5
a $Ca(OH)_2 + 2HCl \rightarrow CaCl_2 + 2H_2O$

b
i Moles $Ca(OH)_2$ = conc × vol = 0.2 × 0.025 = 0.005; Moles HCl = 0.005 × 2 = 0.01; Conc HCl = moles/vol = 0.01/0.0365 = 0.274 mol/dm^3.

ii Formula mass HCl = 36.5; Conc HCl = 36.5 × 0.274 = 10.0 g/dm^3.

(Allow error carried forward from an incorrect calculation.)

Energy changes

Exothermic and endothermic reactions

1
a Endothermic – surrounding temperatures decrease as heat energy is needed by the reaction.

b Exothermic – surrounding temperatures increase as heat energy is released by the reaction.

2
a 15.4°C − 23.7°C = −8.3. The reaction is endothermic as the temperature decrease.

b
i 37°C − 25°C = +12

ii Exothermic

Practical investigation into the variables that affect temperature changes in chemical reactions

1
a

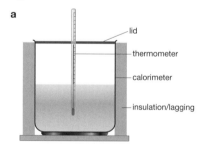

lid; thermometer; calorimeter; insulation/lagging

b To reduce heat loss; to give a more accurate result.

c Two from: The reaction of iron and oxygen is exothermic; The temperature increase is greatest with iron filings; Iron filings are more reactive.

d To make the results valid; oxygen may be controlling the rate of reaction.

2 Possible steps to include: Use an insulated calorimeter; to reduce heat loss; use a thermometer to record temperature; use same equipment throughout; use hydrochloric acid at different concentrations; use same volume of hydrochloric acid; same volume of calcium carbonate; same particle size of calcium carbonate; to ensure the results are valid; temperature increase will increase with concentration; because the rate of reaction will increase; record data on a table

	Concen-tration 1	Concen-tration 2	Concen-tration 3
Initial temperature / °C			
Final temperature / °C			

Reaction profiles

1 A **reaction profile** shows how the energy changes from reactants to products

In a reaction profile for an **exothermic** reaction the products are lower in energy than the reactants because **energy** is released to the surroundings during the reaction.

In a reaction profile for an **endothermic** reaction the **products** are higher in energy than the **reactants** because energy is taken in from the **surroundings** during the reaction.

Chemical reactions occur when reacting particles collide with enough energy to react. This energy is called the **activated energy** (Ea).

2 a Products are higher in energy that reactants; the student is incorrect; the reaction is endothermic.

  b i A – Activation energy.

  ii B – Energy absorbed from surroundings.

  c Catalyst reduces the activation energy:

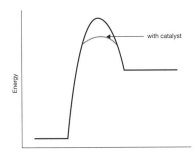

The energy changes of reactions

1 a H–H = 436 kJ

  Cl-Cl = 243

  Sum (bond breaking): 436+243 = 679 kJ

  b 2 × 432 = 864 kJ

  c Exothermic

  d 864 − 679 = 185

2 a 2x (H-Br) → H-H + Br-Br

  b Reactants = 366 × 2 = -732 kJ (breaking).
  Products = 432 + 193 = + 625 (making).
  625–732 = −107kJ = Endothermic.

Chemical cells and fuel cells

1 a Zinc

  b Lemon juice/citric acid

  c

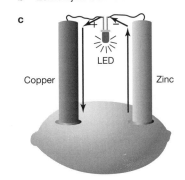

2 9/1.5 = 6 cells

3 a Electrolysis

  b

Chemical cells	Fuel Cells
Can be used anywhere.	Hampered by the need for hydrogen containers.
When non-rechargeable batteries run out, they have to be thrown away and sent to recycling centre.	These will continue to work as long as the hydrogen flows.
Re-chargeable batteries can be charged again and again.	The product of the reaction is water.
Some of the metals used are toxic.	The hydrogen is flammable.

  c At the negative electrode of the fuel cell hydrogen reacts with hydroxide ions to produce water and electrons.

  $2H_2(g) + 4OH^-(aq) \rightarrow 4H_2O(l) + 4e^-$

  At the positive electrode oxygen gains electrons and reacts with water to produce hydroxide ions.

  $O_2(g) + 2H_2O(l) + 4e^- \rightarrow 4OH^-(aq)$

Rates of reaction and equilibrium

Ways to follow a chemical reaction

1 a Size of marble chips

  b Time

  c Volume of carbon dioxide given off (if collected); OR change in mass (if carbon dioxide allowed to escape); OR time for marble chips to disappear (if excess hydrochloric acid).

  d Two from: Mass of marble chips; volume of acid; Concentration of acid; Amount of stirring; Temperature.

2 a Production of sulfur, S, which makes the solution opaque.

  b Concentration of sodium thiosulfate.

  c Two from: Volume of sodium thiosulfate; Volume of acid; Concentration of acid; Amount of stirring; Temperature; Same person doing the timing.

  d Could use a light meter and a lamp; to reduce uncertainty about whether the x is visible or not.

3 Possible steps to include: Measure a fixed volume of (e.g. 50 cm³) of hydrochloric acid; using one of the measuring cylinders and pour it into the conical flask; Put a bung in the conical flask with a delivery tube which goes into an upturned measuring cylinder which is full of water and in a water trough; this allows me to measure the amount of hydrogen gas given off; Cut the magnesium into pieces the same size; put one piece into the conical flask; start the timer; record the amount of hydrogen gas at regular intervals on a table; Repeat for different concentrations of hydrochloric acid.

Calculating the rate of reaction

1 Rate of reaction = Amount of product formed/Time taken

2 a The rate of reaction is constant

  b The rate of reaction is constant

  c The rate of reaction decreases with time

  d The rate of reaction increases with time

3 a $Mg + 2HCl \rightarrow MgCl_2 + H_2$

  b 99/120 = 0.825 cm³/second

  c

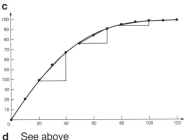

  d See above

  e 30s = 1.8 cm³/s (Allow +/− 0.2)

  60s = 0.75 cm³/s (Allow +/− 0.2)

$90s = 0.15$ cm³/s (Allow +/− 0.2)

f 30s – from graph: 1.8 cm³/s;
110/24 = 0.75 moles/s

60s – from graph: 0.75 cm³/s;
168/24 = 0.03125 moles/s

The effect of concentration and on reaction rate and the effect of pressure on the rate of gaseous reactions

1 For a reaction to happen, particles must **collide** with sufficient **energy**. The minimum amount of **energy** that particles must have for a specific reaction is known as the **activation energy**. The rate of a reaction can be increased by increasing the **energy** of collisions and increasing the **frequency** of collisions.

2 There are more particles; The frequency of successful collisions increases.

3 a C   **b** A

4 a

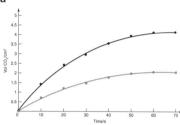

b Rate of reaction starts off fast; slows down as the reaction progresses.

c One (or more) of the reactants has been used up.

d See above (light grey line)

e There are half as many hydrochloric acid particles; reducing the frequency of successful collisions; reducing the rate of reaction.

Rates of reaction – the effect of surface area

1 a B   **b** B

c More particles exposed to the other reactant; increasing the frequency of collisions.

d Sugar is used to make marshmallows; sugar has a larger surface area; the rate of reaction with oxygen under heat would be much higher.

2 a Cut tablets; grind into powder using a pestle and mortar.

b

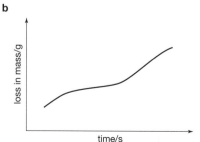

c Collect carbon dioxide bubbles in upturned measuring cylinder;

allow carbon dioxide to escape and measure mass change.

The effects of changing the temperature and adding a catalyst

1 a The particles have more energy so they collide more frequently; and with more energy

b 10°C increase ~doubles rate. So at 30°C = 20s. 40°C = 10s.

2 a It is a catalyst.

b It provides an alternative route for the reaction; reducing the activation energy.

c

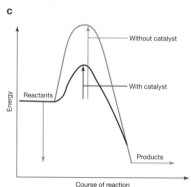

3 a Collect oxygen given off in an upturned measuring cylinder.

b Possible steps to include: Put hydrogen peroxide in a test tube; Use the same volume and concentration for both tests; Put a bung at the top of the test tube with a delivery tube to an upturned measuring cylinder; Add a quantity of liver to the hydrogen peroxide; Record the volume of oxygen produced at intervals; Repeat with the same mass of manganese oxide.

An investigation into how changing the concentration affects the rate of reaction

1 a $2HCl(aq) + Na_2S_2O_3(aq) \rightarrow 2NaCl(aq) + SO_2(g) + S(s) + H_2O(l)$

b As the concentration increases, the rate of reaction will increase.

c The hypothesis will be confirmed/ as the concentration increases the rate of reaction will increase; there will be more particles; more frequent collisions.

d Possible steps to include: Measure out the same volume of different concentrations of sodium thiosulfate /hydrochloric acid into conical flasks; Measure out a volume of hydrochloric acid/sodium thiosulfate; Using the same volume and concentration throughout; To ensure the results are valid; Mark a cross on a sheet of white paper; Put conical flask on cross; Mix reactants; Record the time it takes for the cross to disappear; Repeat for other concentrations.

e Temperature would increase the frequency and energy of collisions; increasing the rate of reaction.

f Cross to disappear – easy and convenient/requires no special equipment; but can be subjective (it is down to an individual's opinion).

Lamp and light sensor – more accurate; because it is not dependent on an individual's opinion; requires additional equipment.

2 a

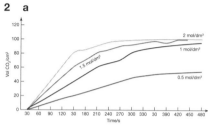

b 0.5mol/dm³ = 0.113 cm³/s
1mol/dm³ = 0.198 cm³/s
1.5mol/dm³ = 0.222 cm³/s
2mol/dm³ = 0.256 cm³/s

Reversible reactions

1 a ⇌

b Reversible reactions can go both forwards and backwards in certain conditions.

c A dynamic equilibrium is when the rate of the forward reaction is equal to the rate of the backward reaction; the concentration of the reactants and products remains constant.

2 a A reversible reaction is one which can go both ways. This means that as well as reactants forming products, the products can also react to give the reactants.

b Exothermic; the forward reaction requires heat so is endothermic; the backwards reaction is always the opposite of the forwards reaction.

c The reversible reaction has reached dynamic equilibrium; both reactions are occurring at the same rate; there is no net change in the volume of carbon dioxide.

The effect of changing conditions on equilibrium

1 At dynamic equilibrium, the rate of the forward reaction is the same as the backward reaction.

2 Temperature; pressure; concentration.

3 If a chemical system is at equilibrium and one or more of the three conditions is changed; then the position of equilibrium will shift so as to cancel out the change; and we get either more reactants or more products.

4 a The reaction would shift to the left; because the forward reaction is exothermic as it gives out heat; producing more nitrogen and hydrogen gas.

b The forward reaction needs enough energy to overcome the activation energy or the rate of reaction will be too slow.

c It provides an alternative route for the reaction – reducing the activation energy; and increasing the rate of reaction; meaning the reaction can be run at the lowest possible temperature which reduces the backward reaction (a compromise temperature).

d There are fewer moles of gas in the products; increasing pressure therefore increases the forwards reaction.

Organic chemistry

Alkanes

1 **a** They are molecules that contain ***only*** hydrogen and carbon.

b They only contain C-C single bonds.

c Any two from: They have similar chemical properties; They have the same general formula; Each member differs by CH_2; Same trend in physical properties.

2 **a** $C_{20}H_{42}$

b C_8H_{18}

3

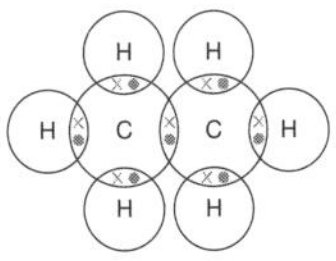

(Correct C-H bonds; Correct C-C bond)

4 **a**

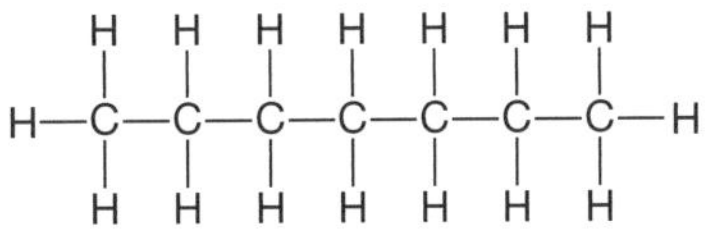

b C_7H_{16}

5 CH_4

6 Pentane

7 C_4H_{10}

Fractional distillation

1 Any 4 from: Crude oil heated; Crude oil evaporates; Vapour rises up fractionating column; Fractions with lower boiling points rise further up column/Temperature gradient in column (hotter at the bottom, cooler at the top); When vapour cools to boiling point of fractions molecules condense into a liquid; Statement relating to bigger molecules having higher boiling points.

2 **a** Fuel for aeroplanes

b $C_{12}H_{26}$

c Bigger molecules so greater intermolecular forces; More energy is needed to overcome these forces.

3 **a** $C_2H_6 + 3½\ O_2 \rightarrow 2CO_2 + 3H_2O$

b $C_3H_8 + 5O_2 \rightarrow 3CO_2 + 4H_2O$

c $C_5H_{12} + 8O_2 \rightarrow 5CO_2 + 6H_2O$ (correct; balanced)

Cracking and alkenes

1 Contain a C=C bond; Molecules made of only carbon and hydrogen.

2 **a** **i**

Pentene + Hydrogen

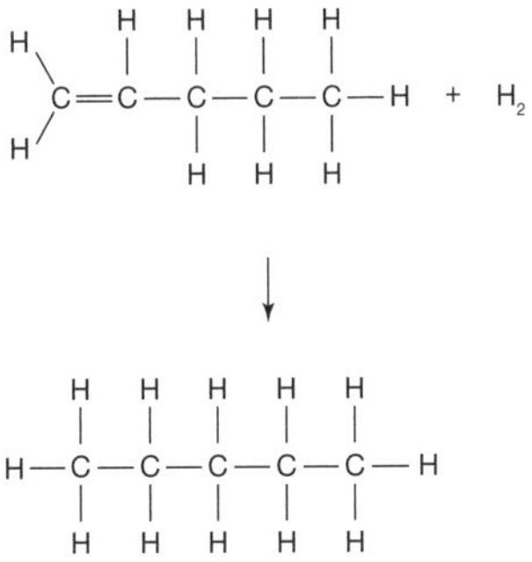

ii

Butene + Steam

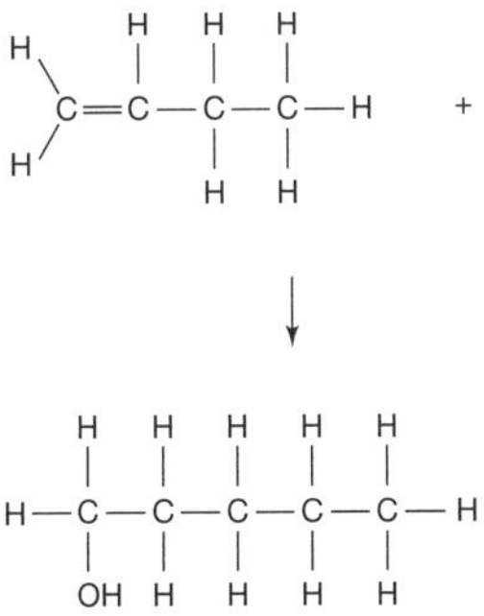

iii

Propene + Chlorine

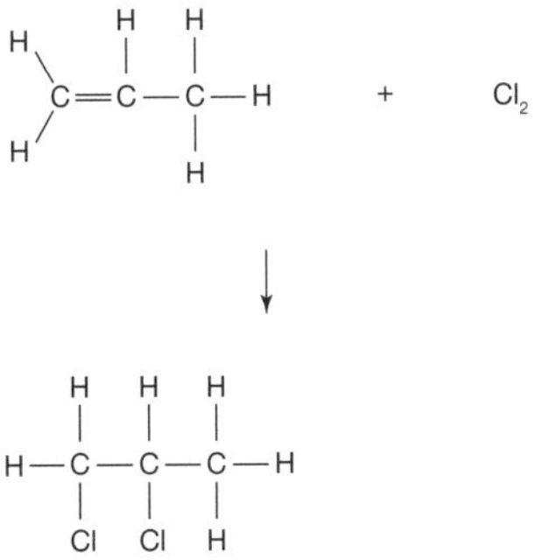

b Only one product/no waste products.

3 **a** $C_8H_{18} \rightarrow C_5H_{12} + \mathbf{C_3H_6}$

b $C_{18}H_{38} \rightarrow C_3H_6 + \mathbf{C_{15}H_{32}}$

c $\mathbf{C_{13}H_{28}} \rightarrow C_4H_8 + C_9H_{20}$

d $C_{14}H_{30} \rightarrow C_4H_{10} + C_6H_{12} + \mathbf{C_4H_8}$

e $C_{14}H_{30} \rightarrow C_8H_{18} + \mathbf{2C_3H_6}$

4 **a** $C_{10}H_{22}$ **b** Fuel/petrol

c It's an alkene.

d Polymers

e $C_{10}H_{22} \rightarrow C_6H_{14} + C_4H_8$

Alcohols

1 **a** B **b** D **c** A **d** C **e** B

2 **a** Methanol + oxygen → carbon dioxide + water; $CH_3OH + 3/2O_2 \rightarrow CO_2 + 2H_2O$

b Propanol + oxygen → carbon dioxide + water; $CH_3CH_2CH_2OH + 9/2O_2 \rightarrow 3CO_2 + 4H_2O$

(multiples allowed)

3 **a** Fizzing; sodium dissolves/disappears.

b Dissolves/forms a colourless solution/miscible.

c The potassium manganate(VII) oxidises the alcohol to form propanoic acid; which turns blue litmus paper red.

Carboxylic acids

1 **a** E **b** A **c** C

d B **e** D **f** C

2 **a** $C_8H_{16}O_2$

b $C_3H_6O_2$; Propanoic acid.

3 HCl is a strong acid; CH_3COOH is a weak acid; HCl fully ionises; CH_3COOH only partially ionises; $HCl \rightarrow H^+ + Cl^-$ or $CH_3COOH \rightleftharpoons CH_3COO^- + H^+$

Addition polymerisation

1

Monomer	Repeating unit	Name of polymer
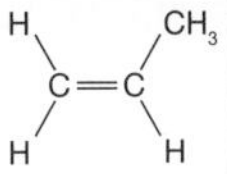 Propene	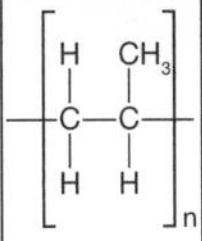	**Polypropene**
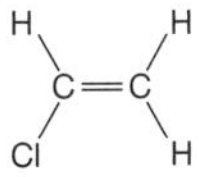 Chloroethene	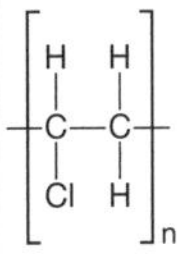	**Polychloroethene**
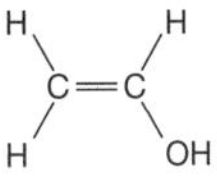 Ethenol	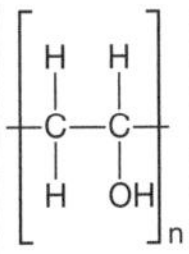	**Polyethenol**
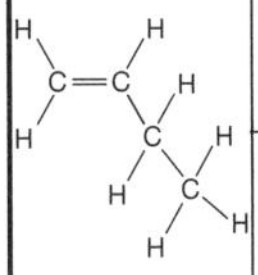 Butene	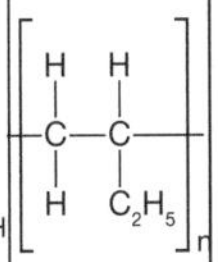	**Polybutene**

2

Repeating unit	Monomer
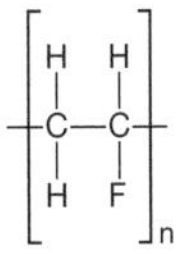	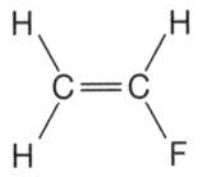
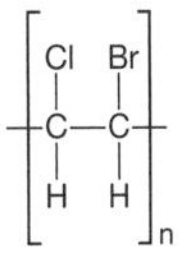	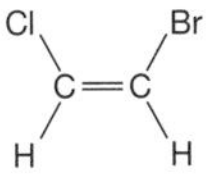

Answers

3 a

$$n \; \begin{array}{c} H \\ | \\ C \\ H \end{array} = \begin{array}{c} H \\ | \\ C \\ | \\ C_3H_7 \end{array} \longrightarrow \left[\begin{array}{cc} H & H \\ | & | \\ C - C \\ | & | \\ H & C_3H_7 \end{array} \right]_n$$

(Correct repeating unit; 'n' on both sides.)

b Polypentene

Condensation polymerisation

1 a A and D **b** C
c Alcohol **d** Carboxylic acid

2 a

$$n \; HOOC — COOH \; + n \; HO - \begin{array}{cc} H & H \\ | & | \\ C - C \\ | & | \\ H & H \end{array} - OH$$

$$\downarrow$$

$$\left[\begin{array}{cc} H & H \\ | & | \\ C - C - OOC — COO \\ | & | \\ H & H \end{array} \right]_n + 2nH_2O$$

(reactants; repeating unit; all 'n' in correct places)

b Water/waste product is formed.

3

$$HO - \begin{array}{ccc} H & H & H \\ | & | & | \\ C - C - C \\ | & | & | \\ H & H & H \end{array} - OH \qquad HOOC - \begin{array}{cc} H & H \\ | & | \\ C - C \\ | & | \\ H & H \end{array} - COOH$$

Amino acids and DNA

1 Two amino acids can join together by **condensation** polymerisation to form polypeptides and **proteins**.

Each amino acid contains two functional groups, a **carboxylic** acid group which has the formula –COOH and an amine group, which has the formula –NH$_2$. The –COOH on one amino acid reacts with the –NH$_2$ group on another amino acid forming a polymer, with the elimination of **water**.

2 a $n \; H_2NCH(CH_3)COOH \rightarrow$ $(-HNCH(CH_3)COO-)_n + nH_2O$ (products; reactants)

b $n \; H_2NCH_2COOH + n \; H_2NCH(CH_3)$ $COOH \rightarrow (-HNCH_2CONHCH(CH_3)$ $COO-)n + 2nH_2O$

(reactants; 'n'; correct product with peptide link)

3 Nucleotides

4 Sugars

Chemical analysis

Testing for gases

1 Hydrogen – a lighted splint put into a test tube of the gas – is extinguished with a 'pop';
Oxygen – a glowing splint put into a test tube of the gas – Relights;

Carbon dioxide – bubble the gas through a solution of limewater – produces solid calcium carbonate, turning the limewater cloudy.

2 a The gas turns limewater turns cloudy **Carbon dioxide**
b The gas bleaches litmus paper **Chlorine**
c The gas extinguishes a lighted splint with a pop **Hydrogen**
d The gas relights a glowing splint **Oxygen**

3 a $CH_4 + 2O_2 \rightarrow CO_2 + 2H_2O$ Bubble through limewater – would turn cloudy.
b $Mg + H_2SO_4 \rightarrow MgSO_4 + H_2$ A lighted splint put into the gas – extinguishes with a pop.
c $CO_2 + H_2O \rightarrow C_6H_{12}O_6 + O_2$ A glowing splint put into the gas – will reignite.
d $HCl + MnO_2 \rightarrow MnCl_2 + 2H_2O + Cl_2$ Litmus paper when exposed to the gas – will bleach.

4 Carbon dioxide gas produced so the limewater will turn cloudy; because it is a combustion reaction involving a fuel and oxygen.
Description of different tests for each gas: hydrogen – lit splint in flame/ oxygen – glowing splint will reignite/ chlorine – bleaches litmus paper; these tests will be negative.

Identifying metal ions using flame tests, flame emission spectroscopy and sodium hydroxide

1 Lithium carbonate – Crimson; Sodium chloride – Yellow; Potassium sulfate – Lilac; Calcium nitrate – Orange-red; Copper phosphate – Green.

2 a Lithium; Sodium.

b i

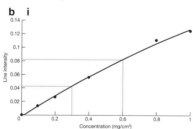

ii 0.3 moles/cm³ (accept within 2 d.p.)

iii Line intensity 0.0.82 (accept within 2 d.p.)

Testing for negative ions (anions) in salts

1

Chloride (Cl⁻)
Nitric acid followed by silver nitrate solution
White precipitate (of silver chloride);

Bromide (Br⁻)
Nitric acid followed by silver nitrate solution
Cream precipitate (of silver bromide);

Iodide (I⁻)
Nitric acid followed by silver nitrate solution
Yellow precipitate (of silver iodide);

Sulfate (SO₄²⁻)
Hydrochloric acid followed by barium chloride solution
White precipitate (of barium sulfate);

Carbonate (CO₃²⁻)
Hydrochloric acid then pass gas formed through limewater
Effervescence and gas turns limewater cloudy/milky.

2 a Carbonate was present; chloride was present from the sodium chloride.
b Hydrochloric acid contains chloride ions; this would give a positive reading to test; regardless of the contents of the salt.
c Silver chloride.
d $2H^+(aq) + CO_3^{2-}(s) \rightarrow CO_2(g) + H_2O(l)$

Identifying ions in an ionic compound

1 a Flame test – calcium gives red flame, lithium gives crimson; OR add sodium hydroxide, if white precipitate forms it is calcium.
b Nitric acid followed by silver nitrate solution; chloride gives white precipitate, bromide gives cream.

2 Positive ion: Flame test – yellow flame if sodium present; Negative ion: Hydrochloric acid followed by barium chloride solution; White precipitate if sulfate present.

3 A – Potassium carbonate; B – Lithium sulfate; C – Aluminium bromide; D – Iron(III) iodide.

4 Hydrochloric acid + calcium carbonate → calcium chloride + carbon dioxide + water; Flame test – brick red; Nitric acid followed by silver nitrate solution; gives white precipitate.

Chemistry of the atmosphere

The composition and evolution of the Earth's atmosphere

1 a Carbonate rock formation; Fossil fuel formation.
b Condensation/formation of oceans OR used in photosynthesis by plants.
c It reduced; carbon dioxide dissolved in the oceans.
d $6CO_2 + 6H_2O \rightarrow C_6H_{12}O_6 + 6O_2$ (correct; balanced)

2 a $2Cu + O_2 \rightarrow 2CuO$
b 21.5%
c To make sure no other variables were affecting the results; to reduce error.

Climate change

1 **a** Climate is complex **or** models are simplifications.

b Results of experiments are checked by other scientists.

c Carbon dioxide; methane; water vapour.

d Any four from: Carbon dioxide – burning fossil fuels in our homes/industry/cars; deforestation;

Methane – cattle farming; rice crops; landfill;

Water – small increases from farming and burning fossil fuels, most is due to natural evaporation; higher global temperatures increases the rate of evaporation.

2 **a** Temperature increases at the same time as CO_2 increases; There is a big increase in temperatures more recently.

b The graph shows a correlation between CO_2 and temperature; it is known that human activity has increase atmospheric CO_2; it is known that CO_2 is a greenhouse gas; recent temperatures are much higher than in the past.

The carbon footprint and its reduction

1 Alternative energy – Renewable energy sources such as solar cells, wind power and wave power do not rely on the burning of fossil fuels;

Energy conservation – Reducing the amount of energy used by using energy-saving measures such as house insulation, using devices that use less energy, reduces the demand for energy;

Carbon Capture and Storage (CCS) – Removing the carbon dioxide given out by power stations by reacting it with other chemicals. The product of this reaction can then be stored deep under the sea in porous sedimentary rocks;

Carbon taxes – Penalising companies and individuals who use too much energy by increasing their taxes reduces the demand for energy;

Carbon offsetting – Removing carbon dioxide from the air using natural biological processes such as photosynthesis. This is achieved by planting trees and increasing marine algae by adding chemicals to the oceans.;

Using plants as biofuels – Plants take in carbon dioxide as they grow, when they are burned they only release the same amount of carbon dioxide. This makes them carbon neutral.

2 **a** Any two from: High use of cars/preference for large cars; developed countries use more energy; high level of industrialisation in USA and Qatar; China and India and developing countries.

b It has **reduced** from 10 tonnes per person to 7.1 tonnes per person.

c Increase in population; increase in industry; increased development has resulted in greater energy use.

Atmospheric pollutants

1

Soot	Global dimming and lung damage	Ensure complete combustion of fossil fuels
Carbon monoxide	A toxic gas which binds to haemoglobin in the blood, preventing the transport of oxygen around the body	Ensure complete combustion of fossil fuels
Sulfur dioxide	Dissolves in clouds to cause acid rain and causes respiratory problems	Desulfurisation of petrochemicals before combustion
Oxides of nitrogen	Dissolves in clouds to cause acid rain and causes respiratory problems	Catalytic converters used after combustion

2 **a** Petrol emits more carbon dioxide/diesel emits less carbon dioxide; diesel emits four times more sulfur dioxide; diesel emits particulate matter, petrol does not; diesel emits slightly more oxides of nitrogen.

b Any two from: Energy and materials are used in construction and transport of vehicles; energy is required to power the vehicles; this energy comes from electricity; which may be produced by burning fossil fuels.

3 **a** Complete combustion = CH4 + 2O2 → CO2 + 2H2O, therefore:

i $CH_4 + 1\frac{1}{2} O_2 \rightarrow CO + 2H_2O$

ii $CH_4 + O_2 \rightarrow C + 2H_2O$

b When 4 moles of coal are burned, 960 moles of carbon dioxide are produced; therefore, 960/4 = 240 moles of carbon dioxide per mole of coal. 240 × 8 = 1920 moles of carbon dioxide.

c Burning coal produces nitric acid (HNO_3) and sulfuric acid (H_2SO_4); causing acid rain which is corrosive/reacts with limestone.

Using resources

Finite and renewable resources, sustainable development

1 The **natural resources** used by chemists to make new materials can be divided into two categories – **finite** and **renewable**. **Finite** resources will run out. Examples are fossil fuels and various metals. **Renewable** resources are ones that can be replaced at the same rate as they are used up. They are derived from plant materials.

Sustainable development meets the needs of present development without depleting natural resources for future generations.

2 Have reactions with high atom economy with as few waste products as possible; Use renewable resources from plant sources; Have as few steps as possible to eliminate waste and increase the yield; Use catalysts to save energy.

3 They reduce the activation energy required for reactions; reducing the use of heat which typically comes from fossil fuels.

4 **a** Company A = 22/25 × 100 = 88%; Company B = 17.5/19 × 100 = 92%.

b Company B has a higher percentage yield so is more sustainable.

Life cycle assessments (LCAs)

1 A life cycle assessment is an assessment of the environmental impact of the manufacture and use of different materials and products.

2 Resources used, production, use and disposal.

3 **a**

Stage of LCA	Plastic bag	Paper bag
Source of raw materials	From ethene, which is produced during cracking of petrochemicals	Come from trees
Production	Simple process involving no chemical change	Consumes water and produces acidic gases and greenhouse gases
Use	Reusable	Damaged by water and more difficult to reuse
End of life	Decompose slowly but produce less solid waste	Decompose quickly but generate more solid waste

b Any two from: Paper bags come from a renewable source whereas plastic comes from a finite resource; Plastic bags are reusable but decompose slowly at the end of their life whereas paper bags can't be reused easily but decompose quickly at the end of their life; Paper bags produce more pollution and consume more water.

4 The supermarket has conducted a selective/shortened/abbreviated LCA, ignoring negative points, e.g. slow decomposition/source materials are finite.

Alternative methods of copper extraction

1 **a**

b It is not pure copper.

2 Smelting and electrolysis use a lot of energy; Copper-rich ores are scarce.

3 a Bioleaching using bacteria; Phytomining using plants; Displacement using iron.

   b i Bioleaching: produces pure copper so needs little further processing; but is slow.

   ii Phytomining: environmentally friendly; but is slow/requires further processing.

   iii Displacement using iron: can use scrap metal; may increase demand for iron.

Making potable water and waste water treatment

1 Water that is safe to drink – harmful chemicals and microbes have been removed.

2 A pure substance is one element or compound; potable water contains other substances like salts and minerals.

3 a

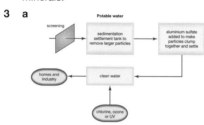

b To sterilise the water.

4 a Reverse osmosis.

   b Distillation separates the water from the salt by heating the salt water until the boiling point of water; this requires energy.

5 a

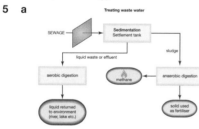

b Removal of harmful chemicals.

Ways of reducing the use of resources

1 a Reduces use of glass bottles; Reduces use of limited raw materials to make other glass products.

   b Separation; Reforming; Melting.

2 a It is magnetic.

   b Steel is made with iron, carbon and other metals; recycling iron in steel uses the amount of iron needed by extraction from its ore.

   c Aluminium extraction uses a lot of energy; which comes from burning fossil fuels – releasing carbon dioxide; recycling aluminium uses less energy.

Rusting

1 Corrosion is the destruction of materials by chemical reactions with substances in the environment.

2 a Test tube 1

   b Rust requires oxygen and water; only test tube 1 is exposed to both oxygen and water; it will rust the most.

   c Iron + oxygen + water → hydrated iron(III) oxide

   d Test tube 2: No water; Test tube 3: No oxygen; Test tube 4: Paint barrier prevents oxygen or water contacting the iron; Test tube 5: Galvanised with a more reactive metal – stops oxygen or water contacting the iron and, as the metal is more reactive, it will oxidise instead of iron.

   e Magnesium or zinc; because it is more reactive; it will react instead of iron.

Alloys as useful materials

1 An alloy is a mixture of metals.

2 a Gold is soft; alloys are harder.

   b Gold ions are arranged in layers; Gold ions can slide over each other.

   c Copper atoms are a different size to gold atoms; disrupting the layers of gold atoms which makes it more difficult for them to overlap.

3 a Car bodywork needs to be hard but still bendable into shape; more carbon makes it strong.

   b Sample A, because it contains more carbon so is hardest.

   c M_r iron = 55.8 – number of moles = 24.80/55.8 = 0.4444 moles. % = 0.444/0.461 × 100 = 96.1%

   M_r carbon = 12 – number of moles = 0.21/12 = 0.0175 moles. % = 0.0175/0.461 × 100 = 3.9% (ignore rounding errors)

Ceramics, polymers and composites

1 a

Borosilicate glass	High melting point	Silicon dioxide and boron trioxide
Fibre glass	Strong and light	Strands of glass fibre and plastic resin
Ceramics	Hard, brittle, electrical insulators, waterproof	Metal ions and covalent structures

b Ceramic

c Glass fibres reinforce the material; plastic resin is the supporting matrix.

d A composite.

e Fibre glass is light; and strong.

2 a i LDPE

   ii HDPE

   iii Thermoplastic

   iv Thermosetting plastic

   b HDPE and LDPE are both produced from chains of the monomer ethene; HDPE has few branches; meaning intermolecular forces are maximised; LDPE has many branches; therefore HDPE is strong and has a higher melting point.

   c Milk bottles are made of thermoplastic so can be melted down to make new products; plastic electrical componenets are made of thermosetting plastic so can't be melted down; thermosetting plastics form strong bonds between strands when they set; thermoplastics have weak intermolecular forces between strands.

The Haber process

1 Ammonia

2 $N_2 + 3H_2 \rightarrow 2NH_3$

3 The reaction is reversible and the forward reaction is exothermic. This means that the backward reaction is endothermic.

4 The conditions used are a temperature of 450°C; a pressure of 200–250 atmospheres; and an iron catalyst.

5 As the forward reaction is exothermic, it would be favoured by lowering the temperature; the problem is that a low temperature would make the reaction slow; compromise is arrived 450°C; forward reaction reduces number of moles of gas; increasing pressure favours forward reaction; an iron catalyst is used to speed up the reaction.

6 a Few molecules of gas in forward reaction; higher pressure favours fewer molecules of gas.

   b Higher temperatures reduce percentage yield of ammonia; but lower temperatures make the reaction too slow.

   c i 300 atmospheres and 400°C = 50%

   ii 200 atmospheres and 350°C = 54% (accept ± 2 percentage points)

Production and uses of NPK fertilisers

1 Plants need compounds of **Nitrogen (N)**, **Phosphorous (P)** and **Potassium (K)** for growth and carrying out photosynthesis. **Fertilisers** containing these three elements are called **NPK fertilisers**.

2

Ammonium nitrate, NH_4NO_3	Ammonia from the Haber process is oxidised to form nitric acid which is then reacted with ammonia
Ammonium hydrogen phosphate, $(NH_4)_2HPO_4$	Mined phosphate rock is reacted with nitric acid to form phosphoric acid, H_3PO_4, which is reacted with ammonia.
Potassium chloride, KCl	Obtained by mining

3 Different crops/plants have different nutrient needs; their soil may be lacking in particular nutrients

4

Fertiliser	Acid	Alkali
Ammonium nitrate	**nitric acid**	ammonia
Ammonium phosphate	**phosphoric acid**	ammonia
Ammonium sulfate	**sulfuric acid**	ammonia
Potassium nitrate	**nitric acid**	potassium hydroxide

5 Atomic mass of phosphorous = 31

Molecular mass of ammonium hydrogen phosphate = 132

$31/132 \times 100 = 23.5\%$

6 Atomic mass of nitrogen (x2) = 28

Molecular mass of ammonium nitrate = 80

$28/80 = 35\%$ $0.35 \times 500g = 175$ grams

$175/28 = 6.25$ moles

Or

N_2 and $(NH_4)_2HPO_4$ have 2 atoms of nitrogen; there is a 1:1 ratio; $500/80 = 6.25$ moles